C000142165

A SPORTSMAN'S JOURNEY

A Sportsman's Journey

Donald C. Jackson

University Press of Mississippi / Jackson

The University Press of Mississippi is the scholarly publishing agency of the Mississippi Institutions of Higher Learning: Alcorn State University, Delta State University, Jackson State University, Mississippi State University, Mississippi University for Women, Mississippi Valley State University, University of Mississippi, and University of Southern Mississippi.

www.upress.state.ms.us

Frontispiece by Robert Jackson

The University Press of Mississippi is a member of the Association of University Presses.

Portions of this work have appeared in altered forms in the following publication: "The Tobacco Patch Hunter," "Duck Tree," and "Postscript Quail Hunting," Mississippi Wildlife Federation, *Mississippi Wildlife*.

Copyright © 2021 by University Press of Mississippi
All rights reserved

First printing 2021

∞

Library of Congress Control Number: 2021946330
Hardback ISBN 978-1-4968-3584-0
Trade paperback ISBN 978-1-4968-3596-3
Epub single ISBN 978-1-4968-3585-7
Epub institutional ISBN 978-1-4968-3586-4
PDF single ISBN 978-1-4968-3587-1
PDF institutional ISBN 978-1-4968-3588-8

British Library Cataloging-in-Publication Data available

To the memory of Nelson "Buddy" Ball, good friend and companion in the woods, on the water, around the table, and in camp. In Buddy's own and often-stated words, "It's been a pleasure."

Contents

A SPORTSMAN'S JOURNEY

Once I Met a Mountain Man

THERE ARE TIMELESS VISIONS THAT STROKE THE HEARTS AND souls of outdoorsmen. They cast spells over us, sending us adrift into the dreamtime. We read the old stories of explorers and adventurers, of naturalists, hunters, and anglers and, somehow, we move beyond the words and find ourselves right there with those folks. As we read we feel the wind and the sun. We can smell the earth. We hear the crackle of fire on a clear cold night, the rushing of streams, the lonesome howls of wolves and coyotes, the cry of a hawk. We stand in awe of the heavens as we watch the Aurora dance. We hold our breath as sheep, moose, elk, caribou, deer, and bear move through the mountains and valleys of our imagination. Full of energy and splendid emotions, we eventually close the book, roll over in bed, and enter into the realm of never-never land. And it only intensifies there.

We are haunted by desire. We believe that it is possible to live what we've read, to be there, absolutely, comprehensively. We hold fast to our dreams, full of faith. They will not die. As we journey through the sunrise of life we look from afar, gazing across mountains and into secluded valleys that are transfigured from words into images, to the sacred places where we know that the wind whispers our name. We believe. We do believe. We do not for an instant stop believing. We shut our eyes and pray. And then the magic happens . . .

The old pickup truck had one working brake, the left front. Tommy Knapp wrestled with the steering wheel to make the sharp, steep,

3

turn off the highway just beyond the little settlement of Denard in Arkansas's Ozark Highlands. Then the truck began its journey, down the side of the mountain on a one-lane rocky trail. Don Flynn and I, still boys in our teens, held tightly to anything we could grab inside the truck's cab. Our fishing gear and other stuff—ice chests, minnow seines, a spare tire, stuff we'd put in the bed of the truck when we'd left Tommy's house in Leslie—slipped across the truck's bed and slammed into the back of the cab. Somehow the truck's one brake held and helped control our descent . . . but just barely.

Tommy was Don's cousin but several years older. The three of us were on a quest that July afternoon, deep into the mountains. We were going to fish for smallmouth bass in the upper reaches of a stream called Archey Fork, a principle tributary of the Little Red River. As we moved down the side of the mountain, picking our way along the rocky trail, I could, from time to time, look beyond the forest toward the southwest. The mountains swept before me, fold upon fold, until eventually they faded into the horizon, a distant blue that melded earth, sky, and dreams. I thought to myself that eternity probably started out there, just beyond that blue.

We forded shallow, clear, gravel-bottom streams. We skirted the edges of limestone bluffs. The old truck never coughed, never slid out of control, never spun or hesitated. It was as if the truck and Tommy were one in being, one in purpose. Deeper and deeper we plunged into a region of North America that apparently had been passed by and seemingly overlooked or considered irrelevant to the purposes of a nation that was churning ahead, full tilt boogie, into a rush away world.

Shadows flickered through the forest. Several deer and one wild turkey flushed beside the road. We stopped once to let a big copperhead cross ahead of us and another time so that a mother raccoon could shepherd her litter of kittens off the lane and out of the way. Spring seeps dripped their treasures into shaded hollows full of moss, ferns, and beautiful mature hardwood trees. The rocky lane narrowed. Branches arched completely overhead. From time to time we had to get out of the truck to move a big rock or branch that blocked our passage. It was obvious that it had been awhile since anyone had traveled this way. There wasn't much talk in the truck's cab. The mountains were the ones doing the talking. We were listening.

It was my first real venture into northern Arkansas's remote backwoods territory. I'd fished and hunted in the hills around my home down in central Arkansas, but, although wild in their own ways, they could not compare with what surrounded me on this Ozark sojourn. I knew creeks and I knew woods. I knew guns and tackle and boats. Even at my youthful age (seventeen years old), I was an experienced hunter, angler, and trapper. And yet, I'd never been on the ground in the heartland of the Ozarks, a region that I ultimately found to be perfectly in harmony with the song that swelled within me . . . perfectly in synchrony with my rhythms. On that afternoon, moving ever deeper through those rugged old mountains, I began to realize that I'd found the place, the region that until this very day owns my heart.

As a younger boy, I'd traveled by car with my family on main highways through the Ozarks, usually to visit my grandparents who lived in the more northern range of the mountains, up in Missouri. But we'd never stopped along the way for me to explore—not even a little. I was a captive in the car and, ultimately, in the little town where my grandparents lived. I longed to somehow fall out of the car on those trips and become a lost boy in the mountains, to live among the people who are as rugged and free and strong and resilient as the land around them. I'd read Jesse Stuart's book, *Hi to the Hunter*, and I was that boy.

I wanted to wander, to be gone, alone in these mountains, for days, for weeks at a time, with a pack on my back, a rifle in hand, and perhaps a dog at my side. I wanted harvest moons filtering through tree branches, casting their spooky shadows across the landscape. I wanted the chorus of coon dogs reverberating among the hollows. I wanted to be part of the culture and world of mountain people, of everything that flows within and from this noble tribe.

Eventually, as a young man in my twenties, all of this happened and in profound and beautiful ways. But on that afternoon with

Tommy and Don, as we made our way down the mountainside, it was all still before me.

I'm absolutely convinced that Tommy knew that he was stoking the fires of a wilderness wanderer, that he was opening the door for a restless soul to come to the place where it belonged. I recall his sideward glances at me as we wound our way through the passages of that afternoon's adventure. I recall the twinkle in his eye. Yes, after fifty years of reflection . . . I'm sure that Tommy Knapp knew, absolutely, what he was doing to me, with me, and for me.

After we drove for more than an hour, the steep lane that we followed began to flatten somewhat. It eventually took us into a large valley that was hemmed in on all sides by mountains. They stood like huge, silent sentinels, as guardians of a sacred place.

This was where the road ended. Nobody lived beyond here. This was "it." There was pastureland that swept across the valley and onto the lower slopes of the mountains. At the far end of the valley was a sturdy barn and a ruggedly beautiful house. A fresh bear skin was stretched, flesh-side out, across one side of the barn.

John Hargis, the owner of the ranch, came off of his front porch to greet us as we drove the truck to the house and turned off the engine. Then quiet, an awesome quiet, enveloped us. With that quiet, there was a stillness that penetrated to the core of my being. There was only the call of a hawk. I felt like I'd been transported back across time, removed from the rest of the world.

John was a soft-spoken man of few words. How could it have been otherwise? Loud talk in these mountains would be a vexation to the spirit. He rarely left his valley, and when he did leave he didn't stay gone long. Constant vigilance was required to care for his livestock. In a time period when black bears and mountain lions were officially considered rare or nonexistent in that part of Arkansas, John regularly dealt with them. I suspected that the government officials who'd declared the critters "not there" hadn't bothered to ask John or other folks who lived and worked in these remote corners of the Ozarks. The bear skin on the side of the barn and the hams and shoulders hanging from the barn's rafters, out of the sun and where the cool breezes could help cure them, were testimony to a different reality, a different realm of being.

During the drive into the valley, Tommy had told Don and me that John didn't live alone out there on the ranch. He lived with his wife, Liz (a local schoolteacher), and an uncle named Wood. From what I gathered, listening to Tommy and John as they visited on that July afternoon, Wood was now somewhere out in the mountains, as he was most of the time. Tommy had told us about Wood, that he was a fugitive from the law and hardly ever left the valley and surrounding mountains. Wood was a mountain man in the purest sense of the word. It was he who had killed the bear. It was he who patrolled the mountains, thinning the deer as needed in order to fill the larder. For Wood, there was no defined hunting season. He shot what he needed when he needed it. Or, when it needed to be done . . . in the mountains or elsewhere.

Lots of people on the "outside" knew that Wood lived with John on the ranch, but nobody talked about him much. They just left him alone and kept conversation about him quiet and carefully among themselves. The story was that Wood had once killed a man, somewhere down in Texas, who'd killed his brother. He'd just stood up in the courtroom as the defendant, a Mexican, was brought in, took aim, and shot the man. Wood escaped from the courthouse unscathed and from the law down in Texas. He'd sought and received refuge on his nephew's remote ranch in the Ozarks.

Back in these mountains he figured he'd be safe. And he was. Nobody in these mountains was going to bother him. Although he most certainly wasn't beyond the reach of the law, there seemed to be no purpose in the law going after Wood. Wood was where he belonged. The law of the Ozarks prevailed over the law of the land. Officially, nobody, including local law enforcement, knew anything about Wood or his whereabouts. People in this part of the Ozarks knew that Wood was not a dangerous man . . . just a man who'd done what he'd thought was the right thing to do. Now, about the only time he went to town and interacted with anybody was for a once-a-year haircut. He conducted his business and then went back home, back to his mountains.

One year, while Wood was in the barbershop, the barber told Wood that he had a "bad place" on his ear and that he needed to have a doctor look at it. Wood went to the local doctor. The doctor said, "Wood, you've got cancer. I can fix it for two hundred dollars or cut off your ear for ten dollars." Wood gave the doctor ten dollars. Those were different times.

A year or so later, in the same barbershop, a young mother brought her little boy into the shop for his first haircut. Wood was in the chair, getting his yearly cut and shave. The county sheriff, an elderly man who knew Wood very well, had just left the shop. Nothing had been said about Wood being there, quietly waiting his turn, as the barber finished cutting the sheriff's hair. The little boy, all smiles and gabble, grabbing at everything in the shop, scattering old copies of *National Geographic* and the newest edition of the local paper, *The Marshall Mountain Wave*, all over the floor, and in general making a nuisance of himself, was a double handful of tribulation for his mama. The turmoil continued unabated and out of control *until* the boy happened to look up and see Wood in the chair. The boy stood transfixed, but only for a moment. Then he screamed, ran to his mother, and started crying. Wood, never one to waste a word, said, "Well, hell. I knew I was ugly, but I didn't think I was *that* damn ugly!" The young mother, her little child in tow, fled from the shop, much to the relief of Wood and the barber.

As Tommy visited more with John, out in the yard beside John's house, I remained quiet. I knew not to say anything about Wood or to ask any questions. The world left Wood alone and Wood left the world alone. It seemed to me that this was as it should be. Just being there, in Wood's refuge, his sanctuary, surrounded by his mountains, and knowing about him, knowing that there were still men like him in the world, was a gift to me.

John then turned around and welcomed me to his ranch with a big smile and a strong handshake. He knew that I knew about Wood. He knew that Tommy had told me the story. Upon reflection,

I think he and Tommy had together planned my Ozark mountain christening and that learning about Wood was part of the catechism.

The gift of knowing about Wood was confirmed and delivered, in trust, by the gift of friendship extended by John's handshake. I silently pledged to myself, out there in front of John's house and surrounded by those mountains, that as long as Wood was alive the trust given to me would manifest itself through my absolute silence about Wood. Wood would be in my heart, and in my mind, but never in my words. I had become, in a few precious moments, an Ozark mountain boy, and Ozark mountain boys keep their counsel close to their chests. I looked at Tommy and Tommy smiled back at me. He understood, absolutely, what had just happened.

Tommy asked John if it would be OK for us to go fishing in the stretch of Archey Fork that went across John's land. John had seen our tackle in the back of the truck but, until that moment, nothing had been said about what we wanted to do that afternoon. Of course he already knew, but still there needed to be the formality. Permission was spontaneous, as was also an invitation to seine some minnows we'd need for bait.

Up until that afternoon I'd never caught a smallmouth bass. I'd never even seen one! But smallmouth bass were our target in that creek, and apparently the creek was full of them. Tommy needed fish for a fish fry back in town that was scheduled for later in the week. Subsequently, we were to fish without reservation and with extreme prejudice.

In reality, the upper reaches of Archey Fork where we would be fishing probably got fished about once every other year or so, if that often. And, from what I gathered, it was Tommy who did that fishing. Although I'm sure there were regulations back then about fishing in Ozark streams, when one considers John and Wood Hargis's world out there in those Ozark mountains, government regulations about such things as hunting and fishing were viewed more as guidance than as rule. We'd get our bait and then fish until Tommy said, "Whoa," or it got too dark to fish.

It never dawned on me, until several years later, that Tommy's purposes on this venture to Archey Fork with Don and me probably had very little to do with fish and fishing—they were only the sacraments that would take us to something greater. All Tommy was doing was setting the stage. He had the gift of understanding how to stoke the fires that burn deeply in the hearts of young men and women . . . and especially the hearts of those who are in love with the mountains and the people who live in them.

Back when my father was in seminary, we'd lived in rural north central Kentucky. There were some pretty creeks there and I was constantly in them, catching salamanders, frogs, crayfish, and small sunfish and staying wet most of the time. When I was ten years old we'd moved back home to Arkansas. I missed those little clear-water creeks back in Kentucky. Where we lived in central Arkansas the creeks were nice, but they were different. They didn't sing songs to me. They had a quieter attitude. Although I adapted to my new world, I missed the songs. They were becoming faint echoes. Up until that afternoon with Tommy and Don, I'd never been in or around an Ozark stream.

When the three of us finally rambled down toward Archey Fork to seine minnows, I started hearing the water sing. I rushed through a scope of woods, drawn by that singing. Then, sparkling in front of me, was Archey Fork. It was just about the most gorgeous creek I'd ever seen—perhaps *the* most gorgeous. It danced across riffles and then grew quiet in the deep holes. I looked into those deeper holes and could see bass cruising and drifting in water that was so clear that it seemed like air. And yet there was a slight green cast to it, a wonderful, pure, green that deepened with depth. Along the edges of the creek there were big boulders and, in some places, vertical rock cliffs. Oaks of various kinds, sycamore, ash, cottonwood, and hickory shaded the water. In the shallows, along the edges of riffles, water willows swayed in the currents.

Don was carrying two minnow buckets. I was carrying the seine and one bucket. Tommy carried our rods and tackle. The bottom of the creek was a mixture of rounded, gray-colored cobble and smooth pebbles of various colors mixed with scattered small patches of sharper-angled, orange and white chert. Out in the pools were sunken, waterlogged branches and logs, but they tended to be on the bottom and didn't seem to inhibit the flow or create obstacles for a wade-fishing angler. It was a classic wadeable stream, cool but not cold, perfect for anglers in jeans and old canvas tennis shoes. The stones were clean and without attached algae. We'd be able to walk on them without slipping.

"Minnows" of all sort scattered as we approached the water. Some of them were brightly colored. Others were silvery. Some had dark stripes along their sides. Most were about as long as our fingers. And that's what we wanted. We unrolled the seine and pulled it through water from waist to ankle deep. It only took three or four passes with the seine to get all the minnows that we would need for the afternoon—about twenty-five or thirty minnows apiece. We threw back the little catfishes (madtoms) and brightly colored ground minnows (darters), keeping only the silvery ones. These silvery ones we divided into the three buckets.

I had no idea regarding the names or conservation status of the fishes we collected from that creek with our seine. Back then, before I studied fishes in college, before I became a fisheries biologist, they were all *minnows*. I never paused to consider whether or not some of them may have been fishes of special concern. When I think back about our collection, and the remoteness of the place where it occurred, I doubt that what we took for bait influenced any species of concern . . . if there were any. At least I hope that was the case.

Tommy then instructed us regarding how to rig our fishing tackle. He told us that the smallmouth bass in Archey Fork were wild fish and not very spooky. Long casts would not be necessary. He tied a single #2 long-shanked gold hook onto each of our lines with an old-style clinch knot. As I recall, the lines were clear monofilament and about ten to twelve-pound test. About eight inches above each hook he pinched on a single small piece of lead shot. That was it.

We were instructed to hook the minnow through the back, above the backbone, just under the dorsal fin. If we hooked the minnow anyplace else it would likely come loose when we cast. And then he reminded us not to try to cast too far. Stalk the bass and more or less "pitch" the bait out in front of them. A thirty-foot cast would be a very long cast.

Don and I both were bass anglers and very familiar with casting artificial lures for largemouth bass in ponds and lakes. Tommy's method for fishing was something very new to us. He said that when we saw or felt a fish take our bait, to release the line on our reels and let the fish run with the bait just a little. The fish would then stop, turn the bait in its mouth, and start to swallow it. That was when we were to tighten up, jerk back, and set the hook. The hooks would be set deep in the fish so he issued both of us a set of sharp-nose pliers for hook removal. He also gave each of us a cord stringer. This was not to be a catch-and-release outing. We were to keep what we caught.

Tommy then told Don to follow him, and the two of them left me there, alone at the edge of the creek, surrounded by beauty and spirit so powerful that I started to shake. I was overwhelmed by where I was and what I was doing. I couldn't control that shaking. It was impossible for me to catch a minnow from the bucket and put it on my hook. For at least ten minutes I just stood there shaking. Finally, I got control of myself and started breathing deeply. The creek continued singing to me. The bass that had hidden while we were seining now began drifting back into the deep, clear-green hole in front of me. A slight wind rustled the leaves of a big cottonwood tree on the bank. I breathed deeply again and tried, this time successfully, to catch a minnow from the bucket and hook it through the back as Tommy had instructed.

Leaving the bucket in the shallows, I slowly moved upstream to a place where I could pitch my minnow out into the pool. When it hit the water, it flashed and struggled and pulled just a little against the line. I gave it slack and watched as it went deeper into the water. Then a shadow rushed from under a root wad and my line started to tighten. As fast as I could I released the bail on my reel and let the fish keep swimming away from me. Then it stopped and I waited.

I wanted to strike back but remembered that Tommy had said to wait. The line moved again and I struck, hard.

A smallmouth bass as long as my forearm cleared the water and ripped across the pool. It had power beyond its size. I'd caught lots of largemouth bass but largemouths this size did not have the strength of this fish. It was my very first encounter with a smallmouth bass, and what a fine fish it was. It jumped several times and then began a bulldog fight down in the pool. I could see it down there, flexing its muscles, bearing down on rocks and logs. I pulled hard to keep it from getting to those places, fearing, rightly so, that the fish would wrap my line around them and break off. Although it seemed like I fought that fish for half an hour, it really was more like two to three minutes. But all of the magic was there. Finally, I got the fish into shallow water and scooped it up onto the gravel. It probably weighed about one pound—a big fish for a small creek.

It lay there glistening on that gravel, a golden-brown jewel with dark stripes on its cheeks and bars on its sides. As I ran my hand along its sides it seemed to feel smoother than a largemouth bass. Its scales seemed smaller. And it had a wilder look in its eyes . . . I can't really describe that look any other way. It was just wilder than I'd seen in any other fish. And I loved that fish. I didn't want to kill it. I wanted to let it go free, back into its pool. But that could not be. I knew that. This was a trip for harvesting, and I'd pledged to help with the goal of getting the basic ingredients for Tommy's fish fry. And so, I put that beautiful fish on the stringer, went back to my minnow bucket, captured and hooked on another minnow and continued with my fishing.

For about two hours I moved upstream, quietly wading, quietly watching the world around me, mesmerized by the magic of moving water, pitching my minnows into little pockets of water near rocks and logs or out into the deeper pools just where the water starts to turn green. The bass tore into the minnows I presented, one after another. And my stringer became increasingly heavier. I knew beyond a shadow of a doubt that this was then and forevermore the place and the fishing that would own me. I might travel the world (which

I did). I might catch many other wonderful fish (which I have). But wading an Ozark stream and fishing for smallmouth bass would be the defining framework of who I really am as an angler. As I write this, more than half a century after that afternoon on Archey Fork, that identity has held steady and unwavering. But it is more than an angler's identity. That afternoon out there wading in Archey Fork, catching those smallmouth bass, I dedicated my life to streams and stream fisheries. That creek and those fish gave me no choice.

Then I heard movement along the stream's bank. It sounded almost like a gentle wind was passing through. A moment later, as I was preparing to put another smallmouth bass on my stringer, a tall and lanky man materialized from the shadows and stood beside me. I didn't question who it was. I knew that it was Wood Hargis. He stood there quietly, looking out across the water. Then he looked up at the sky and then back down to me and the fish.

"You've got enough fish son," he said. "You need to let that one live."

I nodded without speaking, turned away from Wood, and helped the bass gain its equilibrium in the shallow water where I stood. I watched as it swam slowly back into the deep pool of Archey Fork.

When I turned back around, Wood was gone.

I never saw Wood again.

And . . . I've never killed another smallmouth bass.

Tommy, John, and Wood are gone now. With their passing I can share the story. For fifty years I safeguarded it in my heart. I kept my promise . . . the promise that I made to myself as a young man in my teens that afternoon by John's house, a promise never mentioned but clearly known to all three of these men. I've never questioned that.

I also understand, very clearly, that the story has not ended. It never will. All any of us can do is take care of the story for a little while, add what we can to it, and then pass it along. Wood Hargis didn't start the story. There were mountain men before him. In his own powerful way, during a single encounter, and a few quiet words, he passed the story, the song of the mountain men, to me.

Mulberry Season

FOR TWO DAYS A GENTLE SPRING RAIN PASSED OVER NORTH MIS-
sissippi. It brought its blessings, off and on, sometimes steady,
sometimes misty, soaking old leaves that had carpeted the ground
through the winter, nurturing tender new life across the region's
rolling landscapes. As the rain subsided and the sky cleared to a
vibrant blue, it left a sweetness in the air.

I stood alone in the afternoon shadows of a water oak, at the edge
of a pasture on my farm, soaking up that sweetness, looking across
the pasture toward a forested hillside, encouraging my hunter's cadence to stretch, yawn, and come out of slumber. The rhythms were
profoundly deep, profoundly strong. I could feel them reverberating
in my soul. I was ready to be back in the woods again. I was ready
for the break between winter and spring squirrel seasons to end. I
took a deep breath and smiled. Mississippi's spring squirrel season,
the "mulberry season," would open with tomorrow's dawn. And
with that dawn would come the resurrection of a squirrel hunter.

My thoughts swirled back across the years of a hunter's pilgrimage. Although blessed with sixty-five orbits around the sun, I was
once again a boy, a boy with an opening day before me. Excitement
swelled. I could shut my eyes and "be there" again, surrounded by old
friends from my youth, all of us flush with dreams of adventure in
the sunrise of life, prowling the spring woods together, rifles in hand,
engaged in our mulberry season hunts. I allowed these thoughts,
these memories, to gather energy. I smiled again, then went back to
the gate where I'd parked my truck and drove the six miles back to

my home in Starkville, Mississippi, a quiet, southern, college town
. . . where for over thirty years I'd lived and worked as a professor of
fisheries at Mississippi State University. But my soul was anything
but quiet. I had an opening day before me!

When I got home, the stirring, the energy swelling within me,
only intensified as I went to my gun closet and reached for my .22
rifle. I could not help myself. I had to hold it in my hands. It is such
a special rifle to me, a retirement gift from my students, family, and
friends. I checked to be sure that it was unloaded then brought it
up to my shoulder, aimed down the hallway of my home, and let
the crosshairs of the rifle's scope settle on a coffee cup that sat on
my kitchen table. The image was clear and bright, the crosshairs
crisp. Lowering the rifle, I held it out at arm's length, looking at it,
encouraging the intertwining of spirits between hunter and rifle,
man and tool that meld for common purpose. The wood's luster
was beautiful. The checkering was gorgeous. The soft glow of finely
polished metal cast reflections that went directly to my heart. There
would be fine dreams this night.

Dawn crept beautifully upon the landscape as I walked across my
pasture toward the hillside where the hunt would begin. The weight
of the rifle slung across my shoulder felt so good, so right. Slight
wisps of fog gently curled above my pond, dancing like ghosts across
its surface. A pair of wood ducks skirted the edge of the woods,
following the creek that runs along my western boundary, a creek
that leads ultimately to nearby Noxubee National Wildlife Refuge.
The cool air, unusual for mid-May in Mississippi, put a sparkle in
my blood. I blew steam with every breath. My fingers were slightly
stiffened by the chill. My heart, however, was full of a very special
warmth, a warmth that comes to me when happiness blends with
satisfaction. It was a warmth stoked by a sense of rightness that
courses through me when I'm where I'm supposed to be (in the
woods), at the right time (spring morning), doing what I'm supposed
to be doing (squirrel hunting).

There was a deep stillness, around me, within me. The only sounds breaking that stillness were barred owl hoots, the occasional soft calls of sleepy birds readying themselves for another day of frantic, passion-laden activity, and the slight dripping of tiny drops of dew from the upper branches of trees. And in that stillness, with the ground still wet and soft from the rain, I would be able to move as a silent stalker.

As I stepped from the edge of the pasture, past the border of younger trees, and into the still-dusky woods, man the sojourner transitioned to man the hunter. A different rhythm took command. Dormant fires were stoked. I nudged senses to keener perception. I became a predator—calm, focused, smooth, patient, and deliberate.

A small cluster of branches trembled ever so slightly in a tree next to me, about fifty feet over my head. Drops of dew fell gently, hitting the damp leaves at my feet. I immediately became a statue, searching for the source of the nearly imperceptible little micro-storm. A shadow flickered. I saw the squirrel drifting quietly and deliberately along one of the tree's larger limbs. It paused momentarily to survey the world around it. When it paused, I slowly shouldered my rifle, took a steady rest against a water oak's trunk, and put the crosshairs of my rifle's scope on the squirrel's head. Without the scope, it would have been impossible to tell in the early morning light what kind of squirrel it was. With the scope, however, I could tell that it was a fox squirrel. I lowered my rifle.

I do not shoot fox squirrels on my farm. They are Bachman's fox squirrels, Mississippi's big "hill country" squirrels, the squirrels with salt and pepper backs and sides, orange bellies and tails, black heads, and white faces. Bachman's fox squirrels seem to be having a pretty tough time as the smaller but more aggressive gray squirrels invade increasingly more of their domain. So, my focus is on gray squirrels. And I'm glad to give the fox squirrels sanctuary. They are magnificent animals.

Gray squirrels, however, are not magnificent. They are wonderful. They are little ghosts in the woods, darting quickly through shadows and along tree branches; and they are masters of stillness. After more than five decades of hunting, I've come to the conclusion that gray squirrels are, at least for me, the ultimate small game animal in the South. They are about half the size of fox squirrels but at least an order of magnitude smarter and more alert, with extremely well-developed senses of sight and hearing.

A hunter with a rifle will only get split-second opportunities for shots at gray squirrels. If they spot you, chances are you will never see them again. Fox squirrels, on the other hand, tend to forget that you are there. Fox squirrels also forget that they've been shot at. If a fox squirrel hides up in a tree, just sit down quietly nearby, wait about twenty minutes, and it will show itself again. But gray squirrels rarely do this. Miss a shot at a gray squirrel and you most likely won't see that squirrel again. When gray squirrels are gone, they are *gone*.

I saluted the fox squirrel overhead. As I did so it adjusted its perch on the branch and stared down at me. It seemed to know, probably from previous experience with me in the woods, that it was safe. I moved on, deeper into the woods, deeper into the morning . . . deeper into the stillness that wrapped itself around my heart.

Although I'm an ageing man with gray beard and creaking joints, the pace of a squirrel hunt allows me to resurrect a rhythm . . . a cadenced flow to my movements. And I *wanted* to move, to see, explore, ramble, roam, and stalk. I probably could have seen as many, perhaps more, squirrels by sitting under a tree and waiting for squirrels to show themselves. But there was too much to discover in the woods on this spring morning. I could hear the siren's songs calling to me. To stay in one spot was unthinkable on so fine a morning.

Sunlight from the softest of dawns now filtered gently through the trees, probing the woods with misty streams of gold, gently, seductively highlighting the pastel colors of spring. I moved quietly forward, the sun to my back, carefully watching, carefully listening, carefully placing my steps, relaxed but alert for movements in the branches that could be from a squirrel.

Mossy spots were spongy underfoot. Mushrooms of all sorts pushed their heads above the leaves and clung to the sides of old logs on the ground. Warblers, vireos, thrushes, and wrens called. A doe snorted and moved stiff-legged through the woods ahead of me, white tail held high, but not really alarmed. A crow cawed. A sleepy owl gave its final hoots then fell silent.

I felt like a boy thrown into a room of chocolate-chip cookies and ordered to eat his way out. The sweetness of the morning was almost overpowering. I could almost sense elves and leprechauns peering around trees as I passed. I paused, looked more closely, and suddenly realized that one of those "little people" had in fact become a gray squirrel, with only its head visible beyond the trunk of a hackberry tree, twenty feet off the ground and seventy-five feet in front of me.

I was caught flat-footed, in the open, next to a sapling, but thankfully still in shadow. The squirrel knew I was there and what I was, but didn't think I'd seen it. It remained frozen in its position. I slowly raised my rifle. The squirrel's head was still all that I could see. It wasn't moving. The tension of the moment was electric.

The sapling beside me wasn't the steadiest of rests for a rifle shot, but it was all that I had. I mustered sixty-five years of resolve to make muscles steady for what was essentially an offhand shot. The crosshairs of my rifle's scope bounced around the squirrel's head then suddenly came to rest as muscles responded to command. I knew that the magic wouldn't last beyond a second or two. The image was sharp. The squirrel was still etched as if of stone. The crosshairs only moved at the beating of my heart. I started putting a little pressure on the trigger, remembering the lightness of touch required. Then there was the snap of a low-velocity bullet on its way and the soft thump of a squirrel hitting the damp leaves at the base of the hackberry tree. The tail twisted for a couple of seconds then was still. I kept my eyes on the spot and walked directly to the squirrel. It was a mature male, no doubt the prince of his domain, slain by the defender of fox squirrels.

I tucked the squirrel into the game pocket of my hunting vest, ejected the spent brass from the fired cartridge, reloaded, and checked the safety. Beyond this little scope of woods on the hillside, down along a fence line on the western boundary of my farm, not far from the creek, there were several trees with buds and berries that would provide the "soft mast" squirrels seek during spring. I moved on through the woods at a little faster pace, still quiet, still keeping to shadows as much as possible, but not seriously hunting until I got to the fence line.

The morning wrapped itself once again around me. For more than ten minutes I stood beside a big shagbark hickory tree, regaining my focus as a hunter. Then, sixty or so yards down the fence line, I saw branches trembling. My gaze riveted on that spot. For a thirty-second eternity nothing moved. The branches trembled again. A gray squirrel emerged from them and moved along a larger branch, sniffing at the branch as it went. I began my stalk.

This squirrel was busy. It was not focused on things on the ground. I plotted my course. There were several well-spaced trees between the squirrel and me that I could use to move forward in the stalk. Each tree was a small victory as I slowly advanced toward the squirrel. I was careful not to step on sticks or allow branches or briars to scrape against my clothing. I didn't want to do anything to alert that squirrel. The sun was positioned off my left shoulder, so there was no problem with glare. I had on a facemask and was wearing dark green jungle warfare camouflage clothing.

My ultimate objective was to move to a tree that was about half the distance to the squirrel, about thirty yards, then take my shot from there. I didn't want a steep-angled shot. I'm just not steady shooting up at sharp angles. My rifle is tuned for shots up to forty yards but good out to about sixty yards. Thirty yards, with a good rest on the side of a tree, is what I wanted.

It took me over fifteen minutes to get to the "shooting" tree. When I got to it I stood still and regulated my breathing. I opened and closed the fingers of my shooting hand to work out any stiffness, carefully maintaining visual contact with the squirrel, trying to discern a pattern of movement as the squirrel moved along the branches back and forth from trunk to tips. The atmosphere could not have been more intense if it had been an elk, a bear, a caribou, a moose, or a big whitetail buck. I've hunted them all successfully, but that gray squirrel out there at thirty yards, slipping along the branch like a little gray noodle in the shadows on a still May morning, trumped them all.

The squirrel moved back and forth, back and forth, pausing only briefly beside a small clump of leaves, then moving on, back and forth . . . back and forth. The pause at the leaf clump would be my only chance, and if the squirrel's head was behind the clump, there would be no shot. I only do head shots on squirrels.

Slowly, deliberately, I eased into position on the left side of the tree. I chose the left side because from that side my left hand could help me steady the rifle better against the tree's trunk. Sometimes I don't get the choice of sides, but this time I did. The squirrel maintained its pattern as I centered the scope's crosshairs on the leaf clump. I had both eyes open. My right eye was looking through the scope. My left eye was scanning for movement. I'm not some tropical chameleon with eyes that work independently, but still they can do different functions when I'm squirrel hunting.

My left eye caught movement. The squirrel was on the branch and going toward the leaf clump. Then, suddenly, for a fraction of a moment, the squirrel was behind the leaf clump and its head was beyond the clump. I immediately put the crosshairs on its head and squeezed the shot. Nothing happened. The squirrel maintained its position, but was tense . . . very tense. I dared not move to reload. Then it released its grip on the branch and tumbled through a four-second freefall, hitting the ground with a muffled thud, motionless. A perfect shot. Headshot squirrels will sometimes do that—just hang on for a moment before falling.

I went quickly to the squirrel. Even very dead gray squirrels seem to have the ability to vanish on the forest floor. It is possible to look right at them and not see them. They become part of the shadows, part of all that is on the forest floor. I don't look for the squirrel. I look for the squirrel's tail. The squirrel was on a carpet of leaves at the base of the tree. When I picked it up, the only trace of the drama was a small patch of bright blood on one leaf. I turned the leaf over. Then I heard movement overhead and looked up. All of the branches of the taller trees were stirring. Another spring morning was now wide awake, blowing its breath through my woods, teasing the tops of trees, letting me know in no uncertain terms that the hunt was over. Squirrel hunting stops when the morning wind starts.

As the breezes played games with the shadows, and after stretching my back just a little to work out the kinks that had gathered during the stalk, I adjusted the two squirrels inside my hunting vest, tucked my facemask into a vest pocket, unloaded my rifle, whispered a prayer, and drifted slowly, *ever so slowly*, through the woods toward my pasture. And for the record, the pace of that drift had nothing at all to do with the creaky joints of a gray-bearded man. A boy's joints are rarely creaky—regardless of the boy's age—on the opening day of mulberry season.

Crickets Tell the Truth

IT SEEMS TO ME THAT AS A PERSON INCREASES THE NUMBER OF orbits around the sun there's increasing propensity to take a look back over the shoulders. However, retrospective vision can be, and usually is, selective. There's a tendency to polish the jewels and remove the warts. Individual experiences, filtered by recall and interpretation, may not align with the actual facts. As the experiences are recounted, events and places may actually be unrecognizable to persons who perchance were also along for the ride. This is taken to the ultimate, beautiful extreme in southern storytelling, particularly as that storytelling relates to hunting, fishing, and rambling around out yonder in the wilds.

It has been said that in the South there are times when no gentleman will stoop so low as to actually tell the truth. Everybody already knows what it is! Just give us the story! Enough truth slips through the filter to reinforce the story of our humanity within an appropriate context, and that makes people happy as they shuck crawfish tails or fill another plate with barbecue ribs.

When properly projected, southern outdoor storytelling moves us into a richer realm of being that has enough *truth* in it so that folks hearing or reading the tale nod in agreement, enough *experience* in it to make the enterprise fit within a believable framework, and enough *cultural glue* stitching the parts together to make it entertaining. Why else tell the story?

With the passage of years and the retelling of stories, facts are ushered through an evolutionary process that can transcend history, move though legend, and ultimately become myth. Truth is embedded in the myth, but it is the sort of truth that strokes the human heart as much as, or more than, it strokes the human mind. It is truth that is not revealed directly but rather at a tangent—like poetry, like song. We telescope back across the stardust trail that marks our mortal sojourn, through wrinkles in time, piecing together a story that hopefully makes sense . . . at least to the storyteller. And then there are only echoes.

This may all be well and good but there's an issue that's rearing its ugly head, and it has been doing so for a very long time. We all know about it but hesitate to bring it into the light. Regardless of all this pontification about facts, experience, history, legend, storytelling, myth, echoes, celestial bodies, and whatnot, what are we supposed do when it comes to the subject of crickets? How do crickets fit into the framework of humankind's propensity to seek understanding, wisdom, and meaning? The same challenge holds for coffee pots and trotlines, but let's stick to crickets for now.

You see? If you're a southern sportsman you already know the truth . . . about crickets. I don't need to tell you what it is. You know exactly where I'm going with this piece. But you still want the story because it's our shared story even though you and I may never have been together in a boat. It's also a story that has echoed through the ages. You already, right now in this very moment, have images swirling around deep in your oversoul, beyond heart and mind, of places and people who came together as a result of crickets, and you are absolutely aware of significant happenings that occurred when all of the above melded in synergism.

You know all about the old boat that's down by the pond, yes, that one—the one that has the water moccasin living under it—remember? And what about that little pocket of water by the big willow tree, yes, the one that has the old snag by it where the turtles sun themselves—at least the ones that you missed when you slipped up across the pond's levee with your .22 rifle to thin their ranks. The "brim" bed is right there under that willow. It's your secret bed . . .

and everybody else's. And, for the uninitiated, there are no bluegill, sunfish, red ear, or "bream" in the South, just *brim*.

There's a fish fry scheduled for tomorrow night and you're worried sick about it. Thawing out a bag of frozen fillets won't work because the folks coming are real friends, not just guests. They deserve the best, and of course that's fresh-caught brim. You tell yourself, and your spouse, that this is important stuff that requires immediate attention. You sigh, gird up your loins, push aside distractions like mowing the yard and, without hesitation, grab your fishing pole (please, no rod and reel!), a tackle box full of #6 long-shanked wire hooks, cork bobbers, and some split shot. These you pitch into your truck. Then you go to your shed where your cricket cages are stored. You have to crawl across the lawnmower to get to them.

There are important decisions to make regarding those cricket cages. You've got to deal with diversity and variation. You wonder how in the world you got so many of them. Some are wire mesh and plastic. Some are wire mesh and wood. Some are wire mesh and metal. Some are long and tubular. Others are little squat boxes. Some you bought. Some you inherited. Some are the result of spontaneous generation. You have no idea regarding their origin.

I hesitate to talk about other options regarding cricket cages. Nobody, and I mean *nobody*, would dare be seen out fishing with one of those round, white, cardboard cricket containers with a cricket-sized hole in the side that are available at bait shops. Mason jars with nail holes punched in the lids and cider jugs with narrow mouths can work (and have). But drop them and you've got a mess on your hands. Remember?

The wire mesh tubes have a funnel and a cork on one end. The theory is that when you take out the cork only one cricket at a time will come out. That's not ultimate truth but it is true enough most of the time to keep your faith intact. The little squat boxes are open at the top but have a collar that extends down into the box that theoretically keeps crickets from jumping out. Of course, some crickets are athletic and are prepared to bolt for freedom.

This usually happens when you bang the bottom of the cage on your thigh and, while shoving your hand down through the top opening in attempts to catch a cricket imprisoned therein, the other incarcerated crickets sense opportunity and crawl up the outside of your hand, along your wrist, make their leap, and end up in the bottom of the boat.

Immediately you forget your task, shift your focus, remove your hand from the cricket cage, and try to catch the escapees. But your efforts tend to be of no avail because the crickets invariably find and enter the little drain gaps on the inside bottom of the boat under the seats and cannot be captured. Crickets like dark, cool, damp places. They've found paradise under your boat seat. You've known some crickets that have lived in the bottom of your boat for weeks. Go ahead and admit it . . . they sort of became pets, didn't they? From time to time you've thrown them breadcrumbs from your sandwiches. That's OK. We all do it, thinking nobody is looking. It is sort of the equivalent of pitching earthworms back into lawns after the worms have been washed into the streets by heavy rain. Loving life isn't a bad thing.

Now you have your cricket cage, and perhaps two of them. Off you go to the bait shop. The proprietor is wearing a T-shirt with the sleeves cut off and a greasy green John Deere hat. He asks how many crickets you want and you say fifty per cage. You really only need a total of about fifty crickets to get enough brim for your fish fry, but to ask for less than a hundred crickets just isn't done—at least not in polite company.

The proprietor grabs a plastic tube with a mark on it. Supposedly, once upon a time he actually put fifty crickets in the tube one at a time . . . saw how they stacked up, and made his mark. He scoops up a paper egg carton under which crickets are hiding to avoid the light in the cricket bin, shakes some through a funnel into his tube until the crickets get to the mark on the tube, and then pours the crickets into one of your cages. After he repeats that process for the second cage, you pay him and head back to your truck. At the end of your fishing trip you will still have over a hundred crickets in you cages. You remind yourself, with a smile, that this is not "up North." Everything in the South, including truth, perhaps *especially* truth, is relative. That definitely applies to cricket counting.

The bait shop proprietor knows he'll get a fifth of bourbon around Christmas time. And if you catch a cooler full of brim, he'll post your picture on the wall next to the counter. Of course, you'll have to lie about where you went fishing. That's assumed. A photo of you and your faithful fishing partner with a mess of brim has been on that wall for over ten years. Everybody knows that you fish in your own pond, but the faded caption says "County Lake." There may, however, be some truth to that, considering how close your pond is to the road.

Your crickets chirp and sing merrily on the drive to the pond. They are like little gladiators on their way to the Roman Coliseum. They have a mission in life and it leads to their end. They are like the "thorn birds" of Australian legend . . . living their entire lives with but the single purpose of impaling themselves on a thorn bush, and in so doing releasing the most beautiful birdsong in the world. But right now, you're not thinking about that sort of stuff. You're thinking about that boat and the moccasin and the willow tree and the brim bed. But it *is* nice to hear those crickets.

When you get to the pond's edge the turtles plop off the snag and a great blue heron flaps away. Locusts are humming (nobody in the South calls them cicadas). A swamp canary (Prothonotary warbler) flits around in the shadows of some of the larger trees that hang out over the water. You stick your boat paddle under the boat and flip it over. The moccasin slips into the water and you breathe a sigh of relief. Your partner loads his stuff and you load yours. You steady the boat while your partner works his way to the back seat and settles down. You are both well beyond the age where wisdom should have kicked in, so there's a real sense of accomplishment when he's down, finally, on his seat. Then it's your turn. Somehow you get in without stepping on your fishing pole or knocking over a cricket cage. Your partner applauds and you tell him to go to hell— with a smile, of course.

You scull from the front of the boat while your partner rigs up, grabs a cricket from one of the cages, and flips the hook out "just to straighten out the kinks" . . . *sure!* He wants the first fish of the day and he gets it. A fine brim about the size of your hand comes splashing toward the boat. Once in the boat it flops around some on the bottom while your partner searches for his needle-nosed pliers. The tool is lost somewhere down in the deep dark recesses of his tackle box. The brim is nearly dried out and already glassy-eyed by the time he locates the pliers. You tie off your old rusty fish basket, that's right, the one with the wire-spring trap door on the top, and flip it over the side of the boat. In goes the dried brim and you keep sculling out to the willow tree. Somehow the brim experiences resurrection and starts swimming around in the basket, apparently none the worse for wear.

When you get to the willow tree you drop an anchor. Do you remember it? Of course you do. It is an old metal coffee can filled with concrete that has a heavy wire loop made from a coat hanger stuck in the top, embedded in the concrete.

Now that the boat is anchored, you're set for serious fishing except . . . you know that there's no such thing as serious brim fishing. In fact, there's a total disconnect between the word "serious" and the words "brim fishing." The entire enterprise exists in an alternate dimension of being. Of course, using crickets on a fishing pole might be considered more serious than fishing for brim with a fly rod and popping bug, but that's illusion, pure illusion. It's all in how you look at it. Sure, you've got that fish fry staring you in the face. That's certainly serious. But that's *tomorrow*.

Right now, you're just out there on the pond with your buddy. There's a cricket cage on each end of the boat and a treasure trove of "one hundred" crickets (minus one), destiny bound. The boat isn't going anywhere. Between you and your partner there's a fish basket flopped over the side of the boat with the dried out and now resurrected brim in it.

You have fishing poles, not rods with reels. There's no casting. You just swing out a cork and hook on the end of your line. If your hook gets hung up on the snag all you have to do is pull hard and the hook will straighten and come free. You can bend it back into shape with your pliers. You're using heavy enough line (probably 14- to 20-pound test) so that you can grab the line and pull that hook straight when you need to. But, you remind yourself, you've got to be careful when you pull to keep from cutting your hands. It's probably a good thing to wrap your hands in your T-shirt, like a glove, before you grab that line. And, by the way, there is no such thing as 5X tippet or, for that matter, tippet of any size when you're fishing for brim with crickets. Tippet is out of its element in this enterprise. Brim don't care.

You certainly don't want to move from where you are. Not only would moving spook the fish off the bed, it would break the spirit of what's happening in that boat. You're there, settled into the rhythm of the day, the land, and the water, watching a little round cork that, every now and then, gets pulled under the water. You pull back, haul in your fish, take it off the hook, and put it in the basket . . . all without interrupting your train of thought. The crickets—bless their hearts—are chirping again. You grab another one out of the cage closest to you and thread it on, chin to butt, and out it goes, next to the old snag to fulfill its purpose in life.

The brim know, the second the cricket hits the water, that the cricket is absolutely real and telling the truth. It is not some make-believe fabrication of cork, thread, hair, and feathers. The message you are transmitting to those brim is very clear: "This, my dear fellows in the deep, this cricket before you is something that cannot be ignored."

The cricket is kicking and twitching and doing its level best to tell those brim, "Come hither"—and they do. The brim can't help themselves. The siren calls to them and they throw themselves upon the rocks. Slurp, down goes the cricket, down goes the cork.

A brim may have lived a long time in the pond without ever having seen a cricket. Grasshoppers, yes. But crickets, probably not, even though there are crickets right there living in the neighborhood. Crickets also don't go *wilding* as grasshoppers do, fluttering and hopping about among grass stems, losing focus and crash landing on the surface of ponds. Rather, crickets are a more reserved, secretive lot. They live under old boards on the ground around sheds and barns or under wads of moldy hay that the baler failed to pick up when the hay was cut earlier in the summer.

Crickets don't tend to venture forth much into the open, into the unknown. They are homebodies. When you pitch a cricket out into a pond to see if brim will come up to take it (which, as you well know, they will), the cricket has a hard time figuring out which way to go in order to get back to the bank.

This isn't so with grasshoppers. They know the way home and they somehow know about brim. They're careful not to kick too much out there on the surface of the pond lest they attract said predatory denizens of the deep. But then they also know that they've got to kick *some* in order to get back to the bank. The longer they are in the coliseum with the lions, the greater the chance of meeting their ultimate doom. But crickets kick. They are fearless as they announce to all in the watery world that they are there, and they do so with unbridled purposefulness.

Correspondingly, there is no question about the intentions of fishermen who use crickets for bait. They pare away at the superficial, the artificial, the make believe, the tangential, the rind, and the husk until the core elements are all that remain. They take away the fluff. They throw away the wrapper. When they thread on a cricket, they are engaged in announcing unadulterated truth. They are fishing with crickets because they want to catch fish.

And so, as a fisherman who uses crickets in pursuit of brim, you don't even need to tell your story, *but you will* . . . particularly if you live in the South. It's in your blood. You can't help it. And, like it or not, as a cricket fisherman you will, in your storytelling, have credibility beyond the common realm because crickets always tell the truth, and it was you that conscripted them for that mission. It's a matter of association. There's no getting around it. It may be stressful but you've got to deal with it. You are going to have to tell the truth.

The heavy reality of this challenge sort of makes me wonder if crickets should be banished as an ingredient in fishing—at least in the South. Is there too much honesty, too much truth, vested in crickets? But then again, I reckon we ought to just hang on to crickets, say to heck with it, and let the chips fall as they may. It is, after all, *occasionally* appropriate for fishermen to tell the truth. You can always redeem yourself by going bass or trout fishing.

I confess. I like catching fish and eating fish, particularly brim; and, if I'm reading the tea leaves correctly, so do you. Crickets get us there. And besides, there's all sorts of other stuff, beyond the crickets, that goes into making a fishing trip. It's that other stuff, the stuff of stardust trails and echoes, that makes our story ripe for the telling, and especially while we're gathered around a table with platters full of brim fillets and in the company of good friends.

So, please pass the ketchup and let me tell you about a dried-up brim that came back to life when me and old Flynn were out fishing on the "County Lake." You aren't gonna believe this . . .

A Lifeguard's Prescription

"WHOA! WE'RE PULLING OUT. THE ISSUE HAS BEEN RESOLVED! There's no need to fix what isn't broken. You just need to eat more fresh tuna."

I lay flat on my back in a room so cold that you could have hung meat. Pretty nurses flittered about. One of them mentioned that my blood pressure was a little high. I told her that usually happens when I'm around pretty girls. The surgeon, Dr. Steven Carroll, withdrew his stent-placing equipment from my heart and pronounced me to be in good shape. The blockage in one of my coronary arteries had apparently cleared as a result of new medication I'd been taking for the past few weeks.

"I'm adding a new prescription for you. You are to meet me on my boat down in Destin, Florida, for a couple of days of big game fishing. I need to monitor how you do when hooked up with a big yellowfin tuna."

Over the years I've learned that it is usually best to follow doctor's orders. And so began one of the most amazing and unusual doctor-patient relationships I'd ever experienced. Actually, we'd both recognized something had "clicked" between us when we'd first met earlier that summer.

I'd been working as the head lifeguard and waterfront director for a local Boy Scout camp. At age sixty-five, I'd been a lifeguard for fifty years, forty of which had been as an aquatics instructor for the Boy Scouts. The summer I met Steve I'd experienced chest pressure while out in the water teaching some updated techniques to a group of young lifeguards. Then, two days later, I experienced it again, this time with enough severity that I swam back to the main pier of the swimming area and just held on to the side for a few minutes . . . until the pressure went away. That evening while riding my bicycle I felt the same pressure and had to stop and walk the bicycle back home. The next day I was in my primary care doctor's office. Tests were scheduled and run. They were inconclusive. But I knew what I'd felt and so was referred to a cardiologist.

That's when I met Steve. He patiently listened as I explained my health history, my family history (lots of heart problems there), my career as a fisheries biologist, my side work as a lifeguard, and my love for the outdoors and writing about it. He focused very hard on my every word and scheduled more tests.

Then we talked about fishing and he started showing me photographs of his boat and some of the wonderful fish he'd taken over the years. The two of us, huddled around his photographs in one of the examination rooms in his clinic, were like kids in a candy store. We were connected. It was a strange experience for both of us. Later that day I brought him copies of books I'd written about hunting and fishing and rambling in the outdoors.

The laboratory test results came a week or so later and he broke the bad news to me. Yes, there was blockage in one of my coronary arteries, and surgery to place a stent would be necessary. We scheduled the surgery and then talked more about fishing.

Doctor-patient relationships rarely go this way. More typically, doctor and patient live and work in tangential worlds . . . for good reason. There are times when emotional connections, family or friendships, could potentially cloud a professional decision. In fact, I'd been careful about these sorts of relationships in my own profession. Be friendly. Be cordial. Be real. Be absolutely professional. But maintain a respectful distance.

And yet throughout my career there had been exceptions. Occasionally, I'd experienced situations when common denominators make themselves evident and friendships develop in spite of your best efforts. When such friendships emerge and take root, they typically are special gifts that endure across the years. They are treasures of the highest order.

I'd never experienced such a situation in a doctor-patient relationship and neither had Steve. And yet we couldn't deny that there was a bridge between us, a new bridge that needed to be honored. He put me on new medication, confirmed the schedule for my surgery, and told me to be very careful. He also checked his calendar and proposed a fishing trip for the last week of September . . . fishing should be at a peak then.

The surgery was phenomenal. I'd never had any sort of surgery before, so everything was a new experience for me. At one point I asked Steve when he was going to start. He responded, "Don, I'm already at your heart and the stent is ready for placement." Then, suddenly, his exclamation and the pullout. It would have been easy just to go ahead and place the stent, but as he'd said, "Why put something into a heart when it is not needed?" It was the perfect procedure by an excellent doctor.

Final arrangements were made for the fishing trip. On the prescribed day I drove down from my home in east central Mississippi to Destin, Florida. Steve was waiting for me in the parking lot near the fleet of fishing boats when I arrived. He escorted me down to the boat and introduced me to the captain, the mates, and the fellow anglers who'd be fishing with us on this trip.

The boat was beautiful. Named *Bowed-Up*, it had the reputation as being the most successful fishing boat in the fleet. Steve co-owns the boat with Scott Martin, an executive manager with Toyota at the plant in Tupelo, Mississippi. When Steve and Scott are not fishing, the boat and crew hire out as a charter boat. Under the expert direction of the boat's captain, Brady Bowman, the *Bowed-Up* usually comes in as one of the top boats, if not *the* top boat, in tournaments. Their specialty is billfish, both marlin and sailfish, but big tuna, wahoo, and mahi-mahi are also in the mix—as are also the occasional sharks.

We loaded the boat, found our bunks, untied from the dock, and were on our way by mid-afternoon. We had some distance to cover before getting to our fishing area . . . about seven hours. The seas were reasonably calm, mostly just big rollers. The late afternoon sun brushed the sea with gold. The engines purred in perfect cadence. The boat sliced the water. There were fine conversations among all of us as we built the bridges of friendships.

Although I've spent many days at sea during my career in fisheries, primarily working on large ships with the National Marine Fisheries Service, and have fished saltwater a good bit, from the tropics to the sub-Arctic, this was my very first time to be on a vessel equipped specifically for big game. I was fascinated by the rigging and the equipment. I was equally fascinated by the smoothness of operation exhibited by the captain and crew. Everything seemed to move in fluid motion. Everything had its proper place. And to top it all off, there was a constant, prevailing, overarching atmosphere of good cheer. It was a happy boat.

The water shifted colors and became the purest of deep blues. The sky was huge. We were alone in an ethereal wilderness where the measured cadence of a fine boat meets the rhythms of the sea. It is a very special marriage. Some people are born into this wonderful maritime marriage. Others, like me, discover it later in life. Regardless, you take it as it comes to you, and always with respect. You're in a world where you don't belong physically, but where you're absolutely supposed to be spiritually—and you know it!

Without the boat you die. With the boat you avail yourself to experience life in dimensions that wrap themselves beautifully around your heart and fill it with energy. Steve, the heart specialist, knew that this venture at sea was exactly what the old lifeguard's heart needed. As a fisherman he also knew, absolutely, that only at sea can a person so completely blend the spiritual heart with the physical one that it becomes one in being and in purpose. The elements that generate this bonding, this melding, need to be pure. That's what the sea and fishing for big fish is all about: *purity*. The elemental purity necessary to lift a heart to its ultimate potentials exists in the sea as in no other realm. But you must be open to receiving the gifts. You need to be open to what the sea can give . . . and I was. Steve had recognized this from the very beginning, from the genesis of our relationship. He is keenly perceptive, sensitive to the rhythms and murmurs of the human heart, in all dimensions.

The night sky was filled with stars as we moved steadily toward our fishing area. Hours folded across themselves. We entered the timeless dimensions of mariners at sea, linked to the winds, the sky, and the water in ways unknown and unknowable to those who have not ventured beyond the caresses of land. The sea is ultimate wilderness. It is rivaled by none. Every moment spent at sea is a moment of grace.

And so I stood in the dark, feeling the power of this wilderness, listening to the sound of the waves breaking against the bow of our boat, sensing the precious elements that come together in synergy to create an alternate world upon which frail creatures venture in search of denizens of the deep, seeking linkages, seeking meaning, seeking connections that transcend the common realm and that can be used as waypoints for the human sojourn. I have no idea how long I stood there on the stern. Time was a meaningless issue on this sojourn. But, eventually, I turned, made my way to my bunk, and hunkered down for the night's journey into the world of the never-never.

I was awakened by a change in the boat's rhythm as it encountered the seas and a change in the pitch from the engines. I crawled out of my bunk and carefully made my way through the cabin and out to the stern deck. Dawn was sweeping the gray from the sea and replacing it with hints of rose. The smell of freshly brewed coffee, mixed with the salty smell of the sea, flooded the boat's cabin. I poured myself a cup of strong brew and went out to meet the new day.

Standing out of the way in a corner of the boat's stern, I sipped on my first cup of coffee and watched the crew pull out rods and baits, deploy kites, and clip lines from the rods to the kite lines. It was fishing time. Baits were put over the side and allowed to move out to positions prescribed by the kites. There were multiple rigs set up this way. The boat continued to surge ahead as the baits splashed in the distant wake.

I was amazed at the speed we fished. Any fish we'd hook would have to be extremely fast to catch one of our baits. But that's what we were after, fast fish—*big* fast fish. It only takes one such fish to make a trip. As fast as we were going, probably close to fifteen knots, the fish were faster—much, much faster.

Such speed is necessary for big fish to survive in the open ocean. They have a lot of territory to cover, and when they see something to eat, they have to be able to overtake it, quickly, or it will disappear. These big fish are made for speed. They are absolutely streamlined, with grooves in their body to fold their fins into and bullet-shaped bodies tapering to thin caudal peduncles at the end of which are huge crescent-shaped tails for strong thrusts. They have special muscle tissue that, through counter-current heat exchanges, keeps them warmer than the seawater and increases muscle efficiency. They have very big eyes that gather light and help them see forever and beyond. They hear things very far away and can triangulate position with precision. Not much gets by these big predatory fishes in the sea. And, like a grizzly bear in the Arctic, they are not afraid. *They* do the killing. The noise of a boat doesn't seem to bother them. Their focus is on the splash of the bait in the wake behind the boat.

Then—a strike! Quickly the crew retrieved the other rigs as one of the other anglers who'd come to witness the dawn slipped into the fighting harness. There were hooks on the harness that clipped to the reel so that the fish could not jerk the rod and reel out of the hands of the angler. There was a cup where the butt of the rod could go so that there could be more leverage when pulling back on the rod. The short, thick rod bowed. The angler cranked. The fish took line. The angler cranked more. I had never seen so much power in a fish.

There were vibrations that came from the sea, through the line, onto the rod, across the shoulders of the angler, and into the boat. Those vibrations sent messages to the crew: "Tuna!" We were fast to a big yellowfin tuna. And what a fish it was. It had spent its entire life becoming strong and fast. It showed us exactly what it was capable of. It would *not* come to the boat. It went deep and just stayed there. Every inch of line that came back onto the spool of the reel was a

victory . . . inch by inch it came. Then—all was lost as the fish bore
down again to the deep, taking all the recovered line and then some
more. By this time the entire boat was astir. Everyone was up and
anxious to witness the fight.

The first mate, Greg Meyers, brought the angler water to drink.
The rod, built on the lines of a broomstick, was bowed into an almost
perfect U-shape. But everything held: the rod, the line, the reel, the
hook, the angler. After forty plus minutes the angler began to make
significant progress . . . slowly bringing the fish closer to the boat.
The rod was slowly, relentlessly, killing the fish.

There was a flash of silver-blue. The fish was in sight! It came
closer and closer to the boat. Greg grabbed the gaff. Suddenly there
was a lunge and water went everywhere! With a heave the fish was
pulled into the boat. Once onboard, the fish went crazy. The second
mate, Jim Arnold, brought out a club, rushed toward the fish, and hit
it twice, squarely on the head. That ended the fight. A fifty-pound
yellowfin tuna lay glistening on the deck.

I had never seen such a beautiful fish from the sea. I had never
witnessed such a fight. It was a world of dreams. I rushed to the fish
and ran my hands all over it, feeling its life slipping away, marveling
at the compactness, the perfect fit of everything that was that great
fish: the long, tapering pectoral and anal fins, the small, rubbery
finlets along the edges of its caudal peduncle, the stiff tail, the huge
eyes, the steely cheeks and sides, the set of the mouth.

The fish lay there on the deck, cold, pure, shimmering . . . a perfect
jewel. Then Greg came to the fish with a knife, made a cut, and bled
the fish on the deck. This fish was a treasure in many ways. It was
important to bleed it, then get it cooling on ice as quickly as possible.

We put out our baits again and forged ahead in pursuit of more
great fish. We'd tasted first blood, and with that taste all of our hearts
had quickened. We were transformed into warriors and were eager
for the sting of battle. And it wasn't long coming.

Two rods began to sing and there was a rush to take them. I
took one. Scott took the other. Greg and Jim strapped the fighting
harnesses on us and secured the reels to them. The fish ripped line

from our reels as if there was no drag at all. Mine simply would not stop. It just kept going and going and going. I pulled back as hard as I could and the fish pulled harder. I lost track of what Scott was doing. I was focused on the freight train that had itself hooked to every fiber of my being. I momentarily thought about how much line I had out. That, I quickly realized, did absolutely nothing to help me deal with the present tense. And, indeed, the present tense was all that mattered.

Somewhere out there in the sea a big fish was connected to my life and spirit. There was the sea, the fish, and me. That was the entire world. Our lives were joined inextricably. I could "see" the fish in visions from my oversoul as I held onto that rod and turned the handle of the reel: a silver-blue bullet down there in the shadowy world of the deep, pulling ever downward, using its incredible muscles and fins to put power into its dives. It did not want to go where line was pulling it. It wanted only to go any other direction. And, for a while, it did exactly that. It was absolutely in charge of the entire affair.

But fishermen have learned how to kill a fish like that. Just never, ever, take pressure from it. Let the rod kill the fish. Wear it out until its immortal soul succumbs to mortal reality, lactic acid builds, oxygen sags, and muscles finally tire to the point of exhaustion. It will happen, if the gear holds, but it can take time . . . a lot of time for very big, very strong fish in the sea.

If the fisherman tires first and gives a little slack in the line, the fish can bolt and snap the line. A steady pull doesn't typically break line. But the quick bolt on a slack line can do it. So it is mostly a matter of whose heart tires first, who can go the distance, who best transcends pain and exhaustion and prevails, who can keep sustained pressure in the contest.

A fifty-pound fish in the water is much stronger than a two-hundred-pound man on land. The fish has a greater proportion of its body invested in muscle. Subsequently, killing a great fish is more a matter of spirit, ultimately, than anything else. There must be transcendence to win the battle. But the fish has spirit also. Always remember that, and respect that. The fish's spiritual energy is at least as strong as its physical energy. Collectively, the synergism transcends the sum of the energies. Good fishermen, those experienced in such matters, know that the same is true for them. You must have both. One dimension of energy is just not enough to kill a big fish. And it is more than desire . . . it is life itself.

It was with this focus on life that I held fast to my fish. I reached deep into my reserves of energy, focused hard, and lived absolutely in the present tense. I knew that the fish was doing the same thing. I knew that if it could, it would pull me into the sea and send me to my doom. My only advantage was that I was in a boat, not out there in the water. If by some misfortune I were to become entangled in my fishing line and gear and pulled overboard, the fish would win. And if I were able to bring the fish to the surface and alongside the boat, I would win. The boat, along with my ability to stay onboard, was the only thing that tipped the odds into my favor. The boat was the only way that I could be there and live. It was the only thing that made it possible for me to win the battle.

And so I spread my legs just a little for balance, bent my knees, held the rod firmly, and pulled with my back and shoulders. I'd pull back; then, as I moved forward to cock myself for another pull, I'd quickly reel in as much line as I could, keeping constant pressure on the fish. Again and again, I moved forward and pulled back . . . moved forward and pulled back. Slowly the line began to return to the spool of the reel. Slowly the angle of the line sharpened. I lost all concept of time. It didn't matter. I had no more feeling in my arms, but they still worked for me. They held that rod and worked that reel. My back and shoulders kept their cadenced flow, back and forth, back and forth.

I was thankful for being a lifeguard who, although elderly, still had the lungs and shoulders and legs and arms that work for me when I need them. I was thankful also for the focus and ability to transcend fatigue and pain that half a century of lifeguarding had etched into my mind. I was tired, certainly, but in a rhythm . . . a rhythm of life. There was no giving up. Just as in a lifesaving rescue, you don't quit. I could feel my heart pumping strongly, in perfect synchrony with muscles, mind, and spirit. I have never felt more alive than during those precious moments that folded over themselves as I did battle with that fish. Alpha and Omega became one.

From the corner of my eyes I saw Greg move forward with the gaff. Then there was the silver-blue flash, the thrust of the gaff, the spray of water, and the great fish was on the deck. I was transfixed by its beauty and by the beauty of all that surrounded me: the sea, the boat, the wonderful skipper and crew, the fellow anglers who slapped me on the back and congratulated me.

Steve, smiling, handed me a cold beer. "Flushed the system did you?!" All I could do was take a deep breath, suck on the beer, and grin. His eyes were sparkling. He knew, absolutely, the power of his prescription, shared from one lifeguard to another.

Old Trucks Keep Us Connected

THE OLD TRUCK DIED ON A SUNDAY AFTERNOON. JUST PRIOR TO death, all the warning lights indicated that catastrophic failure was imminent. The odometer gently reminded me that we'd shared over 181,000 miles together during the past ten years. I'd had to abandon my old friend out on my pond's levee and hitch a ride with my son who was fishing out there. That evening, heartsick, and looking closely at financial records and calculations, I began the thought processes that I knew would very likely lead to the purchase of a new truck. It was, to say the least, not a pleasant thing to think about. But an outdoorsman needs a truck.

Yet there was something about the way the old truck had died that just didn't seem right. Yes, all the warning lights were on: brakes, engine, tires. But I had practically new tires and brand new brakes. Plus, the engine warning light had been intermittent . . . very likely a loose connection somewhere. Prior to that Sunday afternoon, when I'd cranked the engine, it had always purred beautifully. I'd also been religious to the extreme with regard to oil changes, tune ups, and peripheral issues. I did not want another truck. The one I had suited me just fine.

I have a good friend, Mickey Hayes, who has been a trusted mechanic working with my vehicles for thirty years. I have other good friends at a tire shop: Paul and Kathy Wells, Terry Blair, Mitch McKinney, and Tom Cornelius, who have always made sure that I have the best tires possible and that they are kept in good, safe, working order through tread checks, wheel alignments, and rotations. When Mickey and the tire shop team tell me that my truck is road worthy and ready to go, I forge ahead, out into the world, regardless of what computer-generated warning lights are screaming to me. All of them had recently told me that the warning lights could be reset, but that doing so would cost a lot of money, that the truck was safe—drive it. And so I did, until it died on the farm. It wouldn't start. In fact, the starter would jam and not turn off until I completely switched off the key. It was a horrible sound . . . a horrible situation. I began to mourn the loss of my old truck, my old friend.

Early the next morning, before breakfast, I drove my wife's car to Mickey's garage and left a message with his partner, Scott Singleton, about the truck. Then I began making plans to have the truck towed back into town. I'd hardly gotten home before my phone rang. It was Mickey.

"I'm on my way to your farm. Meet me at your gate and we'll take a look at what's going on with your truck."

It is about ten miles from Mickey's garage to my farm. I'd never even considered the possibility that he'd come out to my farm. Rather, I figured I'd need to get a tow truck to haul my truck back into town. Mondays are busy days for small businesses. My intentions that morning were simply to run a flag up the pole to let Mickey know that I'd be bringing the truck to him. I was overwhelmed by his response.

I snatched a quick breakfast, grabbed a cup of coffee, and drove my wife's car out to the farm. Mickey and I got to the gate of my farm at about the same time. After greetings and a few comments about weather and the upcoming dove season (necessary southern formalities), we took Mickey's truck out across the pasture to where my truck was parked. He cranked the engine a little, then opened the hood, dug out his pocket knife and removed a fuse—the one to my fuel pump. He showed me the fuse. It was burned to a crisp. Then he pried out another fuse with his knife, the one to my trailer hitch, and put it into the slot for the fuel pump fuse. The truck immediately started when I turned the key.

In less than two minutes Mickey had breathed life back into the truck.

"Don, how many miles are on your truck?"

"One hundred and eighty-one thousand."

"I think you're good for another one hundred thousand miles."

"Mickey, are you in a hurry? I'd love to show you around my farm."

"I'm in no hurry at all. Show me your place."

And so, for the next two hours, we drove and stopped to look at things and talked and shared a beautiful late summer morning in east central Mississippi. We talked about land and friends and family and getting older . . . about hunting and fishing and rambling around. We talked about faith and what seemed to be the state of America. We took our time. We fed the bluegill in my pond, and I invited him to bring his little granddaughter out fishing for them. That made him happy and he said he'd do that.

Then I told him I'd drive over to his garage later in the morning to settle up on the repair bill. He told me I didn't owe him anything. He was just being a friend. Getting to spend a morning together on the farm was enough.

The day after Mickey's rescue I got restless. I needed a road trip. I wanted to prowl the South. The perfect trip for that old truck and me, to celebrate its resurrection, would be to make the six-hundred-mile round trip journey all the way across Mississippi and halfway across Arkansas to my "man cave" over in North Little Rock. The two of us, my truck and me, would invite my dog Hank to tag along. Hank loves a road trip. And he loves the man cave. There are lots of dead things with fur, feathers, and scales hanging on the walls.

My man cave is actually a very nice house in a nice neighborhood, the same neighborhood of my youth. I'd had the house for over nine years. It was a gift from an elderly couple who became my adopted aunt and uncle back when I was a kid. They had no children of their own. They'd opened their home and their hearts to me back then. For over fifty years they filled my life with friendship and wonderful counsel. As an adult I took care of them until the very end of their lives. We shared good times. I learned how to deer hunt, shoot guns, fish, and drive a boat with my "Uncle" Al. He was in the stand with me when I shot my first deer, a little spike buck down near Dumas, Arkansas. "Aunt" Frances became increasingly dear to me across the years. After Al died, and for the next ten years, until she also passed away, we took road trips and went to plays, movies, parties, and even dances together. She ultimately moved to Mississippi, into my home, for her final days.

Over the years that old house in Arkansas has assumed characteristics that reflect who I am. There's a piano, fine furniture and art, many of my books, some outdoor gear, an old boat, a canoe, and a quiet place to write. It has a dining room and three bedrooms. It is a house where I can entertain and provide lodging for guests. It has a covered back porch where I can grill outdoors and lots of wall space where I've hung antlers, heads, skins, and fish. Memories are thick in that house. It is my refuge and my sanctuary. It also is a launching platform for my ventures to the Arkansas hills, streams, and duck hunting lands. I have old friends who live in the area. I come to the house to reconnect . . . in multiple dimensions.

A few years ago, however, it dawned on me that as much as I love being in the house and letting it be my writer's haven and the hub of a wheel from which I radiate, the journeys between Mississippi and Arkansas are every bit as precious to me as actually being in the man cave. If I'm in a hurry, I can make the journey in less than five hours by way of major interstate highways. In fact, if it is very early in the morning, when traffic is light, I can make the trip in four and a half hours on these highways. Generally, however, these high-speed highways have too much traffic, including seemingly unending lines of huge trucks, especially between Memphis and Little Rock. When I use these highways, I arrive at my destination exhausted, rattled, and anxious to the extreme. It takes at least one day to fully recover. These high-intensity drives offer little if any opportunity to actually pay attention to the countryside. The driving requires absolute focus—focus to the extreme. The travel is fast, noisy, congested, and dangerous. After several years of these battles, I finally decided that there was no good reason to use these highways. So I changed my routes and my entire mental framework for the trips. The new logistics have been wonderful.

The old truck seemed to understand that adventure was in the wind. It caught the spirit of the trip. When we pulled out of Starkville, Mississippi, it voluntarily shut off the check-engine light . . . all by itself. The entire truck seemed to be tighter. Old rattles evaporated. The brakes were high on the pedal and tight and sure on the receiving end. The engine ran smoothly. The tires hummed beautifully on pavement made wet by the rain from a tropical storm that was sweeping across my little corner of Mississippi. The traction was superb. I smiled with deep satisfaction, both with regard to the truck and the rain. It was a much-welcomed rain, one that would help the wheat I'd recently planted for the deer, a rain that would freshen my ponds. The added water in the ponds would be the critical water I'd need when duck season rolled around later during fall.

Hank was curled on the seat beside me. He is a good traveler. When we travel together he sleeps a lot and also seems to have some internal timer. He knows how long it is between our rest stops. We have special places scattered along the way where he can get out, stretch his legs, and "get comfortable" again. They're secluded little spots, seemingly made just for the needs of an elderly dog and an elderly man. They typically are where we can watch ducks and geese during winter and herons and egrets during spring and summer and shake muscadine vines during fall. The roads are lightly traveled.

Onward we forged across the Mississippi hills. After about twenty-five miles, my first crossroads decision came into view. I took the road less traveled, plunging deeply into the rugged countryside north of Eupora, through little communities where timber operations and small farms (hill cotton, soybeans, corn, and cattle) and isolated homes melt into a background of forests and creek bottoms. The road was a familiar one with a gentle wildness to it. It had been my standard route to the rivers in western Mississippi back when I was a fisheries professor at Mississippi State University. I knew very well the unmarked cutoff roads and the little communities. I knew their stories also. I knew, for example, that in a tiny little crossroads community named Bellefontaine, there was a leather shop that made the saddles for British royalty. Farther up the road I passed another cutoff, one that leads to the upper reaches of Grenada Lake, to the mud flats where teal swarm in September. I'd followed that little road for miles one season, not with a map but with dead reckoning, believing that eventually it would run into the lake, which it did. Where the road ended there was a primitive gravel "boat ramp."

These were federal lands and so they were public. The ramp was therefore, at least in my opinion, public. About a half an hour boat ride from that ramp was the gosh awfullest, most beautiful mud flat you ever saw in your life. Across it was a patchwork of wetland vegetation with occasional clumps of willow trees where a hunter could hide. Two weeks later, while hunting that mud flat with a couple of friends, we "wore out" the teal. It was, and probably still is, a magic place.

Twisting and turning, the truck seemed to remember the roads. It was almost as if it was on automatic pilot, which, in a way, was true. I never gave the route a second thought. It was firmly etched in my memory. The three of us, Hank, the truck, and me, flowed, climbed, and dipped through the misty hills, sometimes driving through dark tunnels where the forest threw branches over the road. I had the truck's lights turned on because of the rain, but even had it not been raining, I'd have had to turn them on to get through those dark forest tunnels. I felt like I was moving through some mystical land. On reflection, I think I was.

It is a land where time seems to have stopped. Old ways persist. People live close to the earth. They move at a pace in keeping with that of the earth, governed more by weather and seasons and hours of sunlight than by clocks. The homes are old. The barns are old. The tractors and implements are old. The land itself is old. The abandoned cotton gins whisper messages from long ago.

But the spirit is fresh. The gardens and pastures are lush. The cattle are in good condition. The deer alongside the road are sleek and healthy looking. The wild turkeys, the raccoons, the opossums, the crows, the foxes, the hawks, and other wild critters are abundant and seemingly thriving. The churches are neat. The churchyards and cemeteries are well kept.

Eventually, I came to the city of Grenada. I reflected on past times. Grenada is a lovely little city with a dark past. Terrible things happened there and in the surrounding area during the 1900s, during times of violent racial strife. Although some of those old echoes still reverberate in the city and surrounding hills, they are, thankfully, fading away. It is a good place now—a safe place now—for everybody. I worked with the fisheries on the nearby lake and river for most of my career. During our days and nights there, my students and I encountered a lot of people from all walks of life, from all social groups, including one person who was very dead in the river. We summoned the sheriff and brought him by boat to the body. We never learned the cause of death. He'd been in the water a very long time.

Once past Grenada I came to another junction. I crossed Interstate 55, the highway that links Jackson and Memphis, and just kept going. The road I was on would take me ever deeper into the country and into the haunts of my past, to and through the little town of Holcomb.

Once upon a time in the 1980s, Miss Teenage America came from Holcomb. When asked by one of the judges what her favorite activity was, she replied, "Hand grabbing flathead catfish from the Yalobusha River." I guess you have to be from the South to fully appreciate the depth and magnitude of her response.

Access to that river via a public ramp is only a couple of miles down the road from Holcomb. I drove my truck down the short gravel road to the parking area at the head of the ramp. Memories flooded me. Letting Hank out to stretch his legs, I drifted along the ramp, down to the water's edge. The river was high and in excellent shape. The water was beautiful, almost clear, with a green cast to it. "Clear," however, is a relative term in Mississippi when referencing river water. If you can stick your hand into the water up to your elbow and see your fingers, the water is clear.

I'd launched boats from that ramp hundreds of times during the thirty years that I conducted fisheries research. I've set literally thousands of hoop nets in that river and caught tens of thousands of fish . . . catfishes of all sorts, buffaloes, gars, suckers, sunfishes, paddlefish, and a variety of less common fishes. I knew the river's moods. I knew the people who prowled it. And I knew and engaged the politics.

My students and I worked hard to get the messages of river stewardship out into the public, with science as our foundation. Although challenges still exist, progress was made. Thinking about those years and what we were able to do for the rivers and the people connected to them made me smile as I stood there on the ramp, looking out across the old Yalobusha River. They were good memories. Those were good years. The Yalobusha River wasn't the only one. I loved them all.

Pulling back onto the highway, I left the river and the hills behind me and headed out across the Delta. This is the alluvial plain of the Mississippi River. The soil is rich and deep. If you spit on the ground you will clone yourself. This is the land of huge farms of rice, soybeans, cotton, and corn. It is the land of fabulous wealth and extreme poverty. It is the land of hardwood forests, sloughs, swamps, muddy streams, backwaters, oxbow lakes, brakes, and hunting camps. It is the land of big deer, crappie fishing, and incredible duck hunting. Faith and culture are deep and profound. The music is everywhere. The Delta has its own. History flows as a current across this land and through the hearts of its people . . . memories endure, across generations.

You're not "from" the Delta unless you have family roots here that go back at least 150 years (or more). The same can be said for other parts of Mississippi as well. Although I've lived in east central Mississippi for over thirty years and my three children were all born in the same hospital in Starkville, Mississippi, all three of them are *from* Arkansas, *and so am I*. We're all (thankfully!) considered "Southerners," but still we're not *from* Mississippi. However, my Chinese Panamanian wife absolutely *is* from Mississippi—no questions asked. Figure that one out. But as I reflect more on this, it makes sense. The Chinese have been in Mississippi, and particularly in the Delta, for a very long time . . . for many generations. Their presence is unquestioned.

The old truck kept on humming along the road through the overflow areas of the Yalobusha River, past the Tallahatchie River, and onto Highway 49. There's a water tower there that's painted like a cotton boll. We turned north to and through Tutwiler, past the prison there that's alongside the road, and met the "Blues Highway" (Highway 61) at Clarksdale. All along the Blues Highway are turnoffs leading to cotton towns like Marks and Jonestown. I mention these two because I have kinfolks from Marks and once got more or less lost on Delta back roads and found myself in Jonestown. Before I retired, I'd go to Marks to access the Coldwater River for fisheries research. It is the most turbid river in Mississippi that I ever worked in and also the most productive in terms of fisheries. There's wealth in Marks, seemingly much more than in Jonestown. Jonestown is primarily an African American town, bright, colorful, and full of life and drama. I was and still am fascinated by the place. The colors and the vibrancy on the streets are etched into my mind. I think also you can still get a good hot tamale there.

The turnoff to Helena, Arkansas, is just beyond the cutoffs to Marks and Jonestown. The bridge crossing the Mississippi River is at Helena. The ten miles of road between the Blues Highway and the bridge is the roughest road of the journey. It is buckled, warped, torn up, and, as it is said locally, "wore out." But my old truck took it in stride, never missing a beat (or a bump).

In spite of the condition of this road, I've always liked this hop to the bridge. I feel the pull of the river. Once I finally come across the levee, into the batture lands, I can sense, comprehensively, the river's power. The land is sculpted by the ebb and flow of flooding. There are backwaters and potholes where water birds prowl, trying to catch trapped fish. Some of the higher ground within the batture is cleared for cultivation, and crops occasionally are planted. It is risky to plant there but apparently worth the risk.

The road is elevated and straight. I tend to look over to the sides more than I should. When I do this the truck weaves a little back and forth across the center line. Other vehicles are doing much the same. It is a sort of dance that all of us do. The river (including its overflow lands) is a captivating force that can pull you off the straight and narrow path . . . literally as well as euphemistically.

I've never been able to decide whether or not I'm in love with the river or scared out of my mind by it. Probably both. When I cross the high bridge over it at Helena, there's great temptation to look down at the river. It is like a siren calling. But you'd better not. It is an old bridge with questionable railing. It is a long fall to the water. If the fall doesn't kill you, the river surely will. Many a head has gone under . . .

Helena: it has been an outpost for civilization for a very long time, a sort of gateway to Arkansas, much as are Vicksburg and Natchez for Mississippi. The one thing that has attracted me to Helena across the years, and particularly back when I was a young man, is that there's a riverboat pilot's school there. There was a time when I was very seriously considering just two career paths: riverboat pilot on the Mississippi River and mail carrier in the Yukon Territories of Canada. I ended up with the consolation prize: university professor. I still think I'd have fit the other two careers better.

You can get a free cup of coffee at the Arkansas Welcome Center just as you get off the bridge. You really should do that, just to get your focus back and let the reality of the river find a proper place in your heart. But the better place (and better coffee) is back on the other side at the Mississippi Welcome Center, which is located where you turn off the Blues Highway onto the river road. As I mentioned before, that's ten miles away from the river. I guess the thought is that, if you're traveling from Arkansas, you've got ten miles to decide whether or not you really want to be in Mississippi. If you do, the coffee is good and the center has a good safe place for a dog to pee (big fenced-in area so the dog won't get run over by traffic). The security guard there served in the Marines during the Vietnam War. He's a wiry little man named Darrel Douglas, with lots of stories. It is worth drinking coffee with him to hear the stories.

During the war he would sometimes crawl into some pretty tight spots to avoid his nemesis, snipers. He no longer hunts or fishes. He's scared of snakes. Considering the other stuff he's done, I find that amazing. He talks about snakes just about every time I pass by. A word of warning is appropriate here. If you're heading *to* Arkansas, drink your coffee at the center, not while driving. The bumps on the road, and your swerving, will spill it all over you. Just drink your coffee and talk with Darrel for a while.

Once you get past Helena, the *West* is all before you. In reality, Arkansas is as far *West* as you can go in America. Beyond Arkansas, you start going *East* again, and you are all the way back *East* by the time you get to the Pacific Ocean. It isn't about geography. It is about mindset. Need I explain?

Arkansas is a beautiful but very strange state. I can talk about it because, remember, I'm *from* Arkansas. Arkansas does not step to the beat of a different drummer. Arkansas never heard the rhythm section at all! It is the only state with a diamond mine. It has rugged hills, fine rivers, good farmland, and good ranches. There's an affinity for fine art, rifles, and hogs. It is also the only state that is mentioned in the Bible: "Noah looked out of the *Arkansas* land." (There was an editorial misprint in the Bible, and the mistake, "ark and saw," was canonized and subsequently couldn't be changed—or so we were told by our Sunday school teachers.) I've always felt pretty good about the fact that I'm from a place that has long been recognized as pretty special. However, considering the text, it could have been that Noah was looking out thinking about leaving it. That's fine too. The fewer people that are in the state, the better.

I always feel like I'm coming home when I get back into Arkansas. People say it is just like Mississippi, but they're wrong. These two states have had a different history. There are certainly some common denominators fifty miles either side of the river, but other than that (and the historical connection to the Confederacy), things are different.

For one thing, being further north than most of Mississippi and further west than all of Mississippi, Arkansas has real seasons. Winter is real in Arkansas. Also, Arkansas has rocks, real rocks—*big* rocks. That does something to the human mind. Again, it is biblical. According to the Bible, things built on rocks are probably going to last longer. I like to stand on rocks. I like to climb on rocks. I like rocks in rivers. The water tends to be clearer in a rocky stream than in streams with sand, silt, and mud bottoms.

It has been said that there are more ducks shot before 9:00 a.m. every morning of the hunting season in Arkansas than are shot the *entire* season in Mississippi. Arkansas has elk and lots of bears. It also has more lakes and streams with smallmouth bass.

People in Arkansas seem to have retained a bit more of the old pioneer spirit and are seemingly a bit more independent in their thinking than is typically the case in Mississippi. And they're not quite as reserved. Subsequently, it is, politically, a "purple" state. Mississippi is bright "red." The Libertarian party is very strong in Arkansas. That in itself is revealing. Most folks in Arkansas simply want to be left alone. I understand.

But Mississippi has saltwater fishing and more writers, poets, and artists. Mississippi also has more hurricanes and, strangely, more Native Americans. While Arkansas has more hills, Mississippi has more forests. Mississippi also has the very last physically unmodified large river system left in the forty-eight contiguous states, the Pascagoula River in southeast Mississippi. It is a national treasure just like Arkansas's Buffalo River, the nation's one and only national river: Buffalo River National Park. Arkansas has more people, and especially more from "up North," particularly in the Ozarks. It has always been that way. A southern accent in some north Arkansas communities is rare music. People from up North are generally terrified by the prospect of living in Mississippi . . . until, of course, they've been in the state for a while. I do not discourage that mindset. Nor do the "immigrants." Just like folks in Arkansas, folks in Mississippi quickly understand the treasures and figure there's probably enough people in the state already. Frankly, I'd rather hunt deer with a rifle than with a shotgun. Ditto for squirrel hunting. Crowds preclude rifles.

I like being from both places. I like going back and forth. I like being a Mississippi writer who does most of his writing in his "man cave" over in Arkansas. I enjoy being a native-born Arkansan with deep family roots and history in that state and a belief (no doubt fantasy) that, because of this, I might be able to run for office in Arkansas and possibly even get elected. I particularly like the reality that "law and order" is more of a *suggestion* in Mississippi than in Arkansas. It tends to be open for discussion. It is tighter in Arkansas.

Mostly, I'm thinking about hunting and fishing in this regard. Maybe it is just because Mississippi is where I now do most of my hunting and fishing and I've just gotten accustomed to the Mississippi framework. And even though I'm not *from* Mississippi, I'm now better known in Mississippi than in Arkansas, at least in my part of the state, and pretty much left alone, on my own land at least. I abide by the rules, but the rules seem reasonable. The rules seem stricter and more complex in Arkansas. When I'm in Arkansas, I have to think about them more . . . a whole lot more.

My truck kept on truckin' through the town of Marvell (where the local police give no tolerance at all regarding speeding). I crept through town. The policeman waved at me. He knows my truck. I'm on this road a lot. I waved back. The speed limit is still 45 mph far out of town. You may think you're through town when you make a big sweeping curve to the right (and you are), but unless you know about the extended zone and act accordingly, the Marvell police will nab you! The sign, by the way, is usually at least halfway covered by vines. Be aware that the Marvell police have a good hiding place not far from the local fish market (it is on the right side of the road going out of town). The market sells buffalo fish as well as catfish. You might as well stop and see what's for sale. Some of the fish are very nice.

Just past Marvell, as I was looking at some recently harvested rice fields and thinking about the duck and goose season on the not too distant horizon, my sister from Iowa called me on my cell phone.

There was no real reason for the call, which is the best kind of call to get. It lasted over forty minutes and took me to and through the town of Clarendon (where, as a Boy Scout, I'd launched a raft once with some buddies and floated fifty miles downstream to St. Charles), across the new bridge over the White River, across the National Wildlife Refuge (where once upon a time I trapped black bears . . . one night capturing six of them!), past the next dog pee spot (and winter snow geese observation post) on the way to Des Arc, and almost to Des Arc itself . . . where Miss Lena sells slices of pie and you can get the best barbeque in the state at Craig's Cafe, which is just after the "communist" house with the big red star on the front and before the minnow farm on the road to Hazen.

I noticed that the check-engine light came back on as the phone call ended. Actually, I think it had been on for a while, but I just decided to pay attention to it after the call. Hazen was eight miles down the road. I figured I could get a fuel pump fuse in Hazen. Between Des Arc and Hazen there's remnant tall grass prairie growing on both sides of the road in certified "natural areas." Arkansas cares about stuff like that. It is something very special to see. My old scoutmaster, Ralph Crowly, and his wife, Ella Rae, are buried in Hazen. I normally stop and say "Hi" when I pass through, but this time I drove straight on, through town and beyond, looking for a place to buy that fuel pump fuse. However, the hardware store in Hazen was closed, empty, and for sale.

So I pushed on to the town of Carlisle, nine miles away. There's an auto parts store there. One man worked at the store. He was well over fifty years old and wore sandals and shorts. Nobody was in a hurry to get anything done. He was enjoying using a magnet to fish out tiny fuses from a tray. I have no idea what those fuses were for. The man wanting them was huddled over the countertop, trying to figure out what he really needed. He couldn't decide so just took several different kinds. There were two younger men, in their twenties, who were asking each other if they still were driving their old trucks. Both said, "Yes." That made me feel good. So was I. They bought some kind of electrical thing and left.

Finally, after twenty minutes of waiting, it was my turn. All I wanted was a 20-amp low-profile fuse. The man in the store led me into another part of the store and showed me a packet of assorted fuses. I told him that's not what I wanted, even though there was one 20-amp fuse in the packet. He asked if I'd like a box of 20-amp fuses. I asked how many fuses there are in a box and he said, "Five." So I bought the box for seven dollars and went out into the parking lot. Hank had his head stuck out the window of the truck and I was proud about that. An old Ford truck with mud on the sides and a hunting dog in the cab (even though there's a dog box in the bed of the truck) is a nice thing to have when you're a stranger in a little Arkansas town. Hank is aware of proper form.

Then the truck decided it had a new lease on life and the check-engine light went back off. It did not need a new fuse. We made the nine miles on to Lonoke in good order, and I cut way down on my speed. Lonoke is close enough to Little Rock that it has a commuter culture. It is about four times bigger than most of the rest of the little towns along the road (over four thousand folks), has government buildings for things like extension services, a fish disease laboratory, and such, and has a city park, a fine school, a walking path on an old railroad bed, and some housing developments with very nice homes. There is money in Lonoke. The local police enjoy the commuter culture, the new housing areas, and the money that's in town. They also like out-of-state license plates. I kept my speed five miles below the limit and was careful not to go through yellow lights.

I eased on through town, then swung around the Joe Hogan State Fish Hatchery. When I was a college student back in the 1970s, I worked one summer at that hatchery. I loved the work, hauling seines through the ponds, driving a tractor, mowing the levees, occasionally getting to go out on a fish-stocking trip, and getting the best suntan of my life. I remembered the ponds, and images of people flashed across my mind. Good folks. A good time. I learned how to eat crawfish there. That's a handy thing to know when you live in Mississippi.

Just past the fish hatchery is Anderson's Minnow Farm, the largest minnow farm in the world. When I was in high school, I hunted ducks on the ponds there, mostly divers like scaup—we called them "bluebills." But now there are signs everywhere saying the place is absolutely posted and no hunting is allowed. I understand, but still, it was (and could be today) a magic place for a high school boy learning about duck hunting.

When I got past the minnow farm, I saw a pickup truck pulled over onto a side road. There was a man sprawled out on the ground behind the truck, all by himself, face down. I immediately pushed my internal alarm button. He looked very sick or perhaps dead. Suspecting a heart attack, I quickly found a turn-around spot and went back to the man. Indeed, he was in serious trouble, but now was standing up and shaking.

The first thing I asked was if he had a health issue and if it was his heart. He said, "No, not my heart. But I'm old, tired, hot, and seriously diabetic. I've been working alone out here on the side of the road for over an hour trying to change a tire on my truck. Nobody would stop to help me. I forgot my cell phone. Left it at home. Can I use yours to call for help?"

I told him that "help" was already here. He couldn't thank me enough and said he was so weak now and so exhausted that he might not be much help, but he'd try. I told him just to go sit down and I'd change that tire.

It was not an easy job. The spare tire was attached by a cable fixture under the truck that was different than anything I'd ever seen or worked with. After almost an hour, I finally was able to get it free and then put it on the truck. But, during the hour, Paul Caraway and I had a marvelous conversation. I was rolling around in the dirt, dust, and gravel, working with those tires and jacks and lug nuts, and all the while we were talking about bird dogs, quail, doves, and quarter horses. I was glad to be able to help Paul, and I thoroughly enjoyed our conversation. In the end, he forced a twenty-dollar bill into my hand in spite of my protests, telling me to have a fine dinner with it. I went to my truck and got a fresh copy of my most recent book, *Deeper Currents*, that I'd brought with me, personalized it, signed it, and gave it to him. We both got back into our trucks, honked our horns, and were on our way.

My truck seemed happy. The engine light was still off. Hank was happy. I was happy. Even the road seemed happy. The sky looked nice. There were billowy clouds. There were farmers on combines harvesting rice from the fields next to the road. Then there was a stretch of road I've always enjoyed. The trees form a canopy across the road, making a tunnel just like the one back in the hills east of Grenada, Mississippi, that I'd driven through that morning.

When I thought about that . . . and about being back in those Mississippi hills, I looked at the clock in my truck. It was after 3:00 p.m. I'd been on the road nearly eight hours! That is nearly double the time it would have taken me had I used the interstate highways. But I wouldn't have traded a single minute of my back roads journey for the fast trip.

Around a bend the road dipped almost to water level alongside Faulkner Lake. The lake was gorgeous. Huge cypress trees grew out through it. In the shallow spots there were all sorts of aquatic plants. Some distance from the road I could see duck hunting blinds. When I was in high school, I'd come to the lake on spring nights to go frog gigging. Those were magic hunts, full of mystery, full of adventure, full of comradeship, full of spirit. I don't hunt frogs anymore, but the memories are with me for a lifetime.

Then we came to the final section of the trip. It required merging back into the traffic, back onto the major highway, but just for about five miles. I "goosed" the old truck as we came off the ramp, got up to interstate highway speed, and we entered the insane flow. Everybody was jockeying for position, weaving in and out of the traffic lanes. Huge trucks roared past us. We were back into the maelstrom, for about ten minutes. When I finally exited that highway on the ramp that led to the neighborhood of my man cave, I said a prayer of thanksgiving . . . for safely delivering me through those final five miles. A couple of minutes later I pulled into the driveway of my man cave. I parked the truck but kept the engine running. I needed a few moments of reflection.

As my heart and my mind swirled in those reflections, I realized that I couldn't have asked for a better day or a better trip. The old truck was happy. The motor purred with a wonderful, smooth cadence. The engine light was still off. The tires and alignments had made driving the truck on those old back roads a dream.

My thoughts ran deeper. There was no question about it. An old pickup truck, a few back roads, a sprinkling of characters along the way, a flow of memories, and a good dog in the cab beside me . . . all had all blended together to form a wonderful gift for the man *from* Arkansas. But I realized that there was an even greater gift, the gift of men like Mickey Hayes and his partner, Scott Singleton, in their garage (and beyond); and the tire shop team, Paul and Kathy Wells, Terry Blair, Mitch McKinney, and Tom Cornelius, who, quietly and without fanfare, keep old pickup trucks (and restless men) on the highways—and, in so doing, they help keep the South connected to its roots. Be sure to include them in your prayers.

The Echoes Linger

FROST CAME LATE TO NORTHEAST MISSISSIPPI. THERE'D BEEN A slight dusting of it during the last week of October, mostly in low spots and on old scraps of hay left in the fields. But that had only been a teaser. Now it was mid-November and, finally, for two nights in a row, there'd been good hard frost, a "meat-hanging" frost, a "hog-killing" frost. It felt good to feel the sparkle in my blood at sunrise, to breathe deeply in the chilled air, to be wrapped in the stillness of a cold southern morning, with geese calling overhead, squirrels barking, and jays scolding each other.

I walked down to my shed as the first rays of sunlight filled my backyard with sparkles. Opening the door to the shed, I could see the deer hanging in the shadows, skinned and ready for processing. It was a big doe by Mississippi standards. I'd estimated its live weight at between 130 and 140 pounds. More typically they run somewhere around 100 pounds, give or take 5 or 10 pounds.

She was the perfect deer . . . exactly what I'd hoped for. She'd been hanging in the shed during those two wonderful frosty nights. Now, today, I'd "make meat," working with my wife in a ritual we've perfected during three decades of marriage. When our children were still home, it was a family ritual, like going out to cut a cedar Christmas tree on our little farm. But now it was just the two of us, full of memories, blessed again with venison taken from our own land. Reflections were deep, very, very deep. The processing of venison on our kitchen table is sacramental.

The deer season was already six weeks old before I could hunt. Weather was the critical factor. I love the quiet beauty of an arrow in flight, its hushed swish followed by the "click-click" as a broadhead cuts through ribs. Then comes the heavy sound as the deer goes to ground, out of sight but not far, and the profound stillness that envelopes me, that penetrates into my heart, as I pick up the blood trail and follow it to where the deer has settled into its final resting place.

But it was not to be this year. It was much too warm to kill a deer during those first weeks of the season. I cannot, I will not, kill a deer in warm weather. I have only my shed to hang meat in and so do not hunt deer unless nights are at least in the forties and preferably in the mid-thirties. Venison is precious. And if by chance I cannot find a deer for a while following my shot, I do not want it to ruin in the heat while I work out the blood trail. I've shot at seventy-six deer in the past fifty-four years (I'm sixty-six years old) and have recovered seventy-three of them. So there was no archery season for me this year . . . and I missed it, terribly.

Next up was the two-week-long primitive weapon season for antlerless deer. The regular gun season would follow, but by then I hoped to have transitioned to quail and ducks. Plus, I would have two of my three children home for the Thanksgiving holidays, the opening week of regular gun season. I didn't want to be out in the woods during the week or so prior to their arrival. Rather, I wanted the woods to settle down and become very quiet and undisturbed.

I'm a retired university professor who no longer wears a watch and who occasionally forgets what day of the week it is. But my children all have their noses to the grindstone in their chosen professions. One son is a landscape architect, one son is an Air Force pilot, and my daughter is a US Peace Corps volunteer. They depend on me to groom our land, so they can come when their schedules allow and reconnect with the rhythms of the hunt, the rhythms of the earth. And that is my highest priority. So, in reality, the first week of the primitive weapon season would be *my* deer season. I had watched the weather, hoping for a front and a high-pressure system that would drop the temperatures.

I reached out and touched the meat hanging in the shed. The cool, dry crust felt good. It was what I'd hoped for. The stiffness of the carcass told me that the meat would be firm as I cut and trimmed. What I had before me was treasure. Sometimes, when the sun and moon and stars align themselves correctly, a bit of stardust settles on a hunter's bounty. It certainly had done so with this doe in the shed.

The deer's hide, with head still attached, lay on the floor of the shed. She had been a mature doe but still in her prime. She had the long nose of an older deer and one of her ears had a ragged spot that made me think that she'd ripped it in flight, or perhaps in defense of one of her fawns. There'd been no fawn with her when I saw her, so I think she was an experienced mother, a doe that had been bred early during the previous rut. I do not shoot does that have fawns with them. I am aware of studies reporting that fawns orphaned in late autumn have good survival. But I do not sleep well if I've killed a doe with fawns, even though those fawns may be nearly as large as "Mama." I think too much about a lonely fawn its first night alone. I am simply not going to be part of that experience.

Yes, she was beautiful in life. She was beautiful as I walked up to her after the shot. She was beautiful as I lifted her head off the ground and felt the warmth of her body. She was beautiful in the bed of my old pickup truck. She was beautiful in my shed. She was beautiful etched in my memories and in my heart. I reached out to her as she hung there from the shed's rafter. I patted her gently, again feeling the wonderful chill of the meat . . . thanking her for coming into my life and giving life to me and to those I love.

Carefully I untied the ropes that bound her to the rafter and, with reverence, carried her across the frosty lawn, up the hill to my patio, where I had a table ready. The journey could not have been more reverent had it been through a cathedral with a boys' choir singing hymns of adoration . . . blessed mother, beautiful doe, giver of life, fanner of flames in a hunter's heart, bridge to the eternal flow of energies in a created world full of spirit.

The knives were ready. I began making the cuts, slowly, deliberately, cautiously. Across the decades, with so many deer, the cuts have been perfected. I believe that we should take that which is our due as hunters but that we should leave some on the bones for other denizens of the wild. It is only fair. They only have tooth, claw, talons, and beak. They do not have the bow or the rifle. And so, I make sure that I share . . . just a little. When there's a question during trimming, I defer to the others in my community who live with me on that land. They get their share. The bones and joints always have a little meat still attached. And, on my land, there's a special place where I take these offerings. Typically, my offerings are gone within hours of giving them. But do I actually "give"? That's probably not the best word for it. "Return" is probably better. It is like a tithe. The coyotes, the foxes, the raccoons, the opossums, the skunks, the mice, the birds of all sorts, come to the tithe and share the bounty of the kill. I would not have it any other way.

First, I removed the shoulders and set them aside. Then I cut away the strap from along one side of the back and placed it in a pan. Then, I cut away the strap from the other side. And I heard whispers. I paused in reflection. I was there again . . .

There she is, in the shadows, waiting, cautious, then quietly moving with grace, stepping out. I am engulfed by the moment of magic and this deer that is blended with so many that have come before her. But always the one in front of me is special beyond imagining. There she is, alert, now looking at me . . . I dare not breathe.

I cut down through the hindquarter, searching for the ball joint, deeper and deeper through the meat, carefully making sure that the cut was clean all the way around the quarter. Then it was free. I paused . . .

The rifle comes up, slowly. The doe puts her head down to graze. There is the soft click of the rifle's hammer as it cocks. The doe does not move.

The second quarter got the same cut, careful and precise. I worked the knife slowly, with focus, and then, realizing that the knife had lost its edge, I laid it aside and took a fresh knife. When I completed the cut, I looked out across my backyard, into the shadows . . .

The rifle's sight settles on the doe, just behind the crook of her foreleg. There is deep breathing. Time stands still.

Then come the ribs. Some don't bother to work with ribs, but I've learned that rib meat from deer is the best of the best. So I sliced between the bones, cutting out the meat between them; then, after all the spaces had been emptied, I went back to trim that which was still on top of each rib. Collectively, this made a triple handful of boneless rib meat, about three pounds that you cannot eat—eating is too slow a process. Rather, you *inhale* it when it is cooked as it should be, slowly and with a sauce having ingredients I refuse to share. A hawk cried overhead. I looked up through the clear sky, searching for it . . .

I take one more breath, let it out, take another, and let half of it out—then the squeeze, steady, smooth, knowing when the trigger will pass its sear. The moment of no return. The blast of the rifle fills the quiet of the woods. The doe is on the ground, then tries to get up, kicks, tries again, falls, and lays still . . . a moment later another kick. That is the last one.

I took another deep breath. The sun was melting the morning frost. The air was sweet and rich in the dampness. Squirrels were ravaging my wife's bird feeders. Blue jays were scolding the squirrels. The jays would clean meat scraps from my patio after I left. Then came the neck meat, tenderloins, and big scraps along the bones— but I reminded myself to leave some for the critters out yonder . . .

I climb out of the tree stand and reload my rifle. I've had "dead deer" get up in front of me and try to run away. But this doe is down for keeps. Slowly I advance, rifle ready. Her eyes are open, unblinking. There is no breathing. She has given herself to me. I shed a tear. I always do.

The work was finished. Had it really been three hours? All of the meat was in pans, and the pans were in the ice chest where the afternoon wasps and flies couldn't get to it. I was full of deep satisfaction for doing it right, honoring the deer with every cut.

It was time for lunch. My wife was calling. She asked, "When will we wrap?" I told her that we'd do it after lunch, after I'd taken a short nap. At 1:30 I woke up and told my wife I was taking the bones and scraps to the farm. Then, when I got back, we could start wrapping. I went to my truck, started the engine, and backed out onto the road beside my house. The forest was calling my name, reminding me that the bones and scraps needed to come home and that my neighbors who share that farm with me were anxiously waiting for my return. I shifted into drive and passed through a wrinkle in time . . .

I make the journey across the pasture to get my truck as the sun hits the top branches of the trees along the western boundary of my farm. Once at the truck, I case the rifle and take off my jacket. The old pickup truck bounces back across the pasture to the trail that leads to the clearing where the doe is laying on crushed leaves. She is a smooth brown mound fringed with white. I dare not drive across the clearing. The ground is too soft. So I park the truck at the clearing's edge and walk across to her. There are no antlers to grab. I grab the two front legs and start pulling. The doe's head swings freely. It is then that I realize that indeed she is a big doe. I do not want to field dress her where she fell. I don't want that smell to linger and alarm deer so close to my stand.

The scraps and bones were scattered on a little flat place near the creek. For twenty-three years this has been the altar where the offering has been taken. I could see a few bones and antlers from past years but most had vanished long ago. I turned back toward my truck and gazed through the woods . . .

She's too big for me to manhandle into the bed of my truck. There's nothing except her front legs or her head for me to hold on to. I lie on my stomach across the tailgate, grab her legs, and lift. That works—except, holding her, I cannot get myself up! So I get a piece of rope from my truck and tie her forelegs and neck together, tightly. Now, standing, I can pull up and back, getting her across the threshold of the tailgate and sliding her into the truck's bed. I grin. There's still a little lead in the elderly man's pencil.

My wife was waiting in the kitchen when I returned from the "bone yard." The countertops were cleared. Tape and white freezer

paper were on the kitchen table. I went to the ice chest and took
the first tray of chilled meat. Bringing it into the kitchen, I carefully
trimmed the cuts and gave them a final inspection before placing
them on the open sheets of freezer paper. We filled eight to ten
sheets with meat, then wrapped, taped, and labeled. Then we filled
another set of eight to ten sheets, until the pan was empty. I went
back out for more meat. There was a gentle breeze . . .

*The drive out into the pasture and selecting a place for field dressing
is a slow, beautiful, and time-honored ritual of respect for the deer. I
carefully slide the doe back out of the truck's bed and onto the soft grass
of the pasture. I do not want to drop her and risk breaking a bone.*

*The first cut is a circular cut around the anus, which, once freed, is
tied off with a piece of trotline cord. Then I roll her over and cut off
her udders. She is dry. Her fawns have been gone a very long time.
Now the split up the middle, first the skin—all the way—then through
the muscle of the abdomen, making sure not to cut organs by holding
the tissue high with one hand and cutting with the other, until I come
to the breast bone.*

The next pan came into the kitchen. These cuts were the roasts
and steaks. Again, I trimmed, making sure that all cuts were across
the grain. The trimmings, however, were good pieces too. They could
be used for stir-fry dishes. The steaks made neat piles. The roasts
were solidly beautiful. The freezer paper beckoned "come hither," and
the pile of wrapped and labeled meat grew on the table . . .

*I reach inside the body cavity of the doe and cut all the way around
the diaphragm, then reach even further, past the heart and lungs, cutting them free. I stick my knife into the ground beside the deer, reach
deeply forward with both hands, and pull hard. Everything comes out
onto the grass. Steam rushes upward into the cool late-afternoon air.
Stepping aside, I wipe my hands clean on the grass. Turning again to
the doe, I flip her onto her belly, holding her foreparts high, so she can
drain. Then I drag her to a clean spot, belly down, and spread all four
legs out to keep her in position.*

Now came the pan of rib meat and the two back straps. These
were the very special cuts. I striped the connective tissue from the

exterior of the back straps, just like stripping the skin off of a fish fillet. All that was left was pure meat, beautiful, clear, clean, unblemished, wonderful, dark red meat. The other back strap got the same treatment. Both were then cut into thirds and each piece individually wrapped. The rib meat collectively made three packages . . .

The sun is setting as I walk from the doe to my pond. Twilight drifts across the landscape. An owl calls. Shadows are deep. Thoughts are deeper. Standing ankle deep in rubber knee boots, I wash my hands, arms, and knife in the shallows. The water is cold and very clear. It makes me think of holy water, baptismal water, in a sanctuary . . . and it is just that. The blood and water join in a sacramental mix that touches my soul. I pause, out there in the pond, water dripping from my hands, and think about the spiritual connections I have with this land, and how hunting here only intensifies and strengthens that connection.

The last pans of chilled meat were brought into the kitchen. These cuts were very good meat. They were big chunks for some of the best dishes: casseroles, stir-fry, even conversion into ground meat for grilling as hamburger or for chili. Finally came two pans of good but tough scrap meat that would go into soups and stews . . .

I can see steam rising from the doe as I walk from the pond back toward her. The sun has set now. Wood ducks are coming to the pond. The coyotes are yelping. When I get to the doe, I use the rope again to get her back into the truck's bed. The night air is cool, so I put my jacket back on. The truck's engine has a fine, smooth-running cadence. The headlights bounce across the pasture and off the edge of the forest. The old bridge across the creek rattles as the truck passes. Then there's the gate, the entryway to my other world.

The wrapped meat was carried from the kitchen, across the carport, and into the storage room where we keep our freezer. Every package was arranged individually so that it would freeze as quickly as possible. There were forty-two of them. They would be rearranged more compactly after they'd spent one night in the freezer. When I had them all in the freezer, I whispered a prayer of thanksgiving, not for finally having finished the task, but rather that I'd been blessed by the privilege of processing this doe. She would feed me, my family, and my friends throughout the coming year ...

I close the gate behind the truck and snap the lock into place. It is time now to transition back into that other world—but I can't. I never can. I'm never the same after a successful deer hunt. A deep stillness settles on me.

I have felt that stillness before. It is a stillness that transcends peace. It links me with earth and God, very much like the overpowering sense of oneness that I feel following Holy Communion in a worship service or mass. All of the component parts are there, including celestial songs, the age-old, treasured, hunter's songs ... the songs that are heard not with the ears but as echoes that reverberate within the human heart.

To Keep a Promise

THE JET RIPPED OVER THE DESERT LANDSCAPE AND UNLEASHED devastating fury on a large concentration of enemy soldiers gathered below. In desperation and futility, moments before being engulfed in a fiery hell, some of the soldiers on the ground rushed about, seeking cover. Others turned to fire their weapons at the jet. But there was no safe cover, and the enemy fire was pitiful. The attack was over in seconds.

After the attack the young pilot banked the jet hard to the left to ensure that it didn't stray beyond the authorized battle zone, and also to do a flyover to be sure that the mission had been accomplished. It was the young pilot's birthday. He was twenty-five years old.

Half a world away an ageing man with a white beard and a slight limp drifted across his Mississippi farm. With him was his dog, Hank, a wirehaired pointing griffon, and the young pilot's dog, Murphy, a one-year-old Brittany spaniel.

Hank was an established hunter with several fine seasons to his credit. Murphy had a hunter's heart and senses and the vitality of youth, but mostly was trying to figure out what was going on with this other dog and this new man in his life. He didn't trust the man and was a bit wary around the big dog. His trust and his love were centered on the pilot who had strangely vanished from his life three weeks earlier. And the mosaic of rolling hills, wetlands, forests, and small farms of northeast Mississippi created a very different world than the sprawling South Dakota landscape where he'd lived.

The older man was gentle with the puppy. He understood the uncertainty and sadness that the puppy was experiencing. He was feeling much the same way.

A military jet passed overhead, returning to a nearby base with its student pilot at the controls. The older man's son had flown such jets during flight training. As the older man watched the jet overhead, his heart seemed to split open ever so slightly. He missed his son, the pilot, the warrior at war. But he also was very proud that the son had chosen this noble path. There was great need and his son had answered the call to service.

Now the only thing that seemed to keep the older man sane was an intense focus on a promise he'd made three short weeks ago. He remembered the final moments with his son the day his son left, the final hug from his son before he got into his truck and backed out of the driveway . . . and then the awesome, overwhelming sense of aloneness the older man felt standing in his front yard, with Murphy on a leash beside him, as the son drove away, down the street, headed to war. As his son vanished around the corner, the older man had whispered again to himself the promise he'd made to his son: "When you come home you will have a good bird dog."

The trainer jet had long vanished from the sky, but the older man could still hear its roar in the distance. Somehow, in ways he couldn't understand, he also could hear the roar of his son's jet on the other side of the world, and the explosions of the bombs in that far away desert. He took a deep breath, straightened himself, wiped his wet eyes, and, for a few moments, watched as the two dogs worked the fringes of the pasture that stretched before him. They seemed to flow over the landscape, poetry and ballet combined, fully engaged in the rhythms that defined their life purposes. Somehow, watching them, the older man found, and entered into, a state of separate peace . . . even as tears flowed.

The older man is me.

So began a pilgrimage of discovery as the two bird dogs and I learned how to nurture and refine the deeper elements in our hunters' hearts, and how, through discipline and practice, to grow stronger, more purposeful, and more precise in the expression in our individual and collective identities. We each brought different skill sets, perspectives, mental and emotional orientations, physical abilities, and mortal limitations into the field. We had to teach one another about these things and be perfectly honest and absolutely pure with one another. We had to learn how to become an integrated team, how to communicate with one another, and—most importantly—how to trust one another.

Hank and I already had all of this worked out between the two of us, but the introduction of Murphy into the equation turned our hunter's world upside down. Frankly, I didn't really worry much about this new framework. Over the course of more than half a century I'd trained lots hunting dogs: pointers, setters, spaniels, retrievers, and Hank the griffon. I understood the differences among the breeds, which could handle heavy training and discipline and which needed a gentle touch. And, within breeds, I knew to watch carefully for different personalities. There was no set formula for success, just a sort of framework that required patience, consistency, encouragement, and love.

A hunting dog needs freedom to develop its own unique style and skill set that work to the ultimate end point of bringing the game to the hunter's hand. But that freedom is granted within the context of discipline and control. The more discipline and control the dog handles on its own, the less external discipline and control must come from the hunter. The hunter, however, also must develop the skills necessary to direct the hunt, handle the dogs, shoot a shotgun effectively under various conditions, and practice his or her own discipline and self control. A dog will quickly understand whether or not a hunter practices what he or she preaches. Respect needs to flow both ways.

Unique and highly personalized relationships evolve between hunters and their dogs. There are personalities involved, and emotions and physical realities. Breeds differ—breeds of dogs, breeds of hunters. The relationships are fluid and dynamic, responsive to changes that are part and parcel to the hunter's world. That's the source of magic in the entire enterprise.

I don't train show dogs or field trial dogs. I train dogs for hunting. I develop hunting companions, not machines or robots. Now I had my son's young Brittany spaniel, a fine dog from a good line of one of the best bird dog breeds ever developed, a breed that lives to please and typically is incredibly intelligent and thoughtful, with superb hunting abilities and fine senses. They are wonderful dogs to train.

Consequently, I had a lot of confidence going into Murphy's training program. I had the time (I'm retired) and the place (I own a small farm). I had access to good, flight-conditioned quail. I'm a fair wing shot, particularly if I shoot instinctively and don't think about it. Everything pointed to success. This was, in my mind, going to be a "slam-dunk" process. I was looking forward to a smooth training program. All the ingredients for success were there . . . or so I thought. But it didn't exactly go as I thought it would. It evolved into a story with currents that run deep, very, very deep. And, had it not been for a fuzzy-faced griffon named Hank, it would have been a very sad and disappointing story.

Hank, the five-year-old griffon, is a classic close-working bird dog, very meticulous and thorough, and an excellent retriever both on land and in the water. He is a pointing breed but not a specialist. He's more of an "all around" dog that will adapt to whatever game is targeted, upland birds or waterfowl or even fur. He will hunt and point rabbits if you ask him to, but otherwise he leaves them alone. He will tree squirrels—if asked. He will track wounded deer—if asked. But his first love is hunting and pointing quail. He takes discipline very well without getting his feelings hurt. Usually, following a problem, we sit down, take a "time out," and have a dog to man talk about things that went wrong. In almost all cases, we come to realize that we both were at fault. We shake hands and move on.

Hank understands bobwhite quail and how to make them behave. He will sometimes break points, circle around, and pin the birds between him and me. And, following a shot, if the bird is hit, it is a rare bird that is not brought to my hand. Hank is obsessed with finding and retrieving shot quail. He is, frankly, a phenomenal hunting dog and also my best buddy in the field.

Murphy, on the other hand, when I got him, seemed to be more of a specialist, a finely bred, high-energy dog that covered ground quickly. In the field he was extremely aggressive, plunging headlong into briars, brambles, and bushes, through barbed-wire fences, and across wetlands. I was concerned that he would run over birds before he caught their scent. I assumed that he would point because Brittany spaniels are bred to do that. But he had never shown me any inclination of doing so. He also showed little interest in retrieving. He would chase and pick up training dummies, both on land and in the water, but then would drop the dummy when he came close to me and simply wander away. He didn't care at all about Hank or what Hank might be doing. He didn't care about anything that I might be doing. He was a loner. But, fortunately, when we were out in the field, he would check in with me from time to time after his long coursing forays across the property. I sensed he didn't want to become a lost dog in this foreign land.

When Murphy came to live with us, he was sad, confused, and unwilling to take instructions from me. He also was extremely gun shy. Just the sight of a gun bothered him. If he heard the sound of a distant gunshot, he immediately shut down and came to walk with me. He would stay close but wouldn't let me touch him. I'd speak to him in a soothing voice to reassure him that all was fine, but he didn't believe me. Even though he didn't care very much for me, he preferred to be with me if there was any shooting going on around us, unless, of course, I was carrying a gun. He loved the hunt—as long as there were no guns.

He was obsessed with chasing anything that had wings: birds, butterflies, horseflies, grasshoppers, bees. I'd catch him watching hawks and vultures soaring overhead. When Canada geese flew overhead, he became transfixed. Robins were his favorite. He would chase and flush them but he would not point. He would not retrieve. He would not come to me or let me touch him. If I tried to put a leash on him, he would dodge away from me. He did not trust me at all. He would do only one thing on command: "Sit." If I told him to sit, his little butt hit the ground hard and he'd stay put until I could get a leash on him. That was the only control I had, and the only way I could get him into a truck to go to or from my farm.

As a very young puppy he had become lost for several days in thick cover and expansive farmland up in South Dakota. Those days of dealing with a lost puppy were very sad days full of stress for my son and for all of us. Then, miraculously, he was found, walking along a farm road. Thereafter he wore an electric collar with a tracking devise so that he could be found if lost again. The collar came with Murphy when Murphy came to live with me. But Murphy hated that collar. In fact, he was terrified of it. If I put it on him, he became a trembling wreck of a dog. I knew that my son had not hurt that dog with the collar, but, regardless, Murphy could not deal with it.

Murphy's sadness, confusion, lack of trust, fear of the collar, and fear of guns threatened to assign him to the world of house pets rather than to membership into the ranks of hunting dogs. But there was something in him that made me keep hope alive. Murphy had some kind of energy deep inside of him that seemed to be trying to come to life. I somehow sensed that in his heart he was a hunter, with the hunter's spirit swelling in his heart like a volcano about to erupt.

Everything about Murphy in the field was beautiful. He loved the runs on the farm. Sometimes, overcome with the sheer joy of being out on a romp, he'd launch himself with all four feet high into the air. He was in love with the hunting but unwilling to be trained by me. His heart and loyalty belonged to a young pilot half a world away. He absolutely would not transfer his allegiance to me.

For weeks on end the training program was plagued with false starts. I tried but failed time and again. I hid the electric collar and never brought it out. If Murphy became lost, I'd just have to try to find him some other way. I bought the softest sounding little "acorn" .22 blanks I could find at a gundog supply store and shot them through a rifle rather than a training pistol. They were still too much for Murphy and only added to his fear of guns.

I tried working with him in the yard, doing the best I could to entice him to play with me. He would have none of it. He would go to my wife when she called and allow her to pet him, but he kept his distance from me. If I put food into his bowl, he would not eat. My wife had to feed him.

It became painfully obvious that I wasn't going to be able to keep my promise. The whole situation was becoming a disaster. Finally, I accepted the reality that I had to relinquish command. I had no choice. I had to turn the entire training program over to Hank. He was my last hope.

Hank, bless his heart, had already figured out that this had to be, that he had to take charge of that puppy. He'd actually begun the process several weeks before my retreat. With gentleness uncommon for a territorial, mature, male dog, he'd befriended the puppy. Slowly, carefully, he helped Murphy emerge from sadness and loneliness through play—gently at first, then more vigorously later—the point that we had to turn the dogs out into the yard to keep them from destroying our kitchen.

Murphy came alive in this play, wrestling, rolling, running, and mock fighting. With the encouragement of Hank and our other dog, a moody and cantankerous old mixed-breed bitch named Daisy with strong beagle genes, Murphy learned the joys of chasing gray squirrels up trees in our backyard. He would run and bark and jump with unbridled happiness. He was a "hunting dog" out there in the yard. When doves or pigeons or flocks of blackbirds came to feed on the ground near our bird feeders, Hank would take Murphy in tow and lead him to the flush. After a run on the farm or a long afternoon of play out in the yard, and after they'd been fed, I'd oftentimes find them curled up together on the same dog bed, even though they each had their own bed. Murphy would have his head resting across Hank and sometimes Hank would have a front leg across Murphy.

The light returned to Murphy's eyes. He had a friend in this big, lonely world . . . a buddy he could trust.

One afternoon, a week or so after Hank officially took charge of Murphy's training, I went out to the backyard with both dogs and began doing yard work with Hank, going through his commands, working on retrieves, and letting him do his favorite thing, go on point with a duck wing tied on a string to the end of a long pole. Murphy sat leashed on the patio and watched.

Hank was flawless. The old "professor" knew that his "student" was watching. Then I leashed Hank and called to Murphy. He looked at me and then at Hank, then back to me. I called again, "Come Murphy." He made a move toward me then stopped and looked back at Hank. Hank looked back at him, smiling as only dogs can smile, lolling his tongue, his fuzzy face cocked in anticipation of good things to come, effectively telling the puppy, "Go ahead. That old man is OK."

Murphy came to me, slowly, carefully, cautiously. He got to within three feet of me, then stopped and looked back at Hank for assurance. Hank got up on all four feet and shook his head, "Go Murphy"—and he did. He came to my arms and I gave that puppy a hug and a thorough petting. He jumped up and put his front paws on my shoulders and licked my neck. Hank barked and tugged at his leash. I released him from his leash and then the three of us walked together around the yard.

I got the duck wing on the pole and whirled it around the yard. Hank made no attempt to point. He held back and let Murphy chase the thing. Then I flopped the wing down onto the grass immediately in front of Murphy and he froze . . . trembling. It was Murphy's first point in my presence. The moment was magic. Hank carefully walked up beside and a little behind Murphy and honored that puppy's point. I stroked Murphy and talked to him softly. He stiffened even more. I pushed on his rear quarters and he pushed back. Through a misty fog of tears, I watched a bird dog materialize before my eyes. I looked at Hank and he shifted his focus from the duck wing to me—and that fuzzy old face of his was all smiles. I reached over to him and said, "Thank you, Professor Hank." He licked my hand and resumed honoring Murphy's point.

Two days later I bought twenty-five flight-conditioned quail and planted six of them out in the fields on my farm, down in tall grass and weeds. I turned both dogs loose at the same time. Hank quickly found and pointed one of the birds. Murphy rushed in and flushed it. Hank let the incident pass with tolerance, grace, and dignity. I said nothing. The puppy flushed every single bird that day and was beside himself with joy. We just let him go with the winds of his soul and feel that joy.

The next day we repeated the process, but this time only Hank was free to find the birds and Murphy was on a long, retractable leash. When Hank pointed, I brought Murphy up to him. Murphy would rush toward Hank, intent on flushing. But every time Hank would turn on him and tell him, in no uncertain terms—with a hard look, a shift in body position, or a low growl—to mind his manners. I held Murphy in check with the leash, but it was Hank who made him stop. When Murphy stopped and had himself under control, with Hank firmly in charge of the situation, I'd lead Murphy up to where he could smell the bird. Then he'd point and watch Hank hold *his* point. I'd flush the bird and we'd watch it sail away. Afterwards we'd move to the next bird and repeat the process.

For the next two weeks we hunted quail this way, with Hank free to find and point birds, Murphy on a long leash, and no gun involved. After all of the birds had been flushed, I'd release Murphy and let him run free. Sometimes he or Hank would find one of the previously flushed birds. Murphy would always flush again. Hank would point. I said nothing. But sometimes I could see that Hank was pretty aggravated with Murphy when Murphy flushed one of Hank's pointed birds.

A week or so later, as the bird hunting season matured into beautiful afternoons full of sky, golden glow, and whispering soft winds, Steve Ball, a friend from Louisiana, came for a visit and to help Hank and me with Murphy's training. We purchased more flight-conditioned quail and then took the dogs out to the farm. We carried a little .410 shotgun with us. When Murphy saw the gun, he hesitated. Hank walked to Murphy and then to me and the gun. Murphy came with Hank. Hank sniffed the gun then looked at Murphy and moved on past the gate. Murphy followed Hank but kept his distance from the gun. We followed the dogs.

Hank pointed. Murphy came quickly to him and paused long enough for me to get a leash on him. We flushed the bird but did not shoot. We repeated this process three more times. Murphy's points improved with every bird. Then we put Hank back in the kennel in the truck and returned to the field with Murphy on the long leash. Murphy looked at me, obviously wondering what was going on with Hank in the kennel. But his desire to hunt overwhelmed those questions. And he was a little excited about finally hunting on his own. Steve and I knew where the birds were planted and led Murphy to the general area for each bird, working him in a way to make sure that he was downwind from the bird.

Murphy found one of the birds and immediately pointed. I firmed up his point and held him tightly on the leash. I asked Steve to walk away about a hundred yards out into the field and, the moment that I flushed the bird, to fire the gun, with the gun pointed directly away from us. I kicked up the bird and Steve immediately fired the gun. Murphy didn't flinch. His focus was completely on the flushed quail.

At this point I consulted with Steve and made an executive decision that would be the "make or break" with this little bird dog. We would shoot over the dog and kill the quail after the flush. Of course, the quail needed to be shot. A missed shot would be problematic. It would be the most important shot of my life.

Murphy pointed again on this, the last of the planted quail. He was staunch, beautifully pointed, textbook perfect. Steve held the leash. I took the gun and walked forward. As I passed Murphy I talked softly to him and stroked him. I then kicked up the bird. It flushed and straightened out, veering just a little to my left—a perfect shot for me. I brought up the little shotgun and fired. At twenty yards there was a puff of feathers and the bird was down! Murphy was still holding his point. I asked Steve to release Murphy from the leash. Murphy had marked the bird down and went immediately to it. His first shot quail, a good point, no problems with the gun—a new bird dog was confirmed!

Murphy was beside himself with joy, sniffing the bird, picking it up, dropping it, picking it up again, and all the while I was petting him and telling him what a good bird dog he was. He was so proud!

That was the beginning. The leash was never used again and a shotgun was always in the mix. I turned the entire program back over to Hank and he was masterful. During the next three months we hunted practically every day. I stopped planting quail. Rather, I'd just take them out to the middle of the farm and throw them to the four winds. The dogs preferred free-range birds and so did I. The birds would get into the most impossibly thick and briar-infested places on the farm. We'd have to work them like wild birds, and they acted like wild birds. We became the team. My job was to kill the birds when they flushed. When I tried to intervene on the finding of the birds, Hank would look at me and basically send the message that I needed to back off and let him handle not only the birds but also his student.

Murphy's learning curve was exponential. He paid attention to Hank's directions but didn't succumb to becoming a "follower." He hunted with a style all his own, but as a member of the team. It was beyond beautiful, old Hank, the "professor," and his "novitiate," Murphy, coursing the fields, the woods, the brushy quarters and fence rows of my farm, working the birds, setting them, holding them until I came, and then going out to get the shot birds.

Hank was the expert, well versed in the ways of quail, knowing how close he could get without a flush. Murphy watched his every move and studied his logistics. When there was something new, Hank would sometimes break point, come back to Murphy, go through preliminary motions, then return to station and continue with the business at hand. I was spellbound watching the professor at work.

When I came in with the gun, I'd get sideways glances from both of them. The messages could not have been more clear: "OK, Mister, kill the bird. You've got the gun. We've done our job." And most of the time I did. I typically was a lone hunter without the safety

restraints needed when hunting with somebody else. I could take
the wild shots. I had 360 degrees of free movement. I let reflexes
take command. I hunted casual, got my gun on the birds quickly,
and then shot slowly. Three or four seconds with a flushed quail is
a very long time, even for a sixty-five-year-old hunter.

The last two months of the bird season Hank, Murphy, and I
worked and shot over 125 quail out there on my farm. Murphy
learned how to track and trail, how to push and set the birds, and
how to mark and find shot birds. As the season progressed into its
last three weeks, a miracle happened. Or, perhaps, it was the dream
of every professor come true. The student surpassed the professor.

Murphy came into a rhythm all his own. He was fast and typically
the first dog to find the birds. He rarely ran over them. His sense of
smell was phenomenal. His points were never false. If he said, "Bird
here, Boss," the bird was *there*. If the quail were nervous, running
birds, Murphy became like a cat on the ground: low, stalking, head
forward, light-footed, careful but secure in what he was doing. He
never rushed a point. He never flushed a bird. He blossomed into
one of the most incredible bird dogs I'd ever experienced.

Hank understood. I could sense that he was very proud of his
student. He knew that Murphy had become a better bird dog than he
was in a lot of ways. He was at peace with that and so was I. Murphy
had a fine nose and was light in foot. He had youth and could cover
the ground very well. He wouldn't retrieve, but that was OK. Perhaps
not retrieving was Murphy's way of letting the older dog command
a dimension of the hunt. And, Hank, the seasoned professional, the
meticulous, close working and thorough bird dog, also found and
pointed his share of birds. When he did, Murphy honored Hank's
points like a champion. Together we became a beautifully balanced
team.

The final week of the quail season approached. The young pilot,
my son, First Lieutenant David Jackson, the central, unwavering focus of a fine bird dog, completed his last combat mission and told us
that he was coming home. I contacted the shooting preserve where
I get the flight-conditioned birds and told them that we needed

twenty-five good quail. They would not let me pay for the birds. They understood what was happening.

My son came home from war. Flags and yellow ribbons were everywhere. A good bird dog met him in the front yard, jumping wildly and barking, a gyrating mass of happiness. The seasoned combat veteran went to his knees and kissed his dog on the forehead.

Two days later father and son walked together across the little Mississippi farm. A crystalline blue late winter sky put a sparkle in their blood. The late afternoon sun caused the pasture to glow. There was a stillness covering the land that wrapped itself around their hearts. The shadowy woods that stretched along the far side of the pasture stood in a shroud of silence than only deepened when a pileated woodpecker called. A gentle breeze whispered to them from the hillside above the pond. A pair of nesting Canada geese called from the pond. A red tail hawk soared overhead.

The two men had made this walk together many times across the years. This was their sanctuary, their cherished refuge. There was little talk. There was no need. Memories swirled around them, bringing them together, once again, in the deepest of currents.

Hank and Murphy moved with grace and dignity across the landscape, coursing the cover, working together as a synchronized team. Murphy found and pointed the first bird. Hank, the old professor, honored Murphy's point with pride in his heart for his student and good friend. My son moved forward to his dog, the shotgun of his youth in his hands. His dog was steady. I stood quietly a short distance away, heart pounding. The bird flushed. My son shot. There was a puff of feathers. A promise was kept . . .

The Most Powerful Fish in the World

BIG FISH ARE FUN TO CATCH, AND PARTICULARLY SO IF YOU'RE not too serious about it. During my sixty-plus years of fishing (fifty of which I was too serious about it) I've caught some big fish. The best ones were those I caught while fishing alone, were released, and I didn't tell a single soul about them. Releasing big fish and not talking about it is sort of like having a big buck whitetail deer show up with a hundred-pound doe at twilight on the edge of a clearing, putting the crosshairs of the rifle's scope on the buck's chest, quietly whispering "bang," and then shooting the doe. All of the magic and most of the power goes away if you say anything to anybody about the encounters.

There are most certainly some big fish out yonder on the prowl! If you tangle with one, you're never quite the same again. One of my most memorable encounters in this regard happened in southeast Alaska. While fishing for rockfish with a good friend one fine May afternoon under an azure sky (rare in southeast Alaska), after a successful black bear hunt, I got hung up on the bottom of the ocean. And then the bottom of the ocean started to move. For about two hours my buddy and I got a fine tour of Prince William Sound as that fish dragged our boat across water so deep blue that it was closer to black. Finally, thankfully, the fish broke off and we were able to find a sheltered cove out of the chop and fix ourselves a lunch. I was terrified by the whole thing (not the lunch, however).

The hard run of a redfish across a marshy flat; the vibrations that come roaring up from yellowfin tuna through the line, across a "broomstick" rod that's bent double, across your shoulders, and on into your heart; the charging acrobatics of silver salmon in a fast river; the explosive encounters with peacock bass in the American tropics, and the brute power of a hammerhead shark that's longer than my pickup truck—all can comprehensively encapsulate an angler's very soul. And let us not forget hookups with sturgeons, groupers, snappers, wahoo, pike, lake trout, and other oversized denizens of wild waters that cause us to drift away ... into the never-never land of an angler's reflections and dreams. I've never hooked a billfish, so I can't speak about them, but people I know who have hooked and caught the things have a faraway look in their eyes that can't be matched.

The fishing doesn't always need to be angling. As a retired fisheries professor who logged his career mostly working in the Deep South's big, turbid rivers, I can say unequivocally that wrestling a hoop net with four fifty-plus-pound flathead catfish in it, all determined to go the other way, is just about as much adventure as I can stand for a day. But on that *particular* day, my perspective regarding adventure didn't matter. Every net (and there were ten of them) was full of big flathead catfish. We'd hit them at the peak of their spawn in Mississippi's Big Black River, and they apparently thought our nets were big hollow logs within which to court their girlfriends. Over the course of the years that followed that day, data evolved into story, then to history, and finally entered the realm of legend ... legend that continues to be shared among my former students who were with me that day, and across the tumbling generations of *their* students, and their student's students. The data is still out there, somewhere, along with a few photographs. It was a long time ago.

And yes, I've caught big catfish with my hands. There's nothing quite comparable to being in complete darkness, with twelve feet of turbid river rushing overhead, sitting on the river's bottom, sucking air out of a tank, trying to hold onto a thirty- or forty-pound catfish that's chewing off your arm while you are trying to remember "which way is up." The thought of wrestling with an eighty- or ninety- or a hundred-pound catfish down in those murky depths scares the do-wattally-squat out of me. Catfish that big (and bigger) do live in those rivers, but the largest we ever saw on the rivers during my three-decade-long career was an eighty-pound flathead catfish that killed itself when it rammed our boat (think Moby Dick!).

Big fish, strong fish, they are certainly wonderful creatures to behold. I love holding them in my arms, close to my chest (except the biting kind), feeling their life pulse, and then, gently, putting them back into the water—where they belong. These big fish can generate memories and form the framework for beautiful and, I admit, sometimes scary dreams.

However, across the years I've learned that "big" and "strong" do not necessarily relate to power—not by a long shot. There are lots of things that are big and lots of things that are strong. But, in my opinion, the key to *power* is the ability to generate and sustain significant influence on the course of events. Some things matter. Some things don't . . . at least not as much.

Since I live in a fisherman's world and want to appropriately acknowledge things that influence the world I have chosen as my operational framework, the world that has defined my career and, in fact, my life, I believe that it is worthwhile that the most powerful fish in world be identified. I feel compelled to step out onto ground where angels fear to tread—before it is too late (my beard is very white). As I do so I am confronted by the thought that I may be considered by some of my fellows as a dangerous element in the community of anglers, or, well . . . at least as an opinionated and biased irritant.

Having long studied angler behavior, and having actually published in scientific journals on the subject, I realize that opinion and bias may be rare credentials in our ranks as fishers, and that having both opinion and bias during my sunset years may relegate me to the edges as a misfit in the tribe. Perhaps it is time to feed me to the polar bears because, taken as a community, fishers of all stripes are all good stewards of objectivity, linear thought process, and decision making grounded in the foundation and framework of sound data and analyses (right?).

And so, in preparation for what I am about to do, you might as well go ahead, load your gun, and lead me to a spot back behind the barn. Nipping this treacherous endeavor in the bud before it metastasizes is, admittedly, a very *reasonable* course of action. I can already hear the howling mob. I can see the flames of torches in the darkening sky and hear the rattle of pitchforks even before the deed occurs.

With a deep breath and unmitigated courage, I am willing to accept my fate, submitting to the purging actions of the first *reasonable* fisherman who steps forward to administer the bud nipping. However, and since I doubt that there *are* any reasonable fishermen (at least I've never met one), I am somewhat emboldened and, subsequently, am going to stand firm with my convictions, not blink, hold steady before fire, and with clear conscience and an unwavering voice proclaim that *the most powerful fish in the world is the twelve-inch bass.*

A twelve-inch bass of any species, when in optimal condition, will weigh about one pound. It has muscle enough to put a strong bow in an angler's rod and send a thrill surging through the angler's heart. A twelve-inch bass typically hits hard and can completely clear the water when it jumps. It's already figured out how to twist, shake its head, and rattle its gills and is perfectly capable of throwing your lure back at you.

It is a dedicated predator, swift, deadly, and focused. It is master of its domain, the apex predator, at the top of the line. Given a chance, it will kill and eat salmon, trout, catfish, suckers, pike, pickerel, all sunfish and minnows, and anything else it can catch, gulp, wad up, and swallow. It will eat mice, baby ducks, turtles, frogs, salamanders, snakes, lizards, and any invertebrate, aquatic or otherwise. Even when not hungry it will kill.

For this reason, no fish can transform a child's day better than a twelve-inch bass. To catch the top-of-the-line predator takes a child to the edge of something so deep in its evolutionary dimensions that echoes of human origins fold around the child's heart and soul. And, in transforming the day, that bass (particularly if it is a child's first) quite likely also transformed a lifetime.

Let's face it: little boys and girls are themselves predators. They have their eyes positioned on the front of their faces and separated by the proper distance to give them excellent binocular vision. This binocular vision allows depth perception that—when coupled with focus and bipedal locomotion (two-legged running) and opposable thumbs (for grabbing and throwing things)—has, through our tumbling generations, equipped them to capture and kill and eat and survive. The poetry can come later.

A youngster who has fished mostly for sunfish or other small non-predatory fish, when first engaged in battle with a twelve-inch bass, will feel that suddenly the whole world is attached out there on the end of the line . . . and it probably is. The fish is not the only thing that is hooked. Life suddenly makes sense to the kid.

This is why young Masai in East Africa kill lions with spears. I'm sure that young Masai would fish for bass if they had any. In fact, I know that the Masai love to fish (although they don't want to touch fish). I have taken them fishing in streams that course the Serengeti; but, alas, there were no bass, only catfish, but we caught the heck out of them on spinners. Catfish on light spinning tackle in an African stream are fun, but it just isn't the same as a Boy Scout or Girl Scout aged eleven years old hauling in his or her first twelve-inch bass.

So powerful is the twelve-inch bass that it can determine careers and the fate of families. It is more powerful than any drug. Encounters with it never fade away. They persist for a lifetime, forever drawing fishers, regardless of age, into the dimensions of pure, clean, wonder and joy that rival those of prayer. It fact, the twelve-inch bass may be one of the most spiritual of all fish. It has grown large enough to be a very real fish worthy of the angler's attention, but not so large that it jerks the rod from youthful hands or creates bad dreams if it wins the battle and escapes.

The twelve-inch bass has saved marriages and lives. It tends to be available for emergencies, or when there is grief, or when decisions are pending, or when some time is needed for reflection and quiet and prayer. They are there when you need something that is worthy of pursuit, but not something so big that it diverts your focus from your purposes.

During my career as a fisheries biologist, when conducting creel surveys of anglers, I've had anglers tell me that if they didn't have a place to go catch these bass, they probably wouldn't be alive. That's powerful stuff folks—mighty powerful stuff.

In this regard, you can catch twelve-inch bass, one after another, *and not interrupt your "fishing."* Twelve-inch bass help you find and keep your rhythm. You can catch and release the fish, knowing that they will probably survive for another encounter with you or someone else, or you can keep them and eat them. When you eat them, they become part of what you are as well as who you are. They are, in every sense of the word, sacramental.

The fillets of a twelve-inch bass fit perfectly into a frying pan. A bass fillet is pure white meat with no bones at all. You can eat them without fear or coaching. You can feed them to friends and family and feel good about giving loved ones a fine meal. It is OK to be proud about that. The entire enterprise is about dignity and meaning and purpose—discovered, maintained, or restored, or all of the above. It is all part of the transformational power of the twelve-inch bass . . . but there's more.

The twelve-inch bass is the fisheries manager's true friend. By professional definition it is a "quality" fish. It is the fish that makes people happy. It is the fish that most anglers will keep. One keeper (quality) fish per hour tends to be the point where anglers shift their evaluation from "poor to fair" fishing to the higher category of "good to excellent" fishing. In consideration of the fact that most anglers fish about four hours per trip (morning or afternoon/evening), fisheries managers have an operational framework within which to work. The truth of the matter is that very few anglers catch a limit of bass. They don't need to do that to be happy.

If there's good water quality and good places for fish to spawn, live, and grow, and enough food of the right kind, a bass can typically reach one pound during its first year of life. They're equipped with the genetics to do that and actually more. But even if it takes two years to reach one pound in weight, that's still pretty good growth.

Fisheries managers know the prescriptions to make this happen. It isn't hard at all. So when you're out on the water where there's bass, you can be pretty sure that the twelve-inch bass is out there with you. It might not bite your hook, but it is there. *Fisheries managers want you to catch that fish.* That's why they are there, the managers and the fish! There may be some rules and restrictions, but they almost never keep you from interacting in good ways with the most powerful fish in the world.

The twelve-inch bass is also the panfish angler's best friend. It can eat a four-inch sunfish and not even blink. It keeps pressure on those sunfish, whacking away at them in ways fishing almost never ever can, and thinning the ranks so that you'll have decent-sized sunfish to catch.

A given body of water can only have a certain carrying capacity (pounds per acre). It is determined by the basic fertility of the water, which in turn translates into fish food. So a given body of water can have lots of very small fish at minimum reproductive size or a few very large fish that are using up lots of energy just trying to support themselves and hardly growing at all anymore.

Good fishery management adjusts the fish population to a place somewhere between these two extremes, determined by what people want to catch. It's called "balance" and is a dynamic situation. If you want a few large sunfish, protect your bass and let them become a "wolf pack" of smaller, slow-growing bass that hammer the sunfish almost to oblivion. The surviving sunfish will grow fast and soon be too large for the average bass to eat. But if you prefer to let the bass get a little larger and catching sunfish somewhat smaller is OK, then harvest a few of the bass and the remaining bass will grow. *But protect those twelve-inch bass (plus or minus an inch or so)!* Harvest the smaller ones and the larger ones, but protect the most powerful fish in the world.

In streams the twelve-inch bass is the prince, and in smaller, wadeable streams it is just about maxed out in size. A twelve-inch bass in skinny water might be nearly ten years old. Yet it commands the kingdom. It does not know that it is small. It is the "tush hog" in its environment. Inch for inch, bass (of any species) in streams seem to be at least half again stronger than their cousins in lakes and ponds. I don't know the reason for this, and I have no idea how to actually measure strength in a fish, but, as an angler, I know that bass are stronger in streams.

Twelve-inch bass in streams will knock the stuffing out of anything so bold as to twitch in their domain. Perhaps it is because they live in a more variable, more dynamic environment and just aren't quite as persnickety as bass in ponds and lakes. But I think it is actually just because they've got no idea that they are small. It's a mind thing. In their world they are at the top of the line, the apex predator. It is sort of like being a grizzly bear in Alaska. A grizzly bear has no concept of fear. Like the bass in a creek, *it* does the killing. Nothing is going to mess with it.

And so, when you put on your old shoes and a pair of cut-off jeans, slither down the bank for a bit of creek fishing, light rod in hand and a pocket box full of little spinners and a few "minnow" type lures, you have entered the realm of twelve-inch bass that have their world already in order and won't put up with intrusion. Put something in front of them and they are prepared to tear the intruder to pieces—and will attack with fury.

Once you've caught a twelve-inch bass or two on your creek fishing venture, something beyond your control grips your soul and gives it a shake. You come to your senses, experience an epiphany, and realize that creek fishing for these bass is THE ultimate calling for the restless angler. All your life you've wondered about where you fit into the scheme of things and now you know. You're a rover, a rambler, a restless sojourner in the wilds. The wild winds that have howled in your soul suddenly become quiet. You surrender to the most powerful fish in the world. You have no choice.

The twelve-inch bass out yonder in those streams becomes a siren calling your name. It lures you ever deeper into relationships with the magic of moving water and life forms that you cannot encounter in any other endeavor. The stream angler will keep moving, keep prowling, keep casting, more and more, later and later, mile after mile, completely lost in the magical vapors of the most powerful fish in the world. There is no cure for this malady.

The twelve-inch bass is *your* best friend out in the wild, wet, and wonderful world of the angler. It is out there working for you, all the time. It is there to bring cheer into your life. It is there to help you have hope for the future. It fills the hearts of children and gives them good dreams. It helps us understand the flow of energy in creation. It helps us to make peace with our place in the universe. It gives us an excuse to be out on the water, which, frankly, shouldn't be necessary but usually is. It can soothe the grief-stricken. It helps us understand relationships between life and environment, between different sorts of fishes, between people and fish, and between people and people. It provides us wonderful meals. It graces the most precious element of creation called time, whether sharing solitude with us or serving as a catalyst in companionship.

The twelve-inch bass is, without question, a fish for every occasion. Its influence on the present and future, around the globe, is profound. Wherever it lives it gives, and gives, and gives. It doesn't ask for respect, but it deserves it. So douse your torches, lay down your pitchforks, and join me in paying homage to the twelve-inch bass. It is, absolutely, the right thing to do for *the most powerful fish in the world.*

The Tobacco Patch Hunter

AS THE AFTERNOON STILLED AND GOLDEN LIGHT BRUSHED THE trees on the other side of the pasture from my stand, I settled into my own stillness, one that ushered in a treasured transcendence, a state of sacred peace that strokes my heart as a hunter. It is a peace that gently and seductively pulls me into its embrace, much as does the embrace of a lovely and loving woman, reminding me, as with such a woman, that I am man. Reflections on that deer stand ran deep . . .

There was a time when there was very little of this peace. I was too young as a hunter—too young as a man—to recognize, much less understand, what was all around me and within me, or how to respond to it. What peace there may have been was covered up by spit and vinegar. It was shoved aside by a full-tilt boogie, absolutely focused, rush-away mindset intent on "bringing home the bacon." It took years for me to learn that *process*, fully engaged, makes *attainment* much more beautiful . . . much more powerful.

I worked hard at being a hunter. I pushed beyond reasonable limits. There was no rest, in fact, no other world, until the deer or ducks or whatever were taken and hauled back to camp or the truck or wherever my base might be. I was deeply and passionately in love. The hunts became my lovers, nearly personified—much as is the case with an unfinished graduate thesis or a developing novel or a piece of land. The intimacy I experienced in my love affairs with the hunts was profound. It was obsession to the extreme. It verged on insanity. And, by the end of the hunting season, I was exhausted and comprehensively spent.

Through those hunts, across the years, I learned a lot . . . about deer as well as other game, about hunting, about the woods, and about myself. Slowly, very slowly, I learned the value of being extremely quiet, but I learned little to nothing about culturing an internal stillness. I also learned the value of patience, but little to nothing about engaging a state of sacred peace. I simply was not tuned in on those frequencies. From time to time I sensed other realms of being as I pursued my life in the wilds, but I didn't pay much attention to any of that stuff. It seemed silly.

I certainly didn't go looking for it—the peace that is. But when it finally folded itself around me and penetrated into my heart and even deeper into the roots of my soul . . . I became a much better hunter. Perhaps even a somewhat better man. The fact of the matter is that I was introduced to the peace I speak of long before I was a hunter. You might even say that I learned about the power of hunting before I even knew there *was* such a thing as hunting (or fishing, for that matter).

As a very young child in rural Kentucky, I'd noticed that older farmers worked differently than younger ones. "Old" was anybody with gray hair around the ears. The amount of gray didn't matter. These old farmers worked hard but with a measured pace, a sort of rhythm. They seemed to be detached from the reality that what they were doing was, in all likelihood, going to determine the difference between "making it" and poverty.

My father was the pastor of a small church in that farming community, and he'd go help his parishioners with their work. I'd tag along, run errands, and work as the water boy. I watched the men carefully. I watched them work their livestock, their corn fields, their hay fields, and their pastures. I watched them in the chicken yards and the milking barns. I watched them slaughter cattle and hogs and chickens. I watched them tend their gardens. But what particularly impressed me was the way that they worked in their tobacco patches.

Tobacco was the cash crop. It was what kept people afloat financially. The value of a piece of land back then (1950s) had little to do with how many acres the farm had. It had everything to do with the "tobacco allotment." A twenty-acre farm with a tobacco barn, ten acres of pasture, and five acres of tobacco allotment was worth much more than a one-hundred-acre farm with a corn field, large pastures, a couple of barns, and a half-acre tobacco allotment.

Working tobacco was hot, dusty, demanding, and oftentimes dangerous work. It was also meticulous and repetitive to the extreme. The older men I'd watch did not rush. They deployed their tools—the knives, the hatchets, the spears, the tractors, the wagons, and their muscles—with what seemed to me to be a mindless, detached attitude . . . as if they, as mortal beings, really weren't there.

But to the contrary, these men absolutely *were* "there" and comprehensively engaged with their tasks and the world around them. They'd be in what was to me a strange state of peace, something I was yet to understand. There was a stillness that radiated from them. I could almost feel that stillness, a sereneness . . . and it confused me. I saw the sweat on their faces and the soaked shirts. But there were no furrowed brows. There was never tension. And there was never a harsh word. The rare conversations were very soft. They tended to be quiet people.

These were men of the earth. They trusted it. And they trusted God. Every action deployed was an act of faith. They knew that they could not *force* nature to conform to their will, individually or collectively. Rather, they worked *with* nature. They were unlettered masters at understanding nature's potentials and limitations. They were in tune with the seasons, the weather, the soil, the plants, the animals, and with themselves. They had achieved synchrony with the rhythms of the earth and lived within its meter.

I am not a farmer and will never be one. I am a hunter, a predator who must move and roam. But I learned from the farmers of my youth, especially the older ones. Now, more than sixty years later, I think I'm beginning to understand, more with each passing day, what it was that those farmers, perhaps unknowingly, taught me.

In fact, the light of these revelations began to glow nearly twenty years ago when I failed to achieve a very personal and private goal of knocking out one hundred push-ups on my fiftieth birthday. I'd done it the day before but could not get the final two push-ups on the prescribed date. I was profoundly disappointed in myself . . . and angry at mortality. The reality check was tough.

My failure to make those one hundred push-ups caused me to take a step to the side of the path and to ask myself what this push-up business was all about anyway. It was, most certainly, a worthy goal, but I'd failed to achieve it. I'd accomplished it several times before that fiftieth birthday, but now was eyeball to eyeball with the reality that I was on the sojourn of becoming an elderly man. What, after all, was the purpose of doing one hundred push-ups? For that matter, what was the purpose of my other exercises and, particularly, long-distance running? Wasn't there another way, another framework, something perhaps deeper or perhaps higher, to guide me on my journeys into the wilds?

The result of all this questioning was that I shifted my exercise program and my mindset. As a woods rambler, a fisherman, and hunter, I did not want my joints to go to pieces like had happened to some of my runner friends. Plus, running had never been fun for me. Although I'd been a runner for over thirty-five years, I'd never enjoyed it or achieved the much acclaimed runner's high—not ever, not one single time. Distance never made a difference. So I stopped running, shifted to bicycling and swimming, and almost immediately experienced the transcendence, the "high" I'd missed in running. I quit push-ups and all the other military-style exercises and shifted to weightlifting, *moderate* weightlifting, with lots of repetitions. And I walked *a lot*.

My newly formulated goals did not focus on achieving end points in the exercise regimes. The exercises were now only bridges leading me to more important goals. What I wanted was to be able to keep up with a bird dog all day long and to drag a deer out of the woods by myself and get it into the back of a truck. I wanted to be able to pick up an outboard motor and secure it to the transom of a boat and be able to sling a canoe onto my shoulders and make a portage. I wanted to be able to swim to safety or help somebody else do so if necessary. I wanted strength, wind, and endurance, but within the framework and rhythm of an ageing man's body. Rather than deny my mortality, I decided to celebrate it. In other words, I wanted to be like an old Kentucky tobacco farmer.

My hunting and fishing were comprehensively transformed. I became smoother, more deliberate, more thoughtful. . . and, strangely, more caring. *How* I handled myself as a hunter and angler, alone or with companions, became the singular most important dimension of my ventures into the wilds. And it wasn't just in terms of how I handled myself physically. It also was how I handled myself spiritually.

I moved in faith. I had faith in my guns and my tackle and my ability to use them. I had faith in my dogs and in our teamwork. I shot less and shot better. I gave fewer directions to the dogs and they hunted better. I cast fewer times and caught more fish. I gave flushed quail an extra second to straighten out and killed more of them. I spent less time deer hunting and had better hunts. I let ducks work my decoys longer and sometimes didn't shoot at all and found that by season's end, I had as many ducks to my credit, and sometimes more, than before my transformation. I invoked an internal stillness and it ushered in the state of sacred peace . . . nothing has been the same since . . .

I took a deep breath, returned from my reflections, recovered my focus, and became again the hunter. Shadows drifted across the pasture before me. Now only the upper branches of the trees retained the golden light. Very purposefully I'd waited until the magic hour before coming to my stand. I'd moved to that stand slowly, in the shadows, like a panther, aware of the wind and the ground before me.

In the northwest corner of my land, on another stand, a friend was hunting. He'd been in that stand for several hours. It had been his choice and was, in my opinion, the best stand on the property. I sent him a text message saying that I was settled into the stand overlooking the pasture, and to please let the magic hour run its full course before walking out.

Fifteen minutes later a buck stepped out of the thicket that runs along the eastern border of my farm and began grazing on wheat about 120 yards from me. He was alert. I read his signals, carefully. I breathed deeply, in cadence with the rhythms of the earth.

Slowly, with very deliberate movements, my senses on their edges, my muscles in absolute control, I brought up my battle-scarred old rifle and braced it between the forks of the shooting stick I'd brought into the stand with me. The crosshairs of the rifle's scope settled solidly on the buck, just behind the crook of his foreleg. I carefully pushed off the rifle's safety.

The shooting stick was testimony to my respect for deer. I also had great respect for the rifle. It was a much-trusted companion of many hunts and was fine-tuned with loads I'd made myself. I knew the rifle *and* the loads, intimately. I knew the synergy between them. I knew the rifle's trigger, the edge of its sear, absolutely. As twilight settled on the land, I also knew the wind. It was my friend. I sensed the stillness. I felt the peace. There was electricity in the air. I squeezed the trigger, gently, smoothly.

At the shot, the buck ran, quartering across the pasture, tail down. I knew he would go down and he did, just behind a big Osage orange tree where the pasture makes a corner and goes up a hillside. He was settled by the time I got to him. I shed a tear . . . I always do.

My friend texted, "Was that your shot?"

"Yes."

"Buck?"

"Yes"

"Your .30-06?"

"Your cigars."

A Bridge across the Creek

A VERY LONG TIME AGO AN ANCIENT MAN DECIDED TO CROSS A creek. Motivation likely determined the means and the schedule of the crossing. Whether driven by fear, anger, hunger, desire, lust, or just plain old curiosity, the impetus to get to the other side was strong. Distance from one bank to the other, water depth and temperature, current velocity, and some sort of time element had to be factored in. All crossings have a degree of risk.

The voice of that ancient man echoes across the tumbling generations of humankind, through my genes, and into my soul. I understand that man. I've been known to strip naked, hold my clothes and boots high overhead, and wade chest deep across creeks during winter. I absolutely had to get to the other side. Cold didn't matter. During warmer seasons, or when confronted by something that has the ability to bite (think grizzly bear), I have crossed deep creeks by swimming with all of my clothes on. Under calmer circumstances, I've crossed narrow woodland creeks using "'coon" logs, albeit with various degrees of success. The pinnacle of my ability to do this occurred several decades ago.

If crossing a particular creek becomes habitual, eventually a regular route is established. We make our own 'coon logs and over time, as need arises, we improve on them. Thus the genesis of bridges of all sorts, for creeks of all sorts. Distance across the creek and availability of materials are primary factors in the determination of how bridges are built and maintained. Generally, we search for the narrowest spot between opposite sides of the creek. Over time, we learn to recognize the places where bridges can be built—and where they can't. Depending on the nature of the crossing, we use different means, different frameworks, different materials, and different approaches to join the opposite sides.

I'm an outdoorsman. I engage the outdoors primarily through hunting and fishing. Accordingly, I approach this business of bridges from those perspectives. The key to the entire enterprise of bridge building is an unwavering dedication to actually construct something that works and, in so doing, to create or reinforce something that is durable and lasting. In this respect, the very best bridge that I know of for crossing creeks that flow across human relationships is a quail hunt.

My selection of this bridge may have something to do with age. When you've logged nearly sixty years in the field with a gun in hand, and fifty of those years have been spent with the same hunting and fishing companions, somewhere along the way you start to figure out what works and what doesn't when you need to span a creek. Walking with an old hunting buddy across the countryside with dogs working the landscape and shotguns in the crooks of your arms is, absolutely, a time-tested prescription for building or repairing a bridge. Particularly so when elevated streamflow has, over time, eroded the stream banks back from where they used to be.

First and foremost, when you start working on this bridge business, it is essential that there be options regarding the tools employed. Solitary activities that require a person to be very quiet (e.g., still hunting for squirrels, deer hunting out of tree stands, fly fishing on a stream, stalking redfish in marshes) might work during interludes, but more typically such ventures generate too much space between the spans. Ditto for situations where there's the intrusion of noise from machines (e.g., outboard motors, ATVs) and their associated forced periods of silence. Silence and conversation are both good tools. But the freedom to speak or not to speak, whenever it seems appropriate, is the imperative.

Silent pillars that trust and respect those on the other side of the creek sometimes create very strong bridges. But equally strong, and the ones that I prefer, are bridges where there's mutual testing of the spans along the way. Almost always the different sides of the creek provide different perspectives that make the bridge stronger than either side originally thought possible. The construction work is a step-by-step process. I've also found it ineffective to try to build or repair a bridge if you're rushed, anxious, distracted, or too focused on shooting something.

So, let's come back to quail hunting. The entire affair is really all about the dogs and the opportunity to be outside rambling around with them. You're out yonder doing what you can to make them happy, opening doors of opportunity and giving encouragement to help them cultivate and maintain a sense of worth and dignity. The dogs are born for the hunt, just like you. But you get more years at it than they do. So there's a bit of an imperative to help them with their little chunk of eternity. This orientation is a good foundation because from it you can build a framework that helps you stop thinking about yourself. And that's the key.

A quail hunt is, fundamentally, a selfless enterprise. *It ain't about you.* It's about the dogs and your hunting partner. You've got responsibilities way beyond yourself. It dawns on you, as you work with and for your dogs and your buddy, that this transcendence beyond self seems to be the nucleus, the "seed" if you will, from which friendships, families, and nations are built and maintained. You look across the "creek" more with your heart than with your eyes, and you see your hunting partner—an old friend of many years. There before you is a man full of grace and spirit and dignity who, for whatever reason, has decided to be out in the hinterlands with you today. As that focus sharpens in your heart, you realize that you've just taken a good turn with your wrench, the jaws of which are tightly gripped to the head of a rusty bolt on the first span of the bridge that crosses the creek. But you say nothing . . . nothing at all. He looks at you and also says nothing. The silence says it all.

You, your partner, and the dogs know that there is mutual interdependency on a quail hunt. The end point is more than the sum of the elements. The dogs find the birds. The hunters shoot the birds.

The dogs bring the shot birds to the hunters' hands. The dogs get praise and security and encouragement and the chance to keep on hunting. Good dog work, good shooting, and good companionship stoke the coals in the hunters' hearts and encourage *them* to keep on hunting—together. But there's more . . .

As members of a team, hunters and their dogs *care* about one another. When I've shot poorly or have stumbled in the field, I've had dogs, as well as my hunting partner, come to check on me. They care. We share sandwiches and water and conversations—all of us (yes, dogs converse quite well!). We stick together. We rest together. We move together. It is this caring, this true, honest, and selfless caring about one another that is a fundamental reality, a recurring lesson that experienced bridge builders on both sides of the creek understand and cultivate in order to engage the magic and meaning and the beauty and sense of awesome purposefulness that collectively define a quail hunt.

I know of no other hunt that requires more trust and respect and good manners than quail hunting. Hunters trust the dogs to search diligently for the birds and, when birds are found, to be careful, to be steady, to honor another dog's point, and to wait on point until the hunters come to flush and shoot. When the birds flush, the dogs trust that the birds *will* be shot. The hunters trust each other to be careful with their shots. You can't shoot quail and simultaneously be looking over your shoulder to be sure that your companion isn't pointing a shotgun at your head or at your dog.

After the shot, if there's a downed bird (and there should be), there is trust that the dog will find and retrieve that bird without mauling the bird with a "hard mouth" or committing the unpardonable, selfish, sin of eating a shot bird. Every time a dog brings a shot bird back to the hunter's hand, the dog is reinforcing the entire concept of selflessness for a greater good. That's the essence of a quail hunt. It is the dogs that keep reminding us about this. That's part of their job.

An old bridge that spans a creek is rarely impassable. It may only need a little work from time to time. Trust and respect—the materials that built the bridge in the first place and maintained it over the years—didn't just happen. They were earned. As quail hunters ramble and roam together, they are, absolutely, checking on and repairing the spans of the bridge. The bolts on the bridge are tightened by the wrenches of selfless actions and oiled by conversations about things that matter . . . guns, loads, gear, dogs, good memories, good friends, land, water, and wildlife. *Other stuff doesn't matter on a quail hunt.*

Those well-oiled turns of the wrench take other forms. Some are verbal. Most are not: a quiet nod or a grin for a shot well made; shots *not* taken in order to let your partner shoot; the sharing of shooting opportunities among points; picking up spent shotgun shells, your own as well as old ones spotted on the ground, along with other litter found on your partner's land, and then tucking the trash into your game vest. Sometimes there is a soft word of praise or a gentle petting given to a dog—done when the giver doesn't think the dog's owner is aware of what's going on. These varied communications are the enduring forces that temper and strengthen the bridge.

After the hunt, you don't linger long. You share a few reflective moments, perhaps sipping a little bourbon together to warm the collective soul, while standing around the tailgate of a pickup truck . . . close but not too close. Then, after a firm handshake, a soft word or two, smiles all around reflecting unspoken grace, and full-faced eye contact, you say, "Goodbye."

You turn, walk over to your truck, load your gear and your dog, and drive away, back to your other world, knowing that the bridge is there, bolts tightened, and that the old bridge still provides a secure crossing that goes both ways. It is a bridge of peace and friendship . . . a sacred space that joins the indivisible.

On the Path of Stillness

WHY DO WE ENGAGE IN OUR SOJOURNS INTO THE WILD? WHAT is it that we seek? Indeed, do we seek, or are we summoned, perhaps pulled . . . drawn by something at once within and beyond the self, some force, some energy that is a thinly veiled linkage beyond time, space, and universe? What is it that we see in the faces of anglers and hunters who have sojourned long in their pursuits and who have evolved beyond their initial motivations?

There is light in their eyes and calmness in their manner, and particularly so when they are afield. They seem to understand the power and beauty of the present tense, but there is something deeper, much, much deeper. The moment seems precious to them. There is an element within these people that lets us know that they have gone past knowledge and understanding and now are in the arenas of meaning.

We carry the original atoms and, it would seem from our restlessness, they are anxious to be about their eternal journey. Life and death are one to atoms. As atoms reconstitute themselves in myriad and diverse patterns, energy is never lost; it just changes form. Atoms, with their internal components and energies, *are* life. Thus, the rocks in the mountains live, as do also rivers, winds, and the cry of a hawk. All is sacred. Do we understand? Can we understand? Do we grasp the meaning?

The metals that form our rifles and shotguns may have been in the blood of ancient beasts. The atoms in hair and feathers and wood and plastics that form the lures we use to catch fish were at one point interstellar dust ... then perhaps part of a primordial stew from which evolved the oceans in time scales that are meaningless to us. The fish we seek came much later. A billion years is a blip, a small part of a moment. When a duck hunter is standing alone in the predawn darkness or a deer hunter is settled into a stand, he thinks about this sort of stuff. So do anglers on lonely beaches or on remote reaches of rivers.

Judeo-Christian theology states that the first creation was time. It was the greatest creation because without time there can be no matter, no atoms, not even subatomic particles, to carry the energy of life. But how can time be defined and, after time was created, where did the energy that is carried in matter come from? What was its origin?

When I posed these questions to an old friend of mine, Dr. Steve Evans, an astrophysicist working for NASA's Marshall Spaceflight Center in Huntsville, Alabama, he told me that before the creation of time there was free energy, the source of everything that is. I pushed him further and asked if there was a name for this free energy. His response: "Yes, it has a name. It is called God."

Steve continued his exchange with me, stating that physicists like himself understand time as relative to resolution ... reference points ... and subsequently impossible to define in absolute terms. Time is only linear when the resolution is small (e.g., mortal and planetary lifespans). Beyond that, time folds across itself into infinite degrees of superimposition that transcend meaning, and so time just "is." Alpha and Omega are one and the same.

I mentioned to Steve that some of the great theologians I studied while a seminary student many years ago had once upon a time been physicists. His response: "You're onto it, Brother." There was no condescension in that statement. He was, as a scientist (and friend), sharing an observation—the first step in science.

I'm not sure if I'm "onto it" or not, but in some of my more reflective moments there's a flow within me that feels like I'm being pulled along a high mountain trail, toward some summit. I think about the physicists, at least the physicists I consider the best ones, who, like Steve, are on the cutting edge between the measurable and the unmeasurable. Science has taken them to that edge, and the only way to go any further is to deal with timelessness (eternity), infinity, and free energy . . . in other words, they have no choice but to become theologians.

For the record, Steve and I went to high school together and were roommates in college. We've shared many pilgrimages. He is an accomplished and experienced hunter and angler, an artist, a chipper of flint, a forger of metals, a maker of spears, and a man of deep faith. He is a distinguished, well-published, and much respected scientist who writes about invisible planets (you don't have to see something to know that it is there), shoots laser beams at the moon to detect how much good old planet earth wobbles and to figure out why, and is the man responsible for working out the equations necessary to take the space shuttle from an elliptical orbit into a circular one (to save gas). He's a pretty practical guy, a blend of primitive man and star child. As a hunter and angler, he is also a spiritual sojourner, a member of the tribe.

The members of this tribe of sojourners, the men and women who prowl the fields and forests and streams and lakes and oceans and tundra and mountains and deserts—with gun and rod in hand—are, like all mortal beings, given a little snip of time salted with a little dose of that free energy. How we handle this mix tends to be a personal choice. Some, like Steve, understand and express it in deep and profound ways. Some just use it up in the context of mortal existence. Some chase it. Some, however, wrap themselves in the folds of time so completely that when they are in transcendental states of being it actually stops . . . and matter doesn't matter anymore. The denominator goes to zero, and they are enveloped by the aforementioned free energy that, while defined, is unmeasurable—but like the unseen planet, it is absolutely real, absolutely there. When this occurs, there is transcendence of the sojourner into the realm of ultimate unmeasurable purity. The light comes on.

In that light, these timeless sojourners come face to face with a profound stillness. They are inextricably one in being with the multidimensional hyper-volume that constitutes universal life. They *are* the fish they catch, the bird or beast they shoot, the mountain they climb, the river they run. Their weapons are, absolutely, extensions of themselves. So are the pieces of metal, wood, composite materials, or stone that come from their weapons at great speed, and the carefully crafted combinations of earth materials surrounding hooks that are cast into waters to entice fish to strike.

The stillness that envelops them is not necessarily quiet, nor is it necessarily peaceful. These sojourners tend to share who they are and they tend to be firm in thought, manner, and deed. Some can, in fact, be pretty rough characters. But, they've been to the top of the mountain, and many just stay there. They willingly become guides. When we encounter these individuals, we sense their deep and vibrant stillness.

Some experience the stillness early in life. We recognize the stillness in the child engaged with clouds and stars and puppies and butterflies and a grandparent's garden, and we know what's happening. We sense it in the young ministers, priests, teachers, attorneys, military officers, tradesmen, musicians, writers, artists, poets, scientists, and persons who are launching themselves into various businesses and have discovered somewhere along the way the power and purpose and meaning of hunting and fishing and have taken up the rod and the gun. Perhaps their life orientations and search modes put them on the fast track to stillness. For many, however, perhaps most, the search for the stillness is a long adventure. We snatch bits and pieces of truth along the way and build a framework that eventually guides us there.

I wonder if it is a unique human endeavor, this sojourn to stillness, or if an earthworm or a flake of lichen also does this. How is a sentient, self-aware element in the universe defined? Do we have the correct universal reference points? Are we speaking the right language that allows us to engage earthworms and lichens during transcendence? Are we in tune with the right forces? I'm not sure, but evidence suggests that we're not there yet. So, just to be on the safe side of the equation, when I see earthworms stranded out in the streets after a heavy rain, I catch them and put them back on the earth beyond pavement—unless, of course, I need them for fish bait. And I leave the lichens on my mailbox, except when they obscure the numbers that identify my address.

And I move ever deeper. A sunrise becomes mind-altering—spirit altering—as it envelopes me with photons that are addled flirts with waves of energy. They join to dance upon my mortal being, my soul, and the universe around me. I lose myself among stars on clear winter nights and, as I soar, I can feel, I can hear, star dust swirling in an unending chorus through the heavens. I watch rusty iron drip from a wound created by other metals that were forged by heat, honed to sharpness, and carelessly engaged by a hand while skinning a deer. The rusty iron dripping to the ground will cycle through eternity in myriad recombinations . . . perhaps in life forms we know, perhaps in life forms we don't or can't know.

Is the knife alive? Warriors and hunters and fishers across the eons of time have sensed life, or perhaps something beyond life, an elemental energy, in their weapons; and they invoked spiritual forces using prayer in various forms and dimensions, including prayers for synergism between being and tool. Is this spirit they addressed actually the essence of the primordial free energy, or is it a derivative of that unmeasurable energy? When hunters and fishers pray, to what extent should their prayers acknowledge the spiritual interconnectedness of all that is within and around them. Although frequently accused of doing so, I do not believe that such prayer is pagan "earth worship." Rather, it is an act of engagement with God, comprehensively.

Subsequently, we should not keep score or engage in contests when hunting or fishing any more than we should measure how much wine we can slurp down or bread we can swallow during Holy Communion. Likewise, hunting and fishing occur in the cathedrals of wild, beautiful, and lonely places where, if we become still enough, perhaps we can hear the wind whisper our names and feel the presence of free energy that transcends self (God?). As in other places of worship, we can sense the holiness and the sacredness of forest, field, prairie, wetland, mountain, desert, tundra, estuary, marsh, river, pond, lake, and sea and engage *with unbridled respect* the lives that dwell therein, whether we know them or understand them or not. The earth will sing to you if you give it a chance. It can also cry.

I have no tolerance for those of my tribe who exhibit and pro-claim disrespect for cathedrals or fellow worshipers. We do not know how the spirit moves in the earthworm, the lichen, the largemouth bass, the catfish, the fox squirrel, the deer, the wood duck, the eagle, the soil, the rock, the water. We do not speak their language. We have different reference points. But to assume that other elements of creation lack spirit or the capacity to engage spirit is ultimate ar-rogance. We don't know. Perhaps, as mortals, moving and expressing our being within dimensions of time, we *can't* know.

It is all about honesty, ultimate honesty, the deepest sort of hon-esty, as creatures, as beings in a created world, a created universe with an operational framework of inclusiveness and interconnect-edness. It is about reverence for life and its various dimensions, including emotions.

It is not wrong to be sad, or even to cry, when encountering or causing death. I cry when I kill or witness a kill. I will quit hunting and fishing when I stop crying at a kill. Tears are beautiful. They tend to be pure. Tears are a very special kind of prayer.

Although hunters and anglers kill, those who are *real* hunters and fishers experience no joy in killing, no joy in death. Joy at death proclaims something dark in the human heart. Rather, for the hunter and angler there is deep satisfaction and a linkage with the infinite when, through the taking of life, purposefully, skillfully, prayerfully, with respect and humbleness, we are engaged in the eternal drama of energy flows. The flow of energy proclaims life, not death.

For the sojourner in stillness there is no victory, no chest thump-ing, no recognition, and no reward save our memories of the en-counter and the flesh that we consume. In humbleness we honor that which we kill by using our weapons skillfully, killing cleanly, carefully processing the game or fish, eating it, and letting it become part of our mortal being. The trophies we hang on our walls, if we choose to do so, are there only to invoke those memories and, in so doing, take the animal or fish that we've killed, and ourselves, into dimensions of immortality . . . engaging the timeless realms of free energy.

This is why I hunt and fish and why I always will. And although I tend to be a solitary hunter and fisherman, I am not alone in my pursuits. I share this pilgrimage with fellow sojourners who enter into the cathedrals of the wild and lonely places for common purpose—common worship.

In the stillness we are one.

Almost Nearly

THE RIVER WASN'T PARTICULARLY HIGH OR LOW. IN FACT, IT WAS as perfect as a river can be. The clear water sent its messages. It swirled around rocks and logs, even those under the surface, letting the sojourner know to steer clear. The channels through shoals splashed and played through their V's, showing the way upstream or down.

I knew the river well. For more than fifty-five years I'd prowled the waters of the White River, from its headwaters, into its maturity, and on to its ultimate merger with the Mississippi. The hills of north Arkansas, where it is born, and the forests, floodplains, and backwaters along its lower reaches are comprehensively integrated into my soul . . . into every dimension of my being. I am a native son of the region. I know the moods of the hills, the forests, and the river. I've fished and hunted, smooth-faced, black-bearded, peppered and white. Every season calls to me, each in its own way.

There is magic in flowing water and in hills. I knew from childhood that they would define my life. Smallmouth bass own my heart where the river sings its songs of youth. Trout restore my spirit when the river resurrects itself time and again below the huge dams that try to kill it. Further downstream, turbid, warmer, and relentless in its power, the river fills me with deep, spiritual awareness, perhaps even a bit of understanding about eternity, letting me know in no uncertain terms that it will win in the end . . . that God, and God alone, has the ultimate say in how stuff gets worked out. In these lower reaches, as I set trotlines for catfishes, or slip into the backwaters for crappies, or hunt for ducks, squirrels, and deer, or as I trap bear, the river's voice is and always has been deep and sure. It has a cadence that resonates with that of my heart.

It is the White River, beyond all others, that has blessed me, and I've known many rivers. I learned respect for currents—about the different ways water moves in channels and among things that get in the way of that movement. I also learned that a river has no respect for those who move upon or in its waters. It will give you great happiness and is absolutely capable of bringing great sadness. I've played on the White. I've watched people die in it. I've seen it ravage the countryside. I've heard its siren's songs . . . songs that I have never been able to resist. The river, in its comprehensive totality as an integrated ecosystem, an almost personified spiritual element, taught me well. And it sent me out into the world as a disciple for river conservation. It gave me no choice.

And so, after a somewhat circuitous route as a world rambler—a journey that incorporated university administration (student housing), professional scouting, Peace Corps, seminary, and homelessness—I settled down (just a little) and, after completing doctoral studies at Auburn University and a post-doctoral post with the University of Alaska, I became a professor of fisheries at Mississippi State University. My primary focus was rivers. For over thirty years I worked with rivers on every continent that has them. (Antarctica doesn't have rivers—yet.) From the arctic to the tropics, from on top to down under, east to west, I was in boats of every stripe. Sometimes others would drive, but mostly I did the driving. Those with me trusted me. They knew I could read the water and make the boat go where it should.

Every river sang its song to me, inviting me to become ever more intimate with it. Some tried to keep me forever. But, during my career, I was always able to avoid the deadly forces—occasionally just barely, but that's all that mattered. I must admit, however, that I sometimes played games with the edges of danger. I was strong. I was fast. I had a good sense of timing. Depth perception was excellent. I was full of testosterone, spit and vinegar. I loved adventuring. I loved the rush of adrenaline.

But respect was always there. I knew that rivers never play games. All of them will from time to time show their angry side. When their anger was extreme, I stayed away from them (except in emergencies). Additionally, I did not travel on rivers when fog swirled and hung thickly over the water. Only under special circumstances did I travel on rivers during the night. If a river is peaceful, night travel can be wonderful, *if* the moon and stars shine brightly enough to give the river enough light. The pilot of a riverboat must be able to see *very* well.

Mortality slips up on a man. Like a river, it is a relentless force. But, unlike a river, a man will play games. He will pretend that all is well when it isn't. He remembers what was and is not thinking clearly about what is. Component parts begin to wear out. The connections become frayed. The man compensates (he thinks) with experience, insight, and perhaps a little wisdom. But, in truth, he is flirting with luck. It is one thing to do that alone. It is quite another to do it with someone else onboard.

I had sense enough during my later years in academia to let my graduate students drive the boats (most of the time). I'd taught them the ways of the rivers and about boats, and they became very good at their work. In fact, I noticed that the more advanced students became teachers themselves, instructing the newer students. They didn't need me to do it anymore. This is how it should be. It filled me with deep satisfaction to watch them do this.

By the time I was in my late fifties and early sixties, it actually got to the point that I hardly went to the rivers much at all. I had absolute trust that my students were handling things quite well. This was a very good thing because, in addition to teaching and research, I was deeply engaged in the administration and politics of academics and science.

Such a chapter can take its toll. It surely did on me. I could become pretty cantankerous during these sunset years. There were also occasional periods of quiet (sometimes not so quiet!) desperation. I missed the rivers. I missed being out on them, driving the boats and messing around with gear and fish and mud and seasons. When I started getting to the limits, the threshold of dissociation with rivers—when I was almost in panic mode and about to go mad and bite myself—I'd start dropping hints to my students that I needed to be in the field "to check on things."

One of my students finally (and bravely) came to me and explained that they didn't need me anymore out in the field, but that they knew that I needed to go, *occasionally*. They maintained a list among themselves for that purpose. When I became overly irritable, hard to deal with, or in other ways weird and abstract and when I started murmuring "in the biblical sense" to myself, whoever was next on the list would invite me to accompany him or her for a day on a river. The brave student said that I was usually OK for about a month after such a trip, and then the next person in line had to put me in a boat, somewhere on a river.

When I was in the boat, my students were courteous, most of the time. But one day a student told me, as I was approaching the boat that was pulled up next to the riverbank and full of gear, "Dr. Jackson, that seat in the middle of the boat is yours. Sit there. Don't move around. Don't touch anything. Do not try to help. I don't want you to screw things up." I asked him if he had a pink parasol for me. It was a good day. We had a good time.

If a professor doesn't die of sickness or accident, quit or get fired, or become a university administrator (heaven forbid!), most of the time retirement happens (sort of). What happens, actually, is that you don't stop, you just sort of fade away. Your former students are all out yonder in the world and most are doing good jobs in the field. Some are professors themselves, with their own students, passing the torch along to new generations of professionals. Some have heard different callings and have moved into careers more precisely in tune with the rhythms of their hearts. The old professor still teaches an occasional course (he loves to pollute young minds!), writes an occasional paper, counsels an occasional student or young faculty member, but stays as far away as possible from administration and politics. The rank of professor emeritus is the best academic rank of all!

I thought I'd hunt and fish more in retirement until I realized that before retirement I was hunting and fishing all the time anyway—that it would be impossible to do more of it. The difference, however, is that in retirement you can go far away for longer periods. There's nobody calling you back for some meeting or whatever. You just up and go away and that's that. You can catch up on stuff when you get back. You don't wear watches or look at calendars (at least not very much).

My son Robert and I have been taking advantage of this new operational framework. Every October we get together for a fishing trip. Sometimes we fish for smallmouth bass in the headwaters of Ozark streams. Sometimes we go to the Gulf of Mexico for saltwater fishing. But mostly, we go to the White River in north Arkansas for trout fishing. The river sings to him just as it does to me.

Yes, the day was perfect. The river was perfect. We'd fished the previous day and done well. The trout were mostly rainbows, but occasionally we'd catch a brown. The boat was a typical White River jon boat, about sixteen feet long, molded fiberglass, with low sides and a 15-horsepower outboard motor attached to the transom. They are perfect boats for the river. They are sturdy and shallow drafted. They probably could follow a sweaty mule up a dusty path. I like them *a lot.*

The previous summer I'd experienced trouble with my eyes, especially my right eye. If it had been primarily my left eye, it wouldn't have been such a concern to me. But I need that right eye in order to shoot my guns. And so I'd gone to the eye doctor and he'd scheduled cataract surgery for me. He wanted to do both eyes at the same time, but I was scared to do that. If something went wrong, I wanted to have one eye left. The surgery on my right eye went well. For the first time since I was ten years old, I had perfect vision in that eye. But there was a problem.

For sixty-five years my brain has worked out the equations that bring messages from my two eyes together and make sense out of it all. Now the messages were all weird and distorted. My "new eye," the one that had surgery, told the brain that whatever I was looking at was high, further away, and to the right. My "old eye" kept sending its regular signals that the object of my focus was low, closer, and to the left. I was never quite sure where things actually were.

I knocked over glasses during meals. I grabbed for things and got a handful of nothing. When I cast a fly or lure, I had no idea of where it might land. When I shot a shotgun, I was pitiful. Prior to the surgery, even with dim vision in my right eye, I was usually hitting at least twenty targets out of every twenty-five. Now I was hitting fewer than ten!

Rifles were different. When rifle shooting, I use my right eye only and look through a scope. I was as good as ever with a rifle— actually better! I had perfect vision and the scope's crosshairs did the thinking for me. The brain didn't need to coordinate binocular vision. Driving—well, it was a challenge. Sometimes my brain got tired of sorting through all the images and started giving me double vision. It was as if I were some sort of tropical chameleon with eyes that worked independently from each other, which, when the brain was tired, they did. I quit driving by mid-afternoon. It was a mess. I didn't tell folks much about these problems. The doctor said they'd go away in a few months. So I forged ahead. And now Robert and I were on the river together, with me driving the boat.

Actually, I was somewhat pleased at how well I was driving that boat. I knew that section of river extremely well and I had an excellent feel for the boat. The river and the boat were old friends of mine. In fact, we'd not experienced a single bump or single miscalculated chute through a shoal. I relaxed. The tension faded. I was "home," doing what I'd been doing out on the river for decades. I convinced myself that all was just fine and dandy. I could focus on the fishing and the hills and my son. After all, this was my domain. I was a seasoned river boat pilot.

The week before our trip, with the river just like it was this day, a man died on this section of the river. There were two fishermen in the boat. It turned over. The river killed one of the men. The other somehow was able to make it to safety.

I shook my head at the news when we'd first arrived at the river resort. The White River is a big, very powerful river here in these reaches. It is not a place to learn how to drive a boat. But it was not angry today. It was not angry a week ago when the man was killed. It was in perfect condition. The accident was surely the result of inexperience. But inexperience is not the only killer on a river. Arrogance also can get you killed.

Yes-sir-re, the *man* (me) was in his element, on holiday with his son, equipped with a new eye and resurrected spit and vinegar. My old hunting dog, Hank, a sixty-pound griffon, was in the boat with us. There was plenty of room. Hank is good in boats and loves fishing. He's been my companion on many river trips.

It was our last drift downstream for the day. It had been a long day. My eyes were getting a little tired . . . particularly the new eye. The sun was turning the hillsides and rocky bluffs to gold. There was just a little chill in the air. There was no wind. The river spoke to us in gentle whispers. We'd just come through the next to last shoal before the final reach to our boat dock. There was a tight bend and below that bend, out in the very middle of the river, there was an old log sticking out of the water. The log had been in that place for at least 15 years. It angled downstream and was big enough to create considerable turbulence below it. Nothing could be more obvious. Beyond that snag were some huge rocks along the left bank. The water was deep around those rocks. There were lots of trout among them.

I positioned the boat so that it would drift between the old snag and the rocks. There was plenty of room. I'd made that very same drift hundreds of times over the years. It was just a matter of timing and getting the boat lined up correctly. Then I'd cut off the motor and start fishing.

Just as the motor stopped and I was reaching for my fishing rod, we slammed into that snag broadsided. I'd miscalculated distance and timing! My eyes and my brain had betrayed me! The boat rode up onto the angle of the log and tipped upstream. Immediately the boat began to fill with water. We were seconds away from capsizing. And, in that current, with those rocks ahead, somebody was going to die—probably all three of us.

I shouted to Robert, "Grab Hank and lean downstream!" He immediately responded accordingly. I leaned also, as hard as I could. The boat was hung on that snag. We were perfectly centered on it. The boat could not swing away from it. By leaning over the side of the boat, we were able to lift the upstream side of the boat to just barely above the surface of the water—perhaps one inch. If we moved at all or shifted weight, we'd flip over into the river . . . into the final moments of life.

Robert had Hank. Hank responded to the command "stay." He knew we were in danger and leaned over the boat just like Robert and I were doing. We were not scared. The privilege of being scared would have to wait. Robert kept his position and kept Hank secured. The river surged beneath us, almost laughing, as if it finally, after all these years, would get me. It had every reason to believe that.

I could not move but knew that, somehow, I had to get my hands on a paddle. It was floating around in the flooded boat out of my reach. I could not change position. I could not shift my weight. But I *had* to get my hands on that paddle and get the boat to swing off of that snag. Unless I did that, we eventually would tire, the boat would capsize, and the river would become a killer, again.

My fishing rod lay before me. I reached for it, carefully. Then, slowly, I moved my arms and the rod out and toward the floating paddle. There was nothing on the paddle that the rod could catch. But little by little I got the paddle closer . . . until finally it drifted into my hands. I dropped the rod and told Robert to keep leaning. As he did that, I paddled in such a way that the current would eventually catch the lower unit of the outboard motor and swing us, stern first, around and off of that snag. But the boat was big and the river very powerful. The boat did not want to swing. I pulled harder with the paddle, fearful that I'd break the handle. Then, slowly, the angle of the boat shifted on the snag. The stern began to shift downstream and, a moment later, we were free. The boat steadied itself in an upright position but was more than halfway full of cold river water. We had two bailing buckets and worked quickly. I could not start the motor until most of the water was out of the boat. To do it too early, with so much water in the boat, would make the water rush back toward the stern and surely sink us. The rocks loomed ahead.

We were about a hundred feet from the rocks when I knew we had no choice. I had to start the motor or else we would crash into the rocks. Robert kept bailing. Hank (bless his heart!) stayed where he'd been told to stay. The motor started, and *very slowly* I drove the boat back out into the middle of the river. We avoided the rocks by about twenty feet. I could almost hear the river sigh, "Well, maybe next time." I also sighed. We'd robbed the reaper . . . just barely.

Once out into the channel, we were able to bail out almost all of the water and be on our way. Hank came to my end of the boat and licked my hand. Then he held my hand in his mouth. I could hear Robert breathing deeply in the chilled air. I drove slowly, forcing my eyes to work together, ordering my brain to work out the differences. As we tied the boat securely in its mooring berth back at the fishing resort, my thoughts raced. I'd nearly killed my son. Arrogance was my sin. I'd played a treacherous game on a river, knowing all the while that I was playing and that a river never does. When it was over, all I could do is tell my son that I was sorry, that I'd betrayed his trust, and to pray . . . a prayer of thanksgiving and apology.

Since that incident on the river—it has been just over one year now as I write this—I have not driven a boat on the White River or, for that matter, on *any* river. I also refuse to get into a boat with anybody else driving on a river. I do not trust them. I also still don't trust myself. My boat and outboard are stored and languishing. My heart yearns to be back upon the currents. The rivers call to me. I want to go . . . back to where I belong. But I won't. I won't go until I'm sure I'm ready. Maybe this year, maybe next. Maybe the year after next.

I'll know when the time is right. It mostly depends on how I'm handling my shotgun. With the passage of time past my eye surgery, my shooting seems to be getting better, just a little. It is a slow process. A double on woodcock in a green ash grove, a double on wood ducks over my brushy little pond at daybreak, or three quail in a row on a golden afternoon will let me know that the equations are very close to working themselves out; the brain is finally sorting out the messages from my eyes and getting them in synchrony with the rest of me. I feel, sometimes, like I'm almost there, almost ready for a river again . . . almost nearly, but (as yet) not quite hardly. Missing a shot at feathers can be a disappointment. Missing a shot on a river, well . . .

An Old Bull's Shade Tree

AS A SPORTSMAN'S BEARD SHIFTS TOWARD WHITE AND HAIR begins to thin on the knob, there are changes in his being that take him into somewhat reflective waters. He becomes more and more like an old herd bull, alone out in the pasture, finding great contentment just moving around in the shade under a tree, occasionally pawing the ground or shaking his horns, flush with memories of how it used to be and enjoying the moment.

The old bull no longer jumps fences or chases small boys out of pastures. He doesn't charge gate posts, tree trunks, or meadowlarks. When he does charge (an increasingly rare event), there is purpose, discipline, and focus. However, it takes a very strong stimulus to rile him anymore. He knows when to go the distance . . . and when not to. Some stuff doesn't matter.

The old bull also very much appreciates the beauty and mystery of the fairer sex and the powerful ramifications therefrom in all of God's creation. However, he has come to an understanding (perhaps there may even be a smidgen of wisdom) that, in many cases, dealing with the temptations of Eve or trying to integrate the differences—not to mention distances—between Venus and Mars into some meaningful end result requires too much energy. It is, primarily, a matter of anticipated return relative to investment. Oftentimes it is better, and usually safer, to shift focus, stay quiet, leave for a little while, and set up shop under a "shade tree."

Similar operational frameworks exist within other relationships. Business, politics, profession, church, extended family, friendships, community, legal matters, and taxes, alone or in combination, can propel an old bull to go to where there's solace and opportunity for reflection and renewal. The shade tree beckons and the old bull has sense enough to pay attention to the call.

This is, fundamentally, why hunting camps, fishing shacks, "man caves" of various sorts, pubs, pool halls, and old diners that serve breakfast twenty-four hours a day were invented. This is why there are greasy, tool-infested garages, workshops, barns, and tractor sheds. These sacred places are, absolutely, *shade trees* where old bulls go alone, or gather, to paw the ground and shake their horns.

It is wise, indeed, to keep one's peace when an old bull begins making moves toward his shade tree. Give him some time and some space. He will eventually come back. It is much better for him to paw the ground out yonder than to do it in or around the homestead.

Keep in mind also that while bulls typically cannot be tamed, they do become somewhat gentler following ventures to their shade trees. This is particularly so with older bulls. When they come back, they will run errands, mow the lawn, help weed the garden, go to plays and community events, fix things, linger over morning coffee, shave and shower every day, remember to wear clean clothes, and stay out of the way . . . at least for a while.

My personal *shade tree* covers an expanse of fifty acres. Located at the interface of red clay hills and the Black Belt Prairie in east Mississippi, on the outskirts of a college town, my shade tree is simultaneously my refuge and sanctuary. It is at the end of a half-mile-long gravel road and surrounded on all sides by pasture and forest lands. I have good neighbors.

During the quarter of a century that I've owned it, it has spoken its messages to me, cleansed my heart, mind, and soul, and given me its bounty. I hunt there. I fish there. I trap there. This is where I take sunrise walks with my dogs and where I listen to coyotes at sunset. This is where I watch hawks soar and where I kick over logs looking for salamanders. This is where I train bird dog puppies and drive a tractor.

I have learned many of my shade tree's secrets and continue to do so. I am no stranger, no intruder, no visitor there. Rather I am a member of the community of living things who call this little part of planet Earth home. And I cherish it. I nurture and protect it. I encourage it to evolve in ways that enhance its beauty and its capacity to sustain diversity of life.

Using my tractor and a small assembly of implements—a mower, a plow, a disk, and a seed spreader—I gently work edges and trails to ensure that wildlife needs are met. I encourage "scruffy" areas and work to create corridors for wildlife movement. I plant and prune, but softly, in appreciation of, and with sensitivity to, native vegetation processes. There are forested hillsides and lowland areas. There are wetlands and cedar brakes. There are thickets and brambles and green ash groves. A large hay field gets cut twice per year: late in summer and just before frost in autumn, after nesting season is over for ground-nesting birds and after young deer and rabbits and other wildlife are old enough to move out of the way as the hay is cut and baled.

There are two creeks and two ponds on the property. I trap on the creeks, mostly targeting raccoons. I hunt ducks on the ponds. The larger pond is also a good fishery, managed primarily for big bluegill and for fly fishing. Largemouth bass are harvested only as needed to ensure good stock structure in the bluegill population. A bass-crowded pond helps me do this.

Over the years my shade tree has given this old bull a lot of joy and has recharged his batteries many times. Long hours on the tractor or on a deer stand or drifting through the woods hunting squirrels—all have worked their magic on me. Sunrise duck hunts and golden afternoons with bird dogs coursing the fields and woodlands for quail and woodcock touch my very soul and fill me with strength and courage. I breathe deeply and feel life surge through my body. My mind clears. I am energized and renewed. I become man again and celebrate the gift, and the mystery, of mortality.

I fully understand that hunting and fishing and the activities leading me into these endeavors, precious though they are to me, are not my ultimate purposes or endpoints. They do not define who I am out there. Rather, hunting and fishing are the bridges connecting this old bull to the vibrancy of present-tense living while simultaneously helping him hear whispers reverberating across the expanse of years past. And, in ways that I do not understand, they give me hope for days yet ahead.

So again and again, as a seasoned hunter, angler, and caretaker of land that I love, I return to my shade tree to engage the power of purposeful living that defines the domain of the old bulls who are integrated within the ranks of sportsmen. It is a domain where respect, courage, and caring, seasoned by reflection, are blessed by enduring dreams that refuse to die.

When I depart from my shade tree, there are echoes that linger. But these echoes didn't originate from me or from my activities. Rather, they are the ageless echoes that reverberate from deep within the realm of the *shade trees* and into the oversoul of old hunters, anglers, and outdoorsmen. It is they, the old bulls, who seem to hear those eternal echoes most clearly, and it is they who seem to grasp their meaning.

The Ghosts of Davis Island

IF YOU HAVE BEEN ON THE BATTLEFIELDS OF VICKSBURG AND
Shiloh or walked the streets of old Savannah or Natchez, it is virtually impossible not to believe in ghosts. If, having ventured into
these realms, you still don't believe in ghosts, you probably have not
walked along vast stretches of coastal Mississippi that were erased
by Hurricane Katrina, or spent enough time on a porch swing with
your grandmother watching heat lightning on hot summer nights.
And if you've done all these things—and you *still* don't believe in
ghosts—then I'm absolutely confident that you've never been to
Davis Island.

Davis Island is a huge chunk of Mississippi, tens of thousands of
acres, that's on the Louisiana side of the river. Before and during the
War Between the States (there was nothing *civil* about it) the island
wasn't an island at all. It was attached to Mississippi, absolutely, and
called Davis Bend. After the war, the river decided all on its own
that it would ramble a bit and change its course. When it did that,
Davis Bend became Davis Island.

The island oozes history. It was the Confederate president Jef-
ferson Davis's plantation. It was his land and, in the hearts of some,
always will be . . . regardless of who owns it. It is now a collection
of very exclusive hunting and fishing clubs. The members of these
clubs guard their island treasures with absolute discipline, knowing
that they are the stewards not only of the island's natural resources
and its cherished traditions of hunting and fishing, but also of its
historical ruins and artifacts.

Over the years, I've developed treasured relationships with the people on the island. We fish, hunt, and break bread together. We explore our deeper currents through fellowship, storytelling, and quieter, spiritual moments shared in the island's lonely places. I'm absolutely convinced that I get to be there with them, on the island, in no small part because I am a southern mystic who engages spirits . . . a man who believes in ghosts.

Hunting ghosts, wood ducks, and squirrels are compatible enterprises that meld together beautifully on Davis Island. And so it was, early on an awesomely still December morning, with misty fog swirling around us, that Steve Ball and I drifted down through the woods to a very special place on the island called Bee-Line Slough. Our plan was to start the day with a wood duck hunt and then to transition to a squirrel hunt. Steve is the caretaker of the island's Palmyra Hunting Club. His father, Nelson "Buddy" Ball, helped found the club back in the early 1970s; subsequently, since childhood, the island has been a big part of Steve's life and identity. Steve is also a spiritual man. I don't think the island gave him much choice in the matter.

When we got to the slough, we carefully waded out to our sentry posts. I settled quickly into my spot to watch the evolution of a new day. Nocturnal shadows were still struggling to maintain their grip among the gray forms of cypress and tupelo. In the predawn twilight only a wren stirred, flitting from branch to log and back to branch again as I stood silently in thigh-deep water against one of the sentinels. The far distant rumble of a riverboat on the Mississippi River served only to intensify the profound stillness. Steve and I did not speak. In fact, we hardly dared breathe for fear of violating the sacred quiet that is the prelude to a wood duck hunt. The only whisper came from stiff wings passing overhead.

We were not alone and I knew it. In this place, down in the slough, not far from where an old riverboat landing once existed, ghosts are thick. Few speak of the ghosts, but those who spend much time on the island—those who are honest with themselves—know absolutely and without doubt that ghosts prowl around the slough and the nearby ruins of the old "home place." In fact, they drift around the entire island. They follow you through the woods on squirrel and turkey hunts. They slip up behind you as you sit alone under a canopy of stars listening to snow geese. They peer over your shoulder as you bend low to free a crappie jig from a snag. They get you lost and then help you find yourself . . . in all dimensions. They sometimes even join the fellowship as drinks are poured or dinner is served in camp after a hunt. I can tell when the ghosts are present. I shiver (and so do others), without saying a word. We know that the shivers are not temperature induced.

The whispers over Bee-Line Slough became more frequent, more intense. I shifted position, just slightly. Steve, standing about thirty yards from me, stood against the trunk of a huge cypress as if etched in stone. In front of us were a few scattered decoys, but in reality they were not needed. We knew that where we stood on that December morning was where the wood ducks wanted to be.

There are certainly other ducks on Davis Island—mallards, gadwalls, widgeons, pintails—but it is the wood duck that has captured my duck hunter's soul and also Steve's. Wood ducks come in hard, fast, and twisting, using the early morning shadows to their advantage. They require instinctive shooting as much or more than deliberate shooting. They typically call as they approach their destinations. But the warning call doesn't help the hunter. In fact, a hunter is rarely, if ever, *really* ready for wood ducks when they come in. The ducks are suddenly there, in front of you, darting among trees and shadows in erratic patterns that generate momentary turmoil, a good bit of shooting, and, typically, very few ducks on the water.

It would be an understatement to say that wood duck hunting and shooting can be profoundly disconcerting or that I am intrigued by it to the extreme. *Addicted* to it is probably more accurate, or perhaps obsessed. But, in actuality, it isn't the challenging shooting that holds me and draws me back to wood duck hunts time and again on Davis Island. In some respects, it isn't even about place and surroundings, although they establish the framework. It is something much, much deeper.

It may have something to do with smell, that rarest and least developed of the senses in the human species. With the possible exception of a tundra bog in Alaska, no place on Earth has the elemental richness of an overflow swamp or slough along the Mississippi River in the Deep South, including Gulf Coast salt marshes. The smell of river backwaters stirs primeval echoes within me, strangely evoking a suspicion that eons ago I was here, in the muck . . . that I've just come back home. The smell serves as a catalyst that ushers me across realms of knowledge and understanding so that there can be flirtation with meaning. It ushers me across the centuries, across the millennia. It is a weird sort of feeling, one that I admit may border insanity, but to deny that it comes to me and that it sort of makes sense (in a mystical sort of way) would make me a liar of the worst sort.

We are told that life probably originated in the sea, but I'm not so sure about this. The essential ingredients and physical forces necessary to create and sustain life are, in my opinion, much thicker in southern mud and muck. This stuff oozes and ferments and reconstitutes itself in a perpetual brew that screams life and evolutionary processes. Life slithers, slips, crawls, jumps, leaps, launches, swims, glides, drifts, squirms, plops, and flies in all shapes, sizes, forms, and means in the South's backwaters. And the perpetual dawning of life, its daily resurrection, its nocturnal reconstitutions, and its integrated, symbiotic, all-consuming forces are like magnets that suck me into the mix, both spiritually and physically. It is the smell, however, that draws me there, that lets me know that I'm where I belong. I'm back in the primordial stew . . . where life and death merge to create incredible potentials. That's the essence of a wood duck hunt on Davis Island—why I'm there, not as an observer but as a participant in the eternal drama. It's the smell of ghosts!

I slithered and wormed my way deeper into the muck and squirmed tighter against the tree I stood beside. The mud sucked at my boots. I knew why. I heard Steve work the action of his shotgun, loading three shells. The shadows were almost gone, but the echoes of my spiritual sojourn continued to reverberate. There was a streak of yellow on the horizon, hinting of dawn. Shooting time was upon us. I also loaded my gun . . . and waited.

A sudden rush of wind, wings, and adrenaline flooded my small spot in the universe. There was no time to think. I do not remember shooting. It was over before I knew it had begun. My dog was on his way to make the retrieve. I pumped an empty shotgun shell from my old battle-scarred gun. After a bit of rummaging around out of sight in some button brush, the dog sloshed his way back to me with a drake wood duck in his mouth. I had not heard Steve shoot. I was too focused on my own intense moments. But, as I looked his way, I saw him carefully hanging a duck in a bush behind the tree where he was standing.

A few minutes later, three more wood ducks rocketed by over-head within range. One fell at Steve's shot. I shot and missed. After Steve went out to pick up his duck and had returned to his post by the tree, a flock of a dozen or so fell in on top of me. I got one of them. And then the sun rose and the wood ducks evaporated.

As sunlight flooded across the slough, I opened myself up, prob-ing for ghosts. I knew that they were around. They always are. I shut my eyes, invoking spiritual realms. I opened them. I opened all my senses, feeling, listening, looking, smelling. There was no wind, but there was a faint tremor on the surface of the water. A bagworm moth cocoon gently rocked as a tiny pendulum in the breezeless air. The expected chill coursed through my body. I smiled.

Life crawled out of the muck on its evolutionary sojourn and, that morning, as hunters, so did we. Wood ducks in hand, we walked from the slough up to where we'd parked our vehicles. There we doffed our waders and swapped our shotguns for .22 rifles. The stillness of the morning was perfect for a squirrel hunt and there was plenty of morning yet before us.

That is another beautiful thing about wood duck hunting. It is over typically before the fox squirrels begin to stir. On Davis Is-land we don't worry about missing the crack-of-dawn gray squirrel movements. There are no gray squirrels on Davis Island. But the fox squirrels are thick.

If forced to choose between wood duck hunting and squirrel hunting, or else die, I'd have to die. I cannot choose. Both stroke me with wonderful connections to the rhythms of the earth. The wood ducks come to me. I must go get the squirrels. Wood duck hunts are about dawns and resurrections. Squirrel hunts are about purposeful living in the present tense. Both occur in the cathedrals of the wild and lonely places. Both generate epiphanies of understanding and meaning. And on Davis Island both take me deep into the realms of ghosts. But I think the squirrel hunts take me deeper. It probably has something to do with where the ghosts come from. There's a lot of history on Davis Island.

For this reason, I do not hunt deer on Davis Island. I cannot stay quietly in one place, waiting, for very long. I am drawn out into the landscape, into the hidden pockets full of mystery, history, and spirits. I must move. I must go. I must seek. I must encounter. My name is called. However, I hear it through my heart, not my ears. The call generates a restlessness that will not be stilled. And, if I am not careful, I can be lost in the land of never-never . . . physically as well as spiritually. A good compass is required in both aspects. Clouds (of all sorts) happen. Coming back home, back to camp, can be a long, trial-laced journey. Squirrel hunts will take you as deep into the wilderness around you and the wilderness within you as you wish to go, and sometimes much further. This is particularly true on Davis Island. Be prepared.

The very first ghost I ever encountered on Davis Island was during a squirrel hunt on a gray November afternoon. I was all alone in a remote corner of the Palmyra Club's property. There was a stillness out there that wrapped itself around me. I was absolutely at peace.

There were a few ridges and also some low spots that I had to work along carefully. My compasses were working in good order. But I didn't use the physical compass, just the spiritual one. Owls called. I listened carefully to their messages. Ducks whistled overhead. Raccoons were out and about. So were deer. I shot well that afternoon and had several squirrels in the pocket of my shooting vest within a couple of hours. Dusk began to settle on the land. The magic of twilight settled on me. I turned to start working my way out of the woods. Then I sensed that I was not alone. I stopped. There was no wind. But there was movement, slight movement, shadowy movement, in the branches of a nearby tree. The shadow darted and drifted among the huge trees that surrounded me. It wasn't an animal or a bird. I waited. I felt the chill. I smelled the presence. I smiled and the ghost also smiled. I did not see it, but I knew it. It moved with me until I got to the edge of the woods, the edge of spiritual dimensions . . . then it was gone.

I walked on through the dark, alongside a big wheat field sprinkled with deer. Across the field, a half a mile away, lights from camp cast a mellow glow under a small grove of live oaks. It melded with the glow in my soul. Quiet enveloped me. It penetrated from the outside in and then evolved into serenity and peace, which reversed direction and worked from the inside out. My boots padded softly on the old dirt road where I walked. I whispered a prayer of thanksgiving for the afternoon's encounters—every one of them. Suddenly the chill returned and again I was no longer alone.

We can pretend that these encounters are not real. But I quit doing that a long time ago. The ghosts are there just to remind us that there are other dimensions than the mortal. That's all. And that's important. I sort of like it when they walk with me on Davis Island.

And so, after our early morning wood duck hunt on Bee-Line Slough, Steve Ball and I went our separate ways to hunt squirrels, each searching for encounters that fit our rhythms that morning— with the squirrels, the land, the forest, the secret places, and, for me, with the ghosts. My dog quietly walked alongside of me. He knows. He understands. Sometimes I think he's more connected to the realms I seek than I am. In fact, as I think about it, I'm sure that he is. Maybe that's the real reason hunters domesticated wolves.

I slipped quietly among the trees, senses alert, and soon spotted the first squirrel of the morning. It was a gorgeous big red-orange fellow. I plotted my course among the trees, selecting a route that would take me to within thirty yards of the tree it was in. I told my dog to stay. He knew the routine. He'd done this many times before. There was no rush. The squirrel obviously had found something in the tree he liked. He'd move around some in the tree, but he never left it.

Finally, I got within range, took a rest for my rifle against the trunk of a tree, centered the crosshairs of my rifle's scope on the squirrel's head, and squeezed off the shot. There was a solid "thunk" as the bullet struck. The squirrel tumbled through a sixty-foot free-fall, hit the ground, kicked a couple of times, and was still. I kept my position just to be sure that there were no other squirrels nearby. Convinced there were none, I retrieved my squirrel, motioned for my dog to come, and moved on into the hunt. An hour later I had three more squirrels. But there had been no encounters with other elements of the realm . . . no ghosts. I thought nothing of it. It can be that way and usually is.

Then a strange feeling flooded me. It caused me to stop hunting, stand still, look around me, and just think about things. I thought about the old plantation, about slavery, about the war, about the triumphs and tragedies, about the suffering, about floods and drought, about hard work, about misunderstandings, about res-urrections . . . about friendships and connections, to the land, to culture, to history. I thought about life and death, about beauty and ugliness. I thought about wood ducks, about fox squirrels, about shotguns and rifles. I thought about the day and the previous night full of stars. I thought about yesterday's sunset and today's sunrise. I thought about ghosts.

There was still an hour or so before the hunt was to end. I had four squirrels to go before reaching the legal limit. But there was this strange feeling that simply would not go away. I took the clip from my rifle and began to reload it. The feeling went away. I put the clip back into the rifle and the feeling came back to me. I removed the clip again and peace returned.

The ghosts of Davis Island are pretty good at reminding me that a spiritual compass always trumps the one in my pocket. On this incredibly still morning, a "breeze" rustled the upper branches of the live oaks near the home place. I could hear the distant rumble of a riverboat . . . and voices echoing from a landing that no longer existed. The old, well-known chill coursed through me. I knew that my hunt that day was over and that it was time for mortals to leave this sacred place again, at least for a while.

Arbor Glow Belongs to Paper Boys

A LONG TIME AGO THE WORLD HAD WHAT WAS CALLED "THE paper boy." This kid was usually somewhere between twelve and fifteen years old, needed money, and had no transportation other than a bicycle or his feet. He had, for the most part, not smelled gas fumes or perfume and thus could still view the world with clarity. His needs were basic and simple: shotgun shells, .22 ammo, and some fishing tackle. There was a lake just down the road from where he lived and woods behind the house. Back in the woods there was a creek.

This boy got up at 4:30 every morning, rain, snow, sleet, storm, or clear sky, and walked up to the front porch of an elementary school, about a quarter of a mile from his house, picked up a bundle of papers, and for the next ninety minutes brought news of the world to around eighty-five households. Then, at the end of the month, after school, he went to those households and collected the fee for newspapers delivered.

If he was careful and made sure that he didn't have more papers in his bundle than households receiving them, and if those households actually paid him for the deliveries, he would earn about fifty dollars every month. Considering that his father worked full time, as did his mother, and that they had four children (the paper boy was the oldest of the four), and they together made less than four hundred dollars a month, the boy's wages were pretty good. The alternative to the paper route was poverty for the boy, or starvation.

You can only skip so many meals at school in order to save your lunch money for fish hooks, .22 bullets, and .410 shotgun shells.

A boy walking alone on the streets of an Arkansas town in the dark hours of early morning, every day, all year long, year after year, with a paper sack across his shoulders, delivering papers to folks in his neighborhood, gets to do a lot of thinking. He gets to see a lot of stuff that goes on when nearly everybody else is still asleep. But most importantly, he develops the habit and the desire to get up early and be about his day while his mind and body are fresh.

Boys who milk cows or bake bread also know about getting up early, but they don't get to ramble about in the world like a paper boy does. Plus, most of the boys of my age that I knew who milked cows or baked bread didn't get paid. They were integral components of family enterprise. Frankly, I'm not sure what the world does now that paper boys no longer are out there, alone, in the quiet and dark of early morning, thinking about important things as they deliver their papers. But I can assure you that the loss is great.

A lot of dreaming and planning and praying and figuring things out happens on a paper route. Seeing a sunrise every single day does magic things to a boy's mind, soul, and heart. Carrying a sack of eighty to one hundred papers that collectively weigh between forty and sixty pounds (depending on the day of the week, Thursdays and Sundays being the heaviest) on your back every day as your body is figuring out how to grow makes a boy strong. The boy only weighs about eighty-five to one hundred pounds. Throwing papers precisely, making sure they go to the exact spot on the porch, the carport, by the window, under a board by the air conditioner, or wherever the customer wants, develops coordination and depth perception beyond belief. A paper boy knows that the US Army got it wrong when it developed a pineapple-shaped hand grenade. The World War II Germans had it right. Put a handle on the thing! And, to this very day, more than half a century later, this old paper boy still wants to stop the man in the car that delivers his morning paper and show that man the correct way to fold a paper so that it can be thrown properly.

Paper boys may not know this, but everything they do equips them to be good outdoorsmen. They know how to endure harsh weather and how to rejoice in good weather. They know how to perform in spite of challenging conditions, and how to improve performance when conditions are in their favor. They learn logistics and distance and timing and accuracy and ballistics as they deal with the different weights of papers they throw, and they know that they must hit the target or suffer from the customer at the end of the month when they try to collect their fee. They learn how to deal with the occasional critter that challenges their advance. They learn how to deal with the occasional person that challenges their integrity and their affairs. But most of all they learn about themselves and how to deal with the person that they look at in the mirror every day.

Paper boys know the seasons. They are the first to hear snow geese traveling under the stars in the crisp autumn sky. They are the first to hear owls returning to their nests with rabbits and skunks to feed their broods in February. They are the first to hear robins begin their courtship songs in the softness of spring. They are the first to see the snakes and the tarantulas cross the streets under the lights as summer folds itself around the world.

Boys who meet the sunrise every day *after* they've completed work understand that faith and hope are essential to the human condition; but to make them meaningful, you've got to do your part and deliver the goods. Grace may be a gift, but good grace comes at a price. You've got to get up, hustle, and meet the day, every day of your life, and do it well. Aspire to excellence. Never, ever make peace with mediocrity. Paper boys understand the power of the rising sun. They stand transfixed and worshipful when the first rays filter through the heavens and brush the tops of trees with gold. They've earned the right to do that. The task today was completed with dignity and good order. Tomorrow will be what it will be. Today is good. "I did my best." Now it is time to get ready to meet the rest of the world.

Old ways die hard. Fifty-five years after being a paper boy, I still meet the sunrise with faith, hope, good cheer, and great expectations. I meet it as ducks circle overhead on whistling wings, as deer slip through the fog near my stand, as squirrels shake the branches of hardwoods on a still morning, as the call of wild geese fills my heart with joy, as bass swirl in the shallows and trout dimple the surface of a stream. I meet it with my dogs as we course my little farm in Mississippi and dew or frost glitters like countless jewels on my pasture. I cannot miss it, any of it. But, especially, I cannot miss the magic moments when the sun first brushes the tops of trees with golden light. I've seen this light on mountain peaks. There's a name for it in the mountains: Alpine glow. But there is no alpine in Mississippi. There are no mountains here. For years I wondered about a proper name for it.

Then, on a special morning, prior to her departure to serve as a US Peace Corps volunteer in Nicaragua, my daughter, Anna, was with me on my sunrise walk across the farm. The gold turned the entire world into a magical fairyland. It had never been more beautiful. I asked her if she'd like to name that glow, considering that as far as I knew it had no name. She did not hesitate.

"Papa, that's *arbor glow.*"

So, it has been *arbor glow* from that day forward.

Arbor glow is a gift to the sunrise people, those who meet their new day in very special ways at a very special time. *Arbor glow* is a promise that is, to me, a sort of reverse prayer that this day will be good . . . the powers of heaven and of earth will join purposefully and with beauty. On days when *arbor glow* graces my mornings, while I'm on my quiet walks across my farm with my dogs or beginning my hunts or launching a canoe or boat, I say a very special prayer of thanksgiving for paper boys, regardless of their age, and for those who gave paper boys the opportunity and the encouragement to meet their days with dignity, grace, good order, and, most importantly, reverence.

Johnny Appleseed got his heavenly orchard. Noah got his rainbow. With all due respect to other people who may get up early, I am absolutely certain that *arbor glow* belongs to the paper boy.

The Restless Wind

IT IS VERY HARD FOR SOME PEOPLE TO STAY PUT. THEY'RE RAM-
blers by nature. Sirens call to them. There is a deep stirring within
their hearts that pulls them out into the world, into the cathedrals of
wild and lonely places. They have no choice but to listen to the songs
in their souls and respond to them . . . to search for their source. A
restless wind is their only compass.

If they don't move, they will wither and die. Their only solace
is the open road, the untrammeled passes, the rivers that flow into
never-never land, wilderness without trails, the forests, mountains,
deserts, grasslands, and the sea. They never arrive because there is
no destiny.

When children drift away from home and yard to follow an old
gravel road or a creek or to explore a woodland on the back side of
a pasture, the motivating forces may not be the frogs, salamanders,
lizards, birds, squirrels, or crayfish, but something much deeper.
There's a good chance that the restless wind is calling to them. The
critters are only sacraments along the way. The children are following the wind.

As they grow older, the wind grows stronger. It does not push.
It pulls. The ventures grow larger, longer, deeper, and eventually
require tools: rifles, shotguns, canoes, tents, packs, fishing tackle.
But, most of all, their ventures require the courage to break free
of bonds that would consign the evolving nomads to imprison-
ment within a settled life. Time and again the nomads experience
the rush of the wind when they escape. It is pure and sweet. They

rejoice in it! Eventually, as they experience the power of breaking into freedom, the wind creates something new and wonderful for them: the dreamtime.

They patiently listen to the wise counsel of family and friends and advisors of every stripe. "Do not throw your life away! Come, join, be one of us. It is safe here." But the dreamtime grows ever brighter, as the restless wind fans its flames. With the dawn, they are off, on their way and gone. They trust the wind more.

Along the way, traveling light, with worn boots and passports, they plunge deeply into the world's currents, then leap from them and keep moving, ever onward, tasting many wines, experiencing the extremes of the human experience . . . love, war, hunger, satisfaction, pain, euphoria, wealth, poverty, health, sickness, fear, peace, anger, happiness, beauty, ugliness, loneliness, God. The restless wind teaches them the arts of moving quickly and lightly with a soft touch across the face of the Earth.

Do not be deceived when it appears they've settled. Look closely. They do not live within a framework, but rather upon a launching platform. All that they were and are is invested in its construction and maintenance. They are now living in the promised dreamtime. Their lives *are* the dreamtime. The world is all before them. Because they do not simply possess it, they own it.

The restless wind grows ever stronger—sweeping across the launching platform—so strong, in fact, that it sweeps up others who, by chance or nature or will, have ventured close to our nomad, close to the launching pad. Some who are swept up quickly drift back to earth, into the settled life. But a few follow the restless wind with the nomad; the nomad now is their mentor. He teaches them how to soar . . . how to navigate with the wind. It is only the proper thing to do.

It is then, seeing those who are in the wind with him, that the nomad sets his wings and pauses in reflection. The new nomads keep on moving out in the main flow of the wind, while the old one drifts to the edges. When he does this (he has no choice), the old nomad realizes that the restless wind that swept him up as a child was ushered into his life by other kindred souls, others who followed the wind. And, like him, they ultimately set their wings and drifted to the edges.

It is quieter near the edges. The nomad listens carefully. Echoes from those kindred souls from the past can be heard drifting on the wind, a wind that now swirls gently around him, probing, teasing, testing. Its tug seems different somehow. It has a new dimension to it, as if it is trying to penetrate deep within his soul, to scour echoes from their resting places and set them adrift, to join with the other echoes . . . on the restless wind.

The old nomad still feels the wind and follows it for a while, just long enough to hear a few echoes, including, occasionally, some of his own, and to set free a few more of them. He's learned to listen ever more carefully, to be sure he's hearing what the echoes are whispering. He's learned to be patient with the world around him and with himself, and to find beauty in the moment. He's learned that the restless wind is eternal . . . and to travel with it is a gift.

Now he understands. The wind's origin is not from beyond. It comes from within.

Under the Lights

A HUSH SETTLED ON THE MISSISSIPPI GULF COAST. THERE WAS no breeze. The water was smooth but still restless from the day. It swelled and withdrew, time and again, gently caressing the sandy beach with a delicate touch, speaking soft messages to any who might care to listen. As the sunset deepened, water and sky tossed gold- and rose-colored light back and forth between them.

The sea was so calm, and the reflections so perfect, that it was impossible to tell where the sky ended and the water began. Then, finally, the sun melted into the horizon and the sky exploded with brilliant colors. The colors, however, faded quickly as twilight gathered strength. Distant shadows that had once been barrier islands now vanished. The gulls stopped calling and began their nightly murmuring. This day was done.

I stood transfixed, out on Pascagoula's public fishing pier that extended off its beaches and into the Gulf of Mexico, my senses flooded by the beauty of watching day transform into night. I could still hear those soft messages from the sea. Then, faintly, as lights began to turn on along the length of the pier, I heard something else. Whispered voices and muffled footsteps filtered through the stillness as the night shift of anglers came to the pier, coming as singles, couples, and in small family groups, and took their positions . . . with what seemed to be a dimension of reverence. As I watched, the members of the night shift seemed to be returning to sacred places, each engaged with his or her rituals.

What was happening on this night was obviously the regular gathering of a tribe. The people seemed to know each other. They apparently had a common denominator, a common identity. They also knew very well, and respected, each other's sacred place along the pier. They gave each other space. There was no crowding, no jockeying. Their greetings were quiet, sometimes only a nod. They were polite. They were helpful. Although social interaction was part of the framework, they were here to fish. Fishing on this pier, on this lovely summer night, was serious business.

My fishing buddy, Larry Deeter, and I had been fishing the tidal marshes near Pascagoula for the previous two days. Our target had been "speckled trout" (spotted seatrout) and "redfish" (red drum). We had the right gear and the right boat. The weather was good. We knew the place, the water, and the techniques. But the fish didn't cooperate. It was just one of those fishing trips where everything was working well—except the fish.

I'd done a lot of work on the Mississippi Gulf Coast, and particularly so after Hurricane Katrina. As a fisheries professor at Mississippi State University, working collaboratively with the American Fisheries Society and the Mississippi Department of Marine Resources, I'd helped with the post-storm restoration of the region's fisheries. While working on the coast, I'd fallen in love with the fishing, and especially fishing for speckled trout and redfish. The region is beautiful. The fish are beautiful. The fishing can be magic. But on this trip with Larry, the fishing had been a bust.

So, I'd suggested that we leave the boat at the hotel, get ourselves some bait shrimp, and go fish with the night shift on Pascagoula's newly reconstructed fishing pier. The pier was open twenty-four hours a day and had good lighting at night. The lights would help us handle our fishing gear and our fish (if we caught any) and also would attract fish. Larry was beyond ready to try something else and said, "Let's do it!"

The first night we fished on the pier, we had very little sense of what we were doing. We had the right rigs and the right bait but didn't have the right feel for the fish when they took the bait. We also started too early in the evening and left much too early that night. Finding the correct rhythm, one that matches the fish, always takes a little time. But still we enjoyed the outing and met some fine folks out there on the pier.

The second night was a very different situation. We got to the pier just a little before sunset and committed ourselves to stay until midnight. That made all the difference. It didn't take long to figure out the fish. They were mostly white trout with a few speckled trout in the mix from time to time. The trick was to wait until you saw a school of trout under your light and then cast into the middle of the school. If you did anything much different, pinfish or crabs would quickly strip the bait off of your hook.

The later it got, the more the fish gathered under the lights. None of the white trout were very large. Most were about twelve inches long. But they are good fish to eat and the right size for that purpose. That seemed to be a very important, almost central, aspect of the fishing. People were there to catch fish, and obviously they were keeping them to eat. They had their coolers partially filled with ice, carefully leaving space for the fish they intended to catch. In that regard, I noted that they kept almost every fish they caught.

I fished for an hour or so, caught a few fish, then shifted my focus to the people around me. They had their stories to tell and were not hesitant to share those stories with me. Many of the stories were about hard lives lived on the edge, of challenges and loss and sadness. The people I visited with out there on the pier came from many backgrounds: Anglo-European, Hispanic, Asian, African American. They did not segregate on the pier. They were all in the same "tribe." They talked of devastation from drug-related violence on the streets, about children and spouses injured and killed by that violence. They talked about fear of government . . . about government seeking to take their children away or government deporting them to a country they have never known. They talked about injury and illness and their inability to get the health care they needed. They also talked with pride about their service, or the service of their children, in the military—and about the importance of education.

The ultimate achievement that they aspired to and coveted was to get a high school diploma or a general education degree (GED). That was the ticket! College was unthinkable—too far away economically and otherwise. Plus, these folks tended to be moving all the time, just following work or the prospects of it. That disrupted education for them and their children. It seemed that a substantial proportion of the children were in grade levels below what they should have been for their ages. What they did *not* talk about was growing old. They also never mentioned retirement.

I talked with their children. The children were not afraid of me. They accepted me as just one more elderly, gray-bearded fisherman out there on the pier. The children I spent time with were bright and articulate. They were full of energy and playful. Their eyes sparkled when they told me about their dreams, what they wished to become . . . someday. Some loved to read. Some loved music. Some loved sports. Some talked of God. They all liked to fish. They knew, absolutely, how to fish from that pier. The younger children, after they'd caught a few fish, played on the pier while their parents continued fishing.

The night deepened. It was late. These children needed to be in bed, well fed, well loved, full of peace and prayer at that hour. How could they perform well at school without a good night's sleep? But here they were, on the pier, while their parents were fishing for food. Their parents understood this very well and were concerned about it. They spoke of it. But there was little choice. They could not leave their children alone at home. And night was the only time that they could fish. These children would very likely eat fish for breakfast.

The parents talked at length with me as we fished together. During the course of our conversations, they asked me what I did for a living. When I told them that I was a retired college professor, they paused, almost in a state of disbelief. What was a college professor doing out on this pier at night fishing for white trout? I told them I was here for the same reasons they were. I liked to fish. I liked to eat fish. I needed a quiet place to be, surrounded by good people who seemed to get along with each other.

They had no idea, nor did I tell them, that they were the reason I entered the fisheries profession in the first place. I'd left seminary and the pastoral ministry to address, through science and political processes, the people who fish for reasons other than fun—the people who have very little voice out there in the world. They did not need to know that I'd supervised graduate research specifically focused on them and their fisheries right here, on that pier (and others), and in the surrounding waters; or that their fishing was published in PhD dissertations and scientific journals . . . that the world knew about them. I did not tell them that I knew who they were, knew of the goodness and the hard work and sense of community and the pain that defined their lives. I did not tell them that I was well aware that they took care of each other, shared their fish with people who could not fish, and that they protected each other while fishing. I did not tell them that I understood that their children were provided "day care" by individuals who took the children fishing and crabbing while the parents were at work, and that I knew that those crabs and fish would be their supper many nights. I did not tell them that once upon a time I was homeless and lived on the streets.

Rather, I just fished with them and played with their younger children. I talked with their older children about schools and careers and about hard work in school and beyond, and what it can mean to them as they become adults. But I was under no illusion.

These kids live in a different world. Theirs is one of many "worlds" that exist on this planet. Sadly, interactions among those worlds are rare and there are very few bridges to join them together. It is easier, and politically more expedient, to build walls. These worlds have little if anything to do with nations or languages or race or religion. Those are easy to transcend. The worlds I'm talking about are defined more by economics, education, and opportunity. And, for the record, environment is a component of opportunity. Environment is the stage, the framework, for life. It defines possibility.

And so, unless *individuals* make an effort to build a bridge and have the courage to walk across it and the fortitude to then live in another world—at least for a little while—they'll never know it or understand the people who call that world home. Thus, I treasure my sojourn as a homeless man on the streets. I didn't choose to live that chapter (although decisions I made took me there), but, having lived it, it is priceless to me. Ditto for the two years I served as a US Peace Corps volunteer in Southeast Asia and for the thirty years spent working in fisheries all around this planet.

I have found that there are good people in every one of the worlds that exist on this speck of stardust. Most are caring, intelligent, creative, and hard-working people. But they are, for the most part, trapped in their worlds. And in these worlds, there is also a darker element, bred of despair, violence, greed, ignorance, and the abuse of power. What happens to the good people when the darker forces take command? What about the people who fish under the lights on a public pier in Pascagoula, Mississippi? What is to become of them? Do they really have a voice? Do they really have alternatives? Many of them cannot even imagine a bridge to another world. Another world is fantasy to them.

But even if there were another world for them and a bridge to it, and they were helped to cross it . . . even then there are deep, perhaps overwhelming, challenges. Also, it is a two-way bridge. The challenges go both ways. Let us not forget that.

The typical Wall Street banker would starve or die of exposure in America's Deep South if given a trotline, an old boat, a shotgun, and a tarp and challenged to "live out yonder" for two weeks. The banker would also perish if all he or she had was a cheap spinning rod and reel, a plastic bag half full of discarded shrimp, a piece of cardboard to sleep under, a cast-off ice chest, and access to a fishing pier on the Gulf Coast.

On the other hand, go to a small wooden-frame house or a second-hand trailer down in the piney woods of south Mississippi, give the resident of that abode $100,000 (quite possibly more than he or she may earn in a lifetime), drop that person into the streets of Houston, Los Angeles, Newark, New Orleans, Seattle, Denver, or Detroit, and he or she also wouldn't last two weeks. The different worlds have different rhythms.

If you're out of synchrony, if you don't know your world, you will not survive. Adaptation takes time . . . sometimes a lifetime. When you finally get into the rhythm of your world, you just don't want to leave. Perhaps you shouldn't. You have, in effect, created a world for yourself and are living inside of it. It works for you. The human species has been doing this for a very long time. There's a word for it: *acculturation*. We adapt.

So it is with the people who fish under the lights on the Pascagoula pier. They live and survive in a world that they and few others (except for their own tribe) know and understand. They teach their children how to do it, how to live within their world. They are resilient. They are tough. They know how to find the "lights" and how to use them. They always have.

As the clock crept near midnight, Larry and I decided that it was time to gather our stuff, our fish, tackle, and other gear, before his truck was turned into a pumpkin, and before the guardians of the "keep" (i.e., the motel) where we were staying were transformed into rodents. We walked off the fishing pier, past the fishermen and their kids, past the lights. I could hear the restless sea still gently stroking the beach and the gulls still murmuring. The breeze had freshened, just a bit. Both of us were quiet, reflective, enveloped by a dimension of timelessness and power that transcended pumpkins and mice. It had been a good day and a wonderful night. Then, as we approached the end of the pier, I turned to look back at the gathering of the tribe out there under the lights. The children were still playing . . . their parents were still fishing.

I think that as a species, as mortal beings infused with the spirit of something beyond time, matter, and place in our hearts (some call it God), we are going to make it. The currents of life are very deep in humanity, and also very strong. Yes, I really do think that we are going to make it—because, within our ranks, there are those who will always find the lights on a pier. And under those lights children will continue to play and their parents will continue to fish. For them, in fact for all of us, there is no such thing as midnight.

Lost in the Booger Woods

WISE OLD HUNTERS, GRANDMOTHERS, AND CEDAR STICK WHIT-tlers perched on front porches at sunset or lounging before a crackling fireplace or wood-burning stove will tell you that all you have to do is spin a person around once and they're likely lost. Being lost is not just a matter of inconvenience either. When our reference points get out of kilter, we are at risk of wandering into the unpredictable and potentially dangerous realms of never-never land. The late British prime minister, Sir Winston Churchill, once said, and I paraphrase, "No man travels so far, or so high, as the one who doesn't know where he is going." True words . . . very true indeed.

Generally speaking, when we realize we don't know where in the heck we are, we are better off if we'll just hunker down for a spell, take stock of the situation, and look closely at the world that surrounds us. That's what they teach Girl Scouts and Boy Scouts. That's what is taught in survival schools. When we aren't sure about our surroundings or what we're about, forging ahead full-tilt boogie can, and usually does, get us deeper in trouble. Pretending that all is well is a poor prescription for the lost. Stop, look, think.

But just try to tell that to a squirrel hunter on a cloudy day. And if that squirrel hunter is a hard-headed, gray-bearded old coot with more than sixty years of woods rambling under his belt, words of caution, regardless of origin, just *ain't gonna matter*. He knows what he's about and where he's going (or so he thinks). He's a squirrel hunter by choice because he loves rambling and roaming. He's a rover who has got to move and be part of all that's going on out yonder in those woods. He's a restless man who has somehow tempered his restlessness a little bit to become the hunter, a silent shade drifting among shadows, a stalker, a predator, a rifleman, a woodsman. Nobody is going to stop him from being out there in it. He listens only to the winds of his soul.

This particular old squirrel hunter especially loves the big spooky "Booger Woods" that flank the Deep South's larger rivers. The soil is incredibly rich in these ancient bottomland hardwood forests. These are overflow lands, subject to nature's forces in all their beauty and power and fury. They are full of old twisting sloughs and bayous, dense cane breaks, thickets, swamps, huge tracks of timber, vines as big around as a man's leg, trees so tall that a shotgun can't knock a fox squirrel out of the upper branches, and all sort of stuff that bites. There's quicksand and mud with no bottom . . . places where you can become a fossil for somebody to chip out of rock a few thousand years from now. The rivers will suck you under if you try to swim in their turbid, swirling, whirlpool-laced currents. And in the quieter backwaters, when the weather is warm, you're really just a snack for some of the alligators that call such places home.

And yet these are magical places of unimaginable beauty. They are beyond "wild." They are wilderness in every sense of the word. They are the seeds from which earth restores itself after civilizations crumble and fade away. Enter with reverence. Move carefully. Move slowly, smoothly. Flow with quiet footsteps. Become one with the forest. Seek, find, and wrap yourself in rhythms of earth, water, wind, and sky. Be aware. Stay focused. Look. Listen. Be thoughtful. Be prayerful.

I am drawn to these primeval forests by spiritual forces that call my name, and within these forests I find my separate peace. And so, on one fine winter's day, I found myself exactly where I belonged . . . and also very lost . . . deep in the Booger Woods of Davis Island, on the western side of the Mississippi River, about twenty miles below Vicksburg.

The somber forest was incredibly still as the gray afternoon began to deepen and slowly merge into dusky twilight. I could hear only the whisper of tiny wings as little birds went about their foraging among the trees. There were no shadows. There was no wind. Clouds hung heavily overhead. There were no features on the landscape to guide me, no hills, no mountains, nothing to give me a sense of place or a broader sense of position. I was too far removed from any road or camp to hear someone passing, or for them to hear me.

When I turned around, trying to recognized anything in the vastness of these woods, I realized that I had absolutely no idea which way was out. The only thing I had to orient me was a barely perceptible, gentle slope, a sort of swale that, frankly, sometimes required a bit of imagination to believe that it actually existed. I was, in no uncertain terms, lost in the middle of a very flat, very expansive, bottomland hardwood forest. "Congratulations, Mr. Squirrel Hunter," I whispered to myself. "You've rambled and roamed yourself into a fine fix. Welcome, *once again*, to the Booger Woods."

The swale ahead of me could mean absolutely nothing, or it could lead to some water somewhere. It was tricky business, but I decided to take my chances. If I followed that swale in what seemed to be a down-slope direction, I might be able to find one of the long-isolated, ancient river channels that grace this wonderful forest. In years past I'd fished in those old channels and hunted along their edges. But I had to be careful. I could end up on the wrong side. If I found water, I pledged to myself that I would not cross it. That's how people get trapped and die in these big woods. And if I did find water, I'd stay on the left side. That would be more or less the west side. The right side could trap me next to the river because the river was high and, as a result, the lower reaches of the channels were flooded out into the woods. That was great stuff for duck hunters who prowl about in boats, but not for a lost squirrel hunter in rubber knee boots.

This whole situation shouldn't have happened. I'd told friends back at camp where I would be hunting and that I had no intention of being out very long, perhaps an hour or so. I would stay close to my jumping-off spot in an area called the "Sand Dunes." Over the years it has become one of my favorite squirrel-hunting places on the island. It is covered with gnarly live oak trees and is open and easy to get around in. Deer like it and so do bears. It is a big, wild, isolated, and remote part of the island. And I'm in love with it.

So I'd grabbed my .22 rifle, hopped onto one of the camp's ATVs, and headed out to the dunes for a short, late-afternoon venture, just to get myself into the rhythm of hunting. I had three days of squirrel hunting ahead of me and wanted to temper myself as a woodsman, to settle down, to clear away some internal dialogue and resurrect the hunter's identity that resides in my heart.

After parking the ATV, I'd drifted down into the live oak grove and, from there, began to hunt along its lower edge. I was enveloped by the quiet, enraptured by the stillness that surrounded me. It penetrated to my soul. I breathed deeply and whispered a prayer of thanksgiving for once again being in those woods.

There had been rain recently. The leaves underfoot were moist and therefore quiet as I slipped along through the woods, senses alert for any movement that could be a squirrel. It wasn't very long, at most only about ten minutes, until I saw my first squirrel. It was a big orange fox squirrel that scuttled around the trunk of a water oak tree about seventy-five yards away from me. The squirrel had apparently seen me but wasn't sure what I was and showed very little concern. I made the stalk and closed the distance to about forty yards. The squirrel worked itself into some of the higher branches of the tree but still presented a clear shot. I steadied my rifle against the trunk of a tree, put the crosshairs of the scope on the squirrel's head, and squeezed off the shot.

The squirrel was hit, fell to the ground, but was not killed. It went twisting and tumbling across the ground with me in hot pursuit. Finally, it crawled up another tree, went out onto a branch, stretched out, and became very still. I took advantage of the situation, steadied my rifle again, and shot the squirrel. It fell, hitting the ground with a soft, heavy thud. I retrieved the squirrel and almost immediately saw another squirrel about fifty yards away. It was a gorgeous black-phase fox squirrel. About one in seven fox squirrels on the island is the black phase. There are no gray squirrels on the island. I wanted that black squirrel badly. Taking one on my first afternoon of hunting would be a very special start.

I made the stalk. The squirrel started moving through a maze of tree branches, jumping from one tree to another. I followed. The squirrel wouldn't stop moving. It took me away from and out of sight of the Sand Dunes' live oaks and into a stand of very large water oaks. It finally stopped, turned, faced me, and started barking. I took a steady aim, put the crosshairs of my rifle's scope on the squirrel's forehead, made the shot, killed the squirrel, picked it up, and realized that I wasn't sure where I was.

From where I stood I could not see the dunes or the live oaks. But I thought I knew where they were. So I tried to backtrack what I thought was the route I'd taken during the stalk for the second squirrel. Somehow, however, during that stalk, I'd apparently moved further than I'd realized. And, as I reflected on the situation, I remembered that the stalk, chasing that second squirrel, had not been in a straight line. It was then that I stopped, looked around, and realized that I had no idea of which way to go. I was lost—even though I was probably less than a few hundred yards from where I'd parked the ATV.

Typically, I carry a compass when I'm hunting. If I'd had my compass, I'd have been able to come out of those woods in fairly short order. I'd seen the compass among my gear as I got ready to leave camp but just hadn't bothered to pick it up and put it in my pocket. I knew better than to go into these woods without a compass. But this was just going to be a short little hunt in an area I'd hunted many times before.

Squirrel hunting in the Sand Dunes was, for me, like walking through a city park . . . or so I thought as I walked out the door of the camp house and mounted the ATV. And it *would* have been like walking in a park if I'd stayed in the dunes and among those live oaks. But once I moved toward that first squirrel of the hunt, away from those live oaks, and then chased it through the woods—with my focus on the squirrel, not the place—with no wind, no sun, no shadows, and no compass, vertigo crept upon me like a tricky ghost.

I didn't realize at the time that this was happening. Then there was the second squirrel, the black one that took me even deeper into the woods and away from the dunes. Now, there was no east, west, north, or south. There were no tracks to follow. All I could see for as far as I could look in any direction was a beautiful forest full of huge trees and an occasional brushy area. And it was beginning to get dusky, just a little.

There was no sense of panic. But there was an uncomfortable realization that I was probably going to be spending a rather long and cold night in the woods if I couldn't extract myself from them in fairly short order. I also didn't want folks back in camp to have to spend their night in the woods looking for me. I knew they'd do that if I failed to come back to camp within an hour of sunset. Looking for me would be a dangerous task for all of them, moving around in the dark like that. If I just hunkered down, they'd come and find me—eventually. But, if I set a course and kept with it and paid attention to what I was doing regarding the lay of the land and water, I felt that I'd probably come to something that would lead me back to camp. Even though it was getting dusky, I figured I had at least an hour of sufficient light to get things into proper order.

It was a tricky decision: to move or not to move. My training said, "Stay put." But my experience said, "Get going." I've traveled in wild places, wilderness places, all over the world. And mostly I've done it alone. I've done it in tropical jungles of Asia and Latin America. I've done it in tundra and mountains and bogs across Alaska many times. I've done it in East Africa and in the Central Australian Desert. And I've done it lots of times in the wild and wooly places across the southern United States.

I've spent some long, lonely, and sometimes very uncomfortable nights in these places when conditions turned against me. But I've always been able to figure out a way to get on with the business at hand. I'm not afraid of being out in the wild, alone, and not knowing exactly where I am, or not being able to get to where I'm supposed to be in a more or less timely fashion. It is OK. I work through it. But it is not fun.

I must say, however, that of all the places I've had to navigate across the face of this planet, under all sorts of conditions, the most dangerous places have been in the big river bottoms of America's Deep South. They are the ones, absolutely, that can "get you." I thought about that as I worked through my situation on that dusky winter afternoon. "Be careful. Be thoughtful. You're in a big, wild place, but you've been in big wild places before. You've been in these big river bottoms before. Be deliberate, stay focused, and you will not die."

Yes, I was lost. Yes, I might have to spend a night in the woods. But I wasn't hurt and, although cloudy, it wasn't raining, sleeting, snowing, or blowing. It was cold but not intolerably cold. I knew I'd come out, maybe not that night, but eventually. That reality formed my framework for action . . . and, stepping out, I smiled.

My strategy was to move in reaches, the longer the reach the better. I'd look as far as I could ahead, pick out a mark, usually a particular tree, and focus on it. I'd also mark my beginning spot for each reach. Every fifty steps, approximately every forty yards, I'd check my back mark to be sure I still had it in my field of vision. When I got to the goal mark, whatever it was, I checked my back mark again and then lined up on a new spot ahead, trying the best I could to keep the future mark in a straight line with the original back mark. By doing this, I would, hopefully, keep myself from moving in a circle. I wanted to make linear progress as much as possible.

Sometimes I had to make detours around logs or some other obstruction, like a small puddle of water or a tangle of brush, vines, or thorns. When this was necessary, I was very careful to keep both ends of my reach in view and line up again as soon as I could. My general direction was along the swale that I hoped would lead to water, one of those old river channels. I knew that somewhere out there were two of those channels . . . assuming I was headed their way. The channels were not exactly in line with one another but almost so. If I missed one of them, then I had a decent chance of hitting the other one. But on the other hand, if I was not going toward those channels, there was a likelihood that I'd eventually hit one of the roads I'd traveled earlier that afternoon to get to the Sand Dunes.

I moved ever deeper on my journey. I was surprised at how long the afternoon was lasting. It seemed that the overhead clouds were not quite as dark as they had been earlier in the afternoon. This was good. I needed as much time and as much light as I could get.

After about forty-five minutes, the woods erupted with life. Squirrels were everywhere, scratching tree trunks, crashing through overhead branches, rustling on the ground, digging and probing. Deer flashed in front of me. Wood ducks whistled and called as they flew over me. From time to time I'd spot raccoons. It dawned on me that I was apparently in a part of the island that was not often frequented by hunters. But I wasn't hunting critters. I was hunting for a way out of the Booger Woods.

It was then that dusk began to win the battle with the day. It was hard to see more than fifty or sixty yards through the woods. My reaches shortened, but I kept moving. Mystery oozed from the woods and drifted up from the waters in vapors real and imagined. It was so quiet. I just kept moving. My reaches shortened to thirty yards, then to twenty. I'd been walking for about an hour and a half and, in my estimates of number of reaches covered, figured that I'd moved about two miles, perhaps a little less. It was almost "hunkering down" time. I would not travel in the dark.

Then, ahead, was a strange form. At first, I thought it was a log on the ground, but then I saw a square corner. It was a boat! And then I saw other boats pulled up alongside of it. I knew where I was. I was at the "Blue Hole" access point on one of the old river channels that had been my goal. There was a road from that access point, back through the woods, to the main road that led to camp. When I got on the Blue Hole access road, there was more light. I could travel faster now and in less than twenty minutes was at the intersection with the camp road.

A friend, Marty Brunson, was in a deer stand at the intersection. I was sorry to have disturbed his hunt during the final magic moments of a hunter's day. But he sensed something was wrong because of how I'd come out of the woods. He knew I'd planned to hunt the Sand Dunes. Those dunes were very far away from where he sat on his deer stand. I waved and moved on past him about fifty yards and settled down in the woods. Almost immediately I saw the ghost-like shadows of deer drifting by Marty's stand. But he did not shoot. They did not fit his criteria for that day.

Then it was dark, absolutely. Marty climbed down from his stand and walked over to where I was hunkered down in the woods. I explained what had happened, but he'd already figured that out. My trek through those woods, on that gray afternoon, and finding that boat landing in the gathering darkness was almost a miracle. He understood that. He understood also, and very clearly, that a very stressful night had been avoided for all of us in the camp.

Now that it was over, I was a bit shaken by the entire affair. "Spooked" is perhaps a better term for how I felt. I slung my rifle across my shoulders and crawled onboard Marty's ATV, with him in front as driver. My thoughts swirled in a vortex of what could have been. My pensiveness, an intense reality check, only grew stronger as we traveled together on those back roads to the Sand Dunes to retrieve the ATV that I'd used that afternoon.

When we got to the Sand Dunes and my ATV, Marty asked me if I was OK. I assured him that I was. Marty turned and started back toward camp. I let my ATV's motor warm a little, even though it wasn't necessary to do that. I just didn't want to hurry. Then, after a few minutes of sitting there on the ATV, I drove slowly back toward camp. When I got to the main road leading back to camp, I could see the tail lights of Marty's ATV dancing far ahead of me and occasionally disappearing in the distance. I kept my slow pace. I needed some time to collect myself.

I slipped into another realm of being. It was deeply spiritual. The more I thought about my sojourn through the Booger Woods that afternoon and evening, driving alone now on the road, with the ATV dipping and diving and forging ahead toward our camp, headlights dancing across the road in front of me, with the occasional deer standing, eyes glowing, in the fields alongside the road, the more my thoughts centered on the smallness and fragility of a human life.

It was then that I finally passed the threshold into very real fear and started to shake so violently that I had to stop the ATV, get off, and walk around for a few minutes. I could taste the fear in my mouth. The shaking would not stop. I focused hard, breathing deeply, and forced myself to push open a gate that would lead me to a very calm, very quiet place in my heart.

This wasn't a new sojourn. I knew about that gate and the quiet place and how to get there. I'd experienced all of this many times . . . this post-event fear and the eventual, incredibly powerful, post-fear calm. I'd experienced these forces, these emotions, so many times during my career as a fisheries biologist, working on the big rivers across the South and around the world, through storms, through floods, through encounters with nature and men that could have quickly ended life. There is no time to be afraid while the events are happening. Rather, when things get intense and there are very real and sometimes very dangerous challenges, I've always experienced a clarity of mind and a focus (and sometimes physical strength) beyond anything I've experienced in life's broader framework. There is just no time for fear when things are happening and you are, absolutely, on your own—and action is mandated in no uncertain terms. Fear is a luxury reserved for *after the fact.*

The after-the-fact fear and the following calm I was experiencing after my sojourn through the woods that afternoon was the same as I'd experienced once in Africa after escaping from soldiers at war, soldiers who had proclaimed me as an enemy mercenary. Why they didn't kill me on the spot will always remain a mystery to me. And my escape was a miracle. The war was raging and I was in the wrong place at the wrong time. It was the same state of being, the same fear and calm, I'd experienced on the shore of a very large river in Alabama, alone, on a winter's night, under the stars, after losing all feeling in my legs, arms, and shoulders in the frigid water, holding onto a capsized canoe and then, very deliberately, letting go of that canoe, knowing that if I didn't let go and try to get to the riverbank quickly, I'd die in the rapids that were churning just downstream from where I was. It took a very long time to get to the shore of that river. I didn't get scared until I crawled up out of the water. And then there was the calm. It was the same taste of fear, the same state of being, and the ultimate calm that I experienced when an Alaskan brown bear decided to stop his charge only a few feet in front of me, popping his jaws to let me know he meant business; and when a leopard backed away from me one morning in the Malaysian jungle; and when a very upset mother elephant in Kenya came to an abrupt halt only fifty feet in front of me and, after shaking her head at me, thundered away in the scrub brush with her calf close to her side; and when somehow I was able to steer a small sailboat away from attacking pirates on a dark and moonless night in the Straits of Malacca off the coast of Indonesia; and when, crippled in the Central Australian Desert, I crawled into a sheltered place among the rocks that would be my home for three weeks as I healed. Following each of these events, I had taken those deep breaths. And now, following my exit from the Booger Woods of Davis Island, I took those breaths again, regained control, stopped the shaking, and moved ahead in life.

Some folks may think that stories of such ventures into the wilds, and of the emotions that follow them, might be tales just a bit over-blown. To this, I have no response other than to be in the company of others who, across the years, have also engaged the cutting edges of rambling off the beaten paths. Most folks of this tribe know, absolutely, what it's like to be a bit befuddled after a frolic through *their* Booger Woods, regardless of continent, latitude, longitude, or elevation. Such sojourns into never-never land typically are, at a minimum, experiences that make me think of ashes and hymns and as yet unborn grandchildren . . . and about how much I enjoy a shot of good bourbon, fine shotguns, and sunrises—reality checks that are incredibly motivating.

When I told the story in camp later that evening, before the fire, bourbon (thankfully!) in hand, and then again around the dinner table, another dear friend and fellow hunter, Nelson Ball, got up from the table, went to his bunk, and shortly returned with a compass and a whistle tied on a long loop of duck decoy line. He very ceremoniously slipped that loop of line around my neck, tugged on it gently, and sat back down at the table to finish his supper . . . without a word. The other hunters around the table nodded. They knew all too well: "Spin a person around one time, under the right circumstances, and they're lost."

Ice Fishing with Alligators

I'VE ALWAYS BEEN INTRIGUED BY ICE FISHING. THE ENTIRE enterprise is fascinating. In the South, just about the only fishing most folks do during winter is trout fishing below some of the region's big dams. We figure that everything else is hunkered down, not moving, and probably not biting. Then, by February, it is almost spring, and so there's a bit of walleye fishing in some of the rivers. And, if spring actually does come early, crappie likely are getting cranked up in the shallower lakes about then. But regardless, our lakes rarely become frozen over. Those that do freeze are typically smaller ones, and even they never have ice thick enough to allow you to safely get out on it.

And so, over the years, I've just read about ice fishing and looked at pictures of people doing it. From my readings, it seems to me that ice fishermen, considered collectively, are a rare breed of anglers who fish with funny little rods or some sort of weird rig that tips up a flag when fish are nibbling at the hook. Ice fishermen have to bore a hole through the thick ice, either with a sort of chisel or some kind of auger. The hardier (or perhaps mentally deranged) anglers seem to be heavily dressed, point their backs to the wind, and sit over their holes, out in the open. Those who have tipped over onto their sides when there were gusts of wind are the ones who have frozen to death.

The more sophisticated ice fishermen, or perhaps the smarter ones, build little shanty shacks that provide some shelter from the elements. Most of the shacks are built on sleigh runners so that they can be dragged out onto the open ice and positioned over the deeper holes. Unlike during summer, the deeper holes tend to be warmer in winter than shallower water ("warmer" is a relative term). Some of these shacks are apparently quite luxurious, with shelves for hot chocolate mugs, little stoves, and lights. The lights are necessary because it's dark in the North most of the day during the winter and usually gray after sunrise the rest of the day. The pictures I've seen of folks inside these shacks show many of them in flannel shirts or sweaters. Apparently, it can become fairly warm inside even though the floor is ice (again, "warm" is relative). Anyway, and even though I have the thin blood of a southerner, I have still always wanted to experience ice fishing. I wanted to know what it is like to try to haul fish through a hole, and particularly if the fish is bigger than the hole. There are, however, some reality checks . . . at least there are for me.

As I nudge up against seventy orbits around the sun, my southern blood has not thickened. In fact, I take medicine to make it thinner! The doctors say that I should be very happy when blood flows freely after I've cut myself while cleaning fish. They say that it means my pipes won't clog, so I'll probably live longer and, subsequently, will catch more fish. I'm not sure I can use the word "happy" when I'm bleeding profusely after slicing myself rather than the fish in hand (an increasingly common event as I adjust to a new lens following cataract surgery). But it seems that the medication, in combination with doctor-prescribed bourbon each evening, has kept the ticker ticking without skipping a beat. Regardless, thin blood does little to whet my appetite for below zero weather.

Additionally, while my interest in ice fishing remains undiminished, my desire to travel to far away northern waters and sit exposed to the elements over a hole in the ice has waned. From what I've observed, read, and heard, there's nothing up there in that neck of the woods between anglers and the North Pole but a barbed wire fence, and it's blown down! And so the likelihood of me going ice fishing up North falls into the same league as hunting polar bears on the pack ice off the coast of Alaska and walrus from a kayak in the Bering Sea. It just ain't going to happen on this watch.

But still, I think about ice fishing . . . usually when I'm wrapped in a blanket and nestled down in my favorite chair in my study, doctor's prescription within reach. I tend NOT to think about ice fishing when I'm trying to thaw my fingers after putting out a couple of dozen duck decoys before dawn on a Mississippi pond that's got ice fringing it. In fact, I'm convinced that duck hunting is just another expression of the same mental illness that afflicts dedicated ice fishermen. Nothing is served by exacerbating the affliction with drifting thoughts.

Frankly, I'm afraid of very cold wind and very cold water, and I'm especially afraid when they come together. Thirty years as a river fisheries biologist, one who worked during some very serious winter weather, left its mark on me. Although I had no choice in my work but to be out on those rivers under very dangerous conditions, I minimized risk as much as I possibly could. Thankfully, there were no major mishaps. But there were certainly some close calls! And, usually, when we were out there working on the water, we were too busy to be afraid . . . until we were done for the day. Then we'd get the shakes . . . and it wasn't because of the cold either (at least not directly). Now that I'm retired, and I don't have to do it, I don't go out on the water anymore in cold weather.

So let's forget about the cold wind, the cold water, and all the risks they bring to people on the verge of insanity who seek to avoid cabin fever any way possible. In fact, let's just go ahead and forget about ice and concentrate on the proclaimed, stated, primary focus of the ice fishing enterprise: going to a lake and pulling fish out of it through a hole.

Surely there's some way to do that without the environmental distractions of winter. Surely there must be an alternative. Perhaps there's a way to shift the entire operational framework in such a way that it includes soft, warm breezes full of birdsong, the scent of flowers, and the sparkle of sunlight caressing your face and arms . . . where the only risk involved would be to become so mesmerized by the gentle lapping of water that you become drowsy, fall to sleep with a slight smile on your face, lean back a bit too much on your chair, and fall over backward into the water, which, although infested by alligators, is warm enough that you can usually extract yourself from their domain before they even know you've entered it. In this regard, over the years I've learned that most alligators in America's Deep South don't bite—most of them. So, the risk is really minimal. Just imagine . . . fishing through a hole. That's the key.

The phone rang. "Don, this is Buddy. Come go fishing with me over in Texas. I'm catching the heck out of white perch on Paul's lake."

"When do you want me there?" I answered.

"This coming Friday. How long can you stay?"

"My classes are over at the university Thursday afternoon. I'll leave Mississippi early Friday morning and can be there by mid-afternoon. I don't need to be back until late Monday evening. My classes next week don't start until late Tuesday morning."

"Perfect. See you then."

I'm a retired fisheries professor who occasionally still gets to pollute young minds at Mississippi State University. Buddy Ball is an old hunting and fishing partner who lives in Louisiana. We've shared many good ventures together, particularly on his hunting club over along the Mississippi River south of Vicksburg. Paul Calhoun is a mutual friend who owns a huge ranch in east Texas. On that ranch is a lake that may well have the very best bass fishing in the United States. I've been privileged to fish there on numerous occasions. It is a treasure that's carefully protected.

Paul is a gracious man and an incredible host. He and I have enjoyed wonderful fishing and fellowship together over the years. He's a fun guy to be around. He has a pet hog named Felicia that's half Russian boar and half Vietnamese pot-bellied pig. He's trained her to fall over on her side when he points his finger at her and says "bang!" Paul also flies a fine airplane and can cook the best steaks you've ever cut with a fork. No knife is needed!

Although I'd fished for bass in Paul's lake, I'd never fished there intentionally for "white perch" (crappie). From time to time I'd caught crappie there, but they were incidental to our main focus.

When you're catching six- to eight-pound bass one after another, and occasionally hooking bass larger than that, crappie tend to be the last thing on your mind. I had no idea regarding what might be in store for us.

When I got to the ranch, Buddy was primed and ready to go fishing. Supper wouldn't be until after dark. That gave us a little over three hours to fish. So we loaded our gear and drove down across the ranch, then across the lake's dam, and over to a little lane that led down to the water. There was an old boat at the edge of the water.

We dragged the boat to the water, loaded our gear, and set sail for a "shipwreck" that was anchored about 150 yards offshore. It was really just a couple of old party barges that still sort of floated in a more or less tangled-up arrangement. The decking was rotted and the railings were twisted and broken. One of the barges seemed stable enough to stand on, and that's where we tied up our boat and disembarked.

In actuality, it was a pretty decent place to be. As a fisherman I thought so, and so did the alligator that considered it his basking spot. It wasn't a very big alligator, probably less than six or seven feet long, and it was pretty shy. We shooed it away and planted our flag. The alligator swam out twenty yards or so and initiated his patrol.

The old barges were anchored in ten to fifteen feet of water. There was plenty of room on this one for two fishermen to move around. We had our fishing gear plus two ice chests. Both of the ice chests were about a third full of ice. Cold drinks were in one of them. The other one was to put fish in.

Buddy rigged up ultra-light spinning gear with a small rubber-skirted jig. I used a long, telescopic "crappie pole" with about ten feet of line tied to the end and a jig like Buddy's. I started fishing around the edges of the barge, slowly and quietly lowering my jig down about five to eight feet and gently jerking it around. Buddy, however, used his shorter rod to get his jig down into an open hatchway between pontoons of the barge beside us that was nearly sunken. Almost immediately we had fish on.

I've caught crappie before and have always considered a one-pound fish to be very nice—and certainly a "keeper." But when I finally got my fish up, out of the water, and onboard, I learned what "big" means with regard to crappie. It was well over two pounds. Buddy's fish was bigger than mine! Into the ice chest they went. Back into the water went our jigs. The jigs had not settled before we had crappie on our lines again! Up they came, and both fish were as big as the first two we'd caught. Then the dynamics shifted. For every crappie I caught around the edges of the barge, Buddy was catching two or three from inside his hole. His short little rod with a jig could penetrate into the dark and mysterious depths down below. He was into the mother lode of crappie. He knew all about it from previous trips he'd made out to fish on that barge.

For a while I tried to ignore what was obvious. I continued fishing around the periphery of the barge. I certainly caught fish, and they were big fish. I'd never in my life seen crappie as nice as these. In fact, any crappie we caught that was one pound or smaller went back into the lake. It was incredible. The ice chest for fish was quickly filled and we started putting fish into the other one that held our drinks. But it was Buddy who was stacking them up.

He invited me to come share his hole. At first I resisted but finally said OK. And it was magic. I shifted to a short rod and snaked my little jig down through that hole. The jig rarely made it to six feet before a crappie sucked it in. Then it was all a matter of trying to gently pull the fish up and through the hole. That hole was probably two feet wide and at most four feet long. The fish kept coming, and coming, and coming, through that little hole. And suddenly it dawned on me—THIS is the "ice fishing" I'd long wanted to experience. I wasn't catching yellow perch, walleye, or pike. I was catching *sac-a-lait*, the Cajun's "sack of milk," the southerner's "white perch," which, in my opinion, is the most beautiful and the best eating of all freshwater fish (sorry folks, walleye comes in second).

We probably had at least fifty beautiful crappies in our ice chests by sunset, and not a one of them was less than one pound. We were *ice fishing* in our shirtsleeves, sipping cold beer, watching the alligator, and listening to birdsong. Right before sunset Paul came buzzing over us in his plane, wagging his plane's wings to tell us that supper would be ready pretty soon. Why use a cell phone when you've got an airplane?!

We gathered our stuff and loaded it, our fish, and ourselves into the boat. By the time we made it back to the beach, I saw that the alligator was already swimming alongside the barge. It was a warm evening, but even so, I suspected that the alligator would probably stay in the water rather than climb back onto the barge during the night. It would be spending the night hunting for its supper. And we were on our way to ours.

Paul had the steaks almost done by the time we got back to his house. They were grilled to the glory of Texas and soon became friends with huge baked potatoes, fine bread, and a tremendous salad. Good food, good drink, and good fellowship further warmed the soft spring evening. Talk focused on the lake and the fishing and, particularly, the *ice-fishing* hole. It was a magic place.

For the next two days Buddy and I continued pulling crappie from that hole. It was virtually non-stop action. By the time we were done we'd harvested well over a hundred beautiful crappies. But that harvest was insignificant relative to the fish population in Paul's lake. It's a very large lake of several hundred acres and it is very lightly fished. The crappies in it grow fast! I aged one of the two-pound fish to be three years old. They spawn like scoundrel buggers in that lake. Our harvest could have been a *thousand* fish and *still* not have made a dent in that crappie population. The limiting factor for us was how many packages of fish fillets we could haul home. When that goal was reached, we stopped fishing and, with the help of Buster Roberts, a ranch hand who helps Paul with his property, got our fish cleaned and packaged.

Now, as I reflect on my ice-fishing adventure down in Texas, I'm starting to understand some of the reasons people do it. Ice fishing, North and South, isn't something that's done for sport. Rather, it is for the wonder of just being out yonder on the water, whether that water is frozen or not. Pulling fish through a hole can be done without interrupting good fellowship and good conversation. In this last regard, ice fishing also is all about the periods of silence that enrich fine conversation, and the whispered exclamations that come when you or your fishing buddy feel the fish hooked. And, absolutely, it is about the beauty of that fish when it finally comes up and out of the hole. All of the magic is there!

As far as I can tell, the primary difference between northern and southern ice fishing is that up North you don't need an ice chest to put your fish in and you don't need to shoo an alligator away from your fishing hole. But on the other hand, when we go ice fishing down South, snaking our jigs through some hole in a derelict, half-sunken barge, we don't tip over on our sides when the wind gets gusty and our beer doesn't freeze.

In consideration of these differences, plus the reality that I enjoy soft spring evenings and Texas-grilled steaks after a day of ice fishing, I reckon that including the alligator gets my vote.

Tribute to an Artist

STILLNESS AND FOG CAPTURED THE MORNING, CREATING A sacred hush. In the distance, across the pasture, we could hear Canada geese. Wood ducks ripped by or crash-landed in the little pond before us. Gadwalls, wave after wave, floated into the decoys on stiff, cupped wings. And our shotguns spoke to them.

The dog, his heart filled with the satisfaction of responding to the rhythms of a former self that echoed across the millennia, went out into the pond—again and again and again—bringing the ducks back to us. Some he had to chase and capture. This only intensified the echoes in his heart . . . and in ours. Then, suddenly, as *arbor glow* brushed the tops of trees, the ducks evaporated.

My eldest son, Robert, a landscape architect who lives in Florida and was home for the Christmas holidays, had a big grin across his face that made the Cheshire cat's smile seem like an insignificant joke. Typically, we get one or two little bunches of ducks coming to our pond during a morning's hunt. But today, this magic morning, they'd nearly smothered us. We'd killed two limits of ducks, that's twelve ducks, in less than an hour. The annual goal for ducks from this little pond is twenty. Most years, however, we take somewhere between thirty and forty ducks from it. For us, a four-duck hunt is a good one. Yes, the magic had been there with us on this very special morning.

When it was over, Robert and I were spellbound by what had just happened. There were no words. For a few moments all we could do is look at each other. How in God's creation could words possibly have any purpose after a duck hunt like that? The dog knew it too. He sat beside me, looking at me with penetrating eyes, clearly communicating truth, a truth that merges man with dog, truth which has, across the thousands of years we've hunted together, proclaimed that *this* is what life and death are all about. As hunters and companions in the wild and lonely places, we're one in being and spirit, always and forever; and there is nothing, nothing at all, that can come between us and the day or the hunt or, in fact, the reality that we're doing exactly what God intended for us to do. We are part of something so profoundly deep that even God has to come, right there, into the brush at the edge of a duck pond, to soak up the energy of what he, himself, or she, herself, or *it* created. It is beyond the human capacity to understand . . . it just is.

We gathered our ducks. They were beautiful: the gadwalls with dark feathers aft, russet and herringbone forward, and white wing speculums; the wood ducks with bold patterns and colors on the drakes and humble grays, olive, and blue on the hens.

It was mid-December, the dawn of the very best in America's Deep South. The hunter's moon was in proper order. The stars were lined up. The rhythms of the earth were at full-tilt boogie. The ducks were here. The deer were in rut. The squirrels were working the hardwoods. The woodcock flights were here. The geese were here. The rabbits knew the covers and seemingly were as thick as fleas on a mongrel dog. Quail hunting was cranking up. Life was rampaging across the Mississippi landscape—and we were smack dab in the middle of it all.

Standing in knee-deep water at the edge of my duck pond, with stringers of ducks slung across our shoulders, shotguns in hand, and a wet dog wondering what in the heck was happening, I finally broke the silence. "Son, what do you want to do now?"

There were options. We could go home and reflect on a fabulous morning. We could take a break and come back later in the day, after lunch, for quail and woodcock. Or we could regroup and keep on hunting through the rest of the morning for squirrels or even, perhaps, deer. The choice was his.

Across the years I've learned many lessons from my son. Most of all, I've learned to pay attention to him, to watch him and listen to him carefully. He is a quiet man. He is an artist. The eldest of my three children, Robert has been blessed by deep intellect and an equally deep spiritual dimension. He moves in life with a cadence all his own. He sees what others don't (or won't) see. When in the field, hunting, fishing, canoeing, hiking, camping, or just rambling around, there is light in his eyes. He's happy to be there. Regardless of setting, he engages the world around him comprehensively. He's building bridges. He's transcending the fanfare of common man.

Robert is a very good shot. And yet, when we are hunting together, I never know if he will shoot or not shoot. Sometimes he does. Sometimes he doesn't. I can detect no pattern. Those are his decisions and his alone. When Robert and I are together, we talk a lot about the hunting but almost never about the shooting.

Now, in the aftermath of a tremendous duck hunt (during which he made some outstanding shots), I asked him what he wanted to do. We had our shotguns. I told him I had the proper loads, back in the truck, if he wanted to spend the rest of the morning hunting squirrels. There was still fog over the land. The ground would be quiet with the dampness. Conditions were perfect for stalking. There was no wind. It was cold but not so cold that squirrels wouldn't move. We'd heard them barking and seen them moving while we were engaged in our duck hunt. The squirrels would probably be active all day, but especially during the first one or two hours following sunrise.

Another possibility was a deer hunt. The bucks were in full rut. The magic hours for deer movement during December are between 9:30 and 10:30 in the morning and the thirty minutes before and after sunset. I had the orange vests and the slugs for his shotgun in the truck. Robert stood for a few moments and then softly said he'd prefer a deer hunt.

He was twenty-seven years old at the time and had never killed a deer. He'd hunted deer since he was eight years old and had had many opportunities to shoot one. I knew that several that had come by him across the years had been bucks, and that a few of those bucks had been quite respectable. I knew also that on occasion he'd played games with the deer. He'd let some come very, very close to his stand and then had spoken to them in different ways or tested how much he could move before they were alerted to his presence—how much conversation or movement was necessary before they'd go away, some drifting, some running. Sometimes he'd tell me about these events. Sometimes, when he wasn't aware I was nearby, I witnessed them. But I never asked questions. A father never questions an artist son about such matters. The artist has his own ways, his own reasons, and is connected to a different universe. An artist lives in a special realm of being . . . a precious place in creation. To have an artist son is a gift to a father.

We took our ducks back to my old pickup truck and pulled out the deer-hunting stuff: blaze-orange vests, sitting pads, slugs for his gun. The morning was perfect, but I quietly thought to myself that there would be no deer skinning that day. After nearly twenty years of hunting deer with my son, I knew the way it would go after the hunt.

"Robert, did you see a deer?"

"Yes."

"Any come close?"

"Yes, but not the right one."

And I'd stop the inquiry there. There had always been something else going on in his hunter's heart with regard to deer. I just couldn't put my finger on it. He'd established some code, some ethic that he'd not shared with me. To ask about shooting or not shooting a deer would have been inappropriate to the extreme. I would not to cross that line.

I recommended a particular stand, one I'd recently put up, and guided him to it. When he was settled, I told him I'd take the dog, the ducks, and our duck-hunting gear home, then come back and do a little squirrel hunting on the opposite side of our farm. Although I didn't mention this to Robert, there was no way in the world that I'd deer hunt while he is deer hunting. He wouldn't care if I shot a deer. He's absolutely noncompetitive as a hunter. But I, as his father, would not feel right bringing home any deer other than the one that my son shot. I also told him that I'd send him a text message when I returned to the farm so that he'd know I was back.

Forty minutes later I walked past the farm's gate and drifted down through a little scope of woods alongside a creek where I knew there were a few fox squirrels and an abundance of gray squirrels. When I got to the edge of the woods, I spotted one of the fox squirrels. It was a Bachman's fox squirrel, a big orange fellow with black head and white nose, feet, and tail tip. They are beautiful squirrels and are having a pretty tough time competing with the more aggressive gray squirrels. So I don't shoot fox squirrels on my farm, only grays. I sent a text to Robert that I was on the farm and had just seen a fox squirrel. He texted that a big doe had just passed under his stand and had stopped and looked back over her shoulder. I replied that the buck was coming, to be ready.

About two minutes later I heard a muffled boom coming from across the pasture, from down in the thick woods where Robert was stationed. It was the sort of boom that, when it comes all alone, is deep and hollow and proclaims finality.

I sent a message to Robert, "Was that your shot?"

His reply: "Buck"

That was it. He didn't confirm he'd shot. He didn't say anything about "Buck."

It took me about five minutes to get to Robert's stand. When I got there, he was on the ground, about thirty yards from his stand, standing beside Buck.

Buck, while definitely down for keeps, was still breathing hard, holding onto life in spite of Robert's well-placed shot. I told Robert to finish him off and he did so, quickly, humanely, and with efficiency and compassion. Then all was still. I looked at Robert standing over his deer and saw moist eyes.

"Papa, now I understand what you mean when you say there's sadness mixed with satisfaction when you've killed a deer."

I walked to my artist. With no words at all, I put an arm around his shoulder, just for a moment. Then I turned to look again at

Buck, to *really* look. Up until then my attention had been focused on my son.

Oh, my goodness gracious alive! Buck was huge! His antlers spread tall and wide. There were nine beautiful points. It was bigger than any deer I'd ever killed (as of this writing, 2018, fifty-five years of deer hunting and seventy-four deer killed), and the biggest buck I'd ever seen on our farm. He was absolutely in his prime, with muscles bulging. I estimated his weight at more than 250 pounds. In Mississippi, that's a monster buck. A buck like that would be, for most hunters, the buck of a lifetime. It certainly would be for me!

"Papa, like you said when you texted me, he was following the doe. He came out of that green ash thicket over there, the one where we hunt woodcock. The sun flashed on his antlers. I could see the muscles moving in his shoulders and steam as he breathed. The world stood still and got very small. He was the only thing in that world. When he came out of the thicket, I thought to myself, 'This is my deer.' I waited until he got closer and gave me a good clean shot. When I shot, he went down hard and fast. This is the buck I wanted. This is the deer I've been waiting for."

We stood there together in the Mississippi woods, father and son on their own land, as December sunlight filtered through the branches and danced upon a carpet of wet leaves. Blue jays called. A woodpecker hammered. A pair of wood ducks whistled overhead. The sky was the richest of blues . . . a deep "winter sky" blue. Fog still swirled over the pasture . . . just a little. Sunlight sparkled on the grass. There was a dank, swampy, tartness drifting up from the crushed leaves where the buck lay. It hung heavily in the moist air and mingled with the thick, musty odor of a buck in full rut.

A gentle stirring overhead caught my attention. The wind was whispering. I listened carefully to the whispers and smiled. The whispers called to Robert. Robert also heard the wind whispering. He looked up for a moment and, taking a deep breath, got down on his knees, reached out, and ran his hands along the antlers—every inch of them—from their gnarly bases, along the main beams, and out to the tips of each long and polished tine. Then he stroked the deer . . . *his* deer, an artist's deer, a magnificent animal that he'd waited twenty years to shoot, passing up all others, until this one came busting out of the green ash thicket on a gorgeous December morning, full of life, full of fight, full of wild and wonderful power.

As I watched my son stroke Buck, I could almost see Buck's power being transferred from the deer to the man, the hunter, the artist. Sunlight filtered through the trees as a misty, golden curtain across Robert's shoulders and onto his deer. The light shimmered, just a little, as the wind once again whispered in the branches. The day, the deer, the light, the wind, and the spirits of the hunt all came together at that moment, right there in the woods, in that quiet place tucked back along the edge of a little Mississippi farm, to form a perfect tribute to the most disciplined and patient deer hunter I've ever known. The vision is eternal. The place is hallowed ground.

Tough Guns

HUNTERS TEND TO ACCUMULATE MORE GUNS THAN THEY NEED. It just happens along the way. As the decades fold one into another, cabinets and closets and racks get full of the things. All have their purposes and some have wonderful histories. When we pick them up, we are drawn by some inexplicable force into the never-never land of dreams, fantasies, and memories.

I have never owned a gun that was not durable, at least not for very long. But some of them, even though they have guts and are well made from good materials by the right folks, are of the sort that they should not be subject to the rigors of hard hunting. They are what I call "soft" guns: things of beauty and precision, works of art, or links to history, to be lovingly cared for, protected, and passed on to family and friends. They are reserved for use in controlled situations where weather and terrain can be negotiated with some degree of certainty and minimal risk. When conditions are right, and stars are appropriately aligned, these wonderful guns, taken afield, stroke the hunter's heart and serve as bridges to special people, dogs, and places . . . past and present. But still, they are *soft*.

Classic double-barreled shotguns; finely tuned, precision, high-velocity "varmint" rifles; and an Olympic-grade .22 squirrel rifle: all of these sport beautiful metal and wood finishes and fall into this category. Included also in this group is my grandfather's Remington Model 11 "hump-backed" shotgun. He hunted geese with it on Mississippi River sand bars using live decoys in the early 1900s, and with that gun (using a second, differently-choked barrel), he followed many a bird dog through the Arkansas Delta. I never knew him but am told that I look and act like him. He died when my father was twelve years old. Decades later, when I inherited that old shotgun from a much-loved uncle, it had a broken stock and was covered with rust. I replaced the stock and had the metal refinished and blued. It still shoots but I never use it. It is too precious.

There's also a retired Marlin .30-30 lever action, my first deer rifle (bought used for sixty dollars in the 1960s). It was my constant companion when I was a black-bearded young man prowling the Ozark highlands of north Arkansas. I hand-rubbed a linseed oil finish onto its gorgeous, fine-grained, black walnut stock. I used to shoot that rifle very well, and I killed lots of deer with it. But now my eyes are not good enough to use the peep sight I put on it, and I refuse to put a scope on a lever-action rifle. A scope destroys the balance, the beauty, and the romance of lever-action rifles.

The bottom line is that although I own lots of guns, most of my hunting is done with three "tough" guns: a 12-gauge Remington Model 870 Wing Master pump shotgun, a 20-gauge Remington Model 11-48 semi-automatic with an adjustable Poly-Choke on the barrel, and a .30-06 Winchester Model 70 bolt-action rifle with a rugged, low-power scope. All three of these guns are old, scratched, and worn, with many years of use under their belts . . . just like me. They all have fine-grained walnut stocks and good steel. These materials and the workmanship that bonded them have stood the test of time.

I've killed deer with all of these guns. In fact, my very first deer (at age twelve) was killed with the 20 gauge. I've carried the pump gun and the .30-06 all over North America. I've killed thousands of ducks, piles of geese, a few grouse and ptarmigan, and God only knows how many squirrels with that pump gun. I've taken over fifty deer with the .30-06, as well as bear, moose, elk, and several caribou. It is on its fourth scope. I've re-blued the barrel and action three times. The 20 gauge is fast and deadly as a bird gun. It also has hammered its share of ducks, a few geese, and lots of rabbits.

Like the pump gun, most of its blued steel receiver is worn down to silver metal that glows with a rich patina.

These are the guns that go with me when the hunt is very likely to be demanding to an unpredictable extreme . . . which is almost always. They are the guns that I depend on. I care for them and keep them clean and well oiled, but I don't coddle them. Scratches and worn metal are their badges of honor. They have been with me in mountains, tundra, muskeg, swamps, salt marshes, fields, woodlands, and forests of all sorts. They've been in bush planes, jeeps, old trucks, boats, and canoes. They've been checked as airline baggage more times than I can remember. I've dropped them all in mud and water and sand. I ran over the pump gun once with my pickup truck. It survived unscathed. I've had to go diving in deep sloughs, ditches, and flooded timber for the pump gun after tripping over logs, stepping into holes, or slipping down mud banks on duck hunts. I just slosh that old gun around in the water to get the grit out and keep on hunting. But when I get home, I take it apart and give it a thorough cleaning.

I've used the pump gun and the .30-06 as walking staffs to help me scale steep mountainsides in Alaska and in the Rocky Mountains. I've used both of them as emergency boat paddles. I've slept with the rifle in my sleeping bag on Alaska hunts—rounds in the magazine but none in the chamber—wishing that the hole in the rifle's barrel was bigger because there are things up in Alaska that bite and stomp. But I have confidence in that rifle. It speaks with authority. When fed the right ammunition, it is a "tush hog" of a rifle and *will* put big game on the ground—in short order.

As for the 20 gauge, well . . . it shoots itself, thankfully. I can be in the thickest briar- and brush-infested, tangled mess of a place imaginable, wrapped in vines, trying to get to my bird dog on point, when, suddenly, the gun goes off and a bird drops. Oftentimes, I can't recall the flush or the gun coming up for the shot. But then the dog retrieves the bird to my hand and I stand in wonderment. I don't know or understand or, in fact, care how it happens. It just happens. That gun invokes a special sort of magic . . . all instinctive and reflexive and spontaneous.

When I hunt alone, which I usually do and, frankly, prefer, I've been known to shoot that 20 gauge from the hip, to crouch, twist, or fall deliberately and roll, shooting from a kneeling or prone position, taking advantage of 360 degrees in an n-dimensional hyper-volume free-fire zone as a quail or woodcock zips through the branches. Four seconds is an eternity to a bird hunter. But that gun is lightning fast, allowing me to get on the bird quickly and then to shoot slowly (a relative term).

Quite frankly, however, at my age (currently sixty-nine years old) I probably shouldn't be doing this sort of shooting. Jungle fighter tactics are best reserved for younger warriors. But I'm addicted to it . . . and to that old 20 gauge. When we hunt together, we become one in being and purpose. And together we emerge from our hunts ripped, ragged, scratched, torn, and victorious—regardless of the toll on birds. The primary difference between us is that the gun doesn't bleed.

Bird hunting like this isn't for the timid hunter who is prone to deliberate, thoughtful shooting. There's just no time for that, nor do conditions allow it. My bird hunting and the shooting are all about eyeball-to-eyeball confrontations with scoundrels. "Sir Robert" (aka bobwhite quail) is no longer a gentleman (and perhaps never was), and when I hunt him, I'm not much of one either. These are hard but lovely hunts that require a no-nonsense, fast-shooting, *tough* gun.

Both of my *tough* shotguns now jam if I load them with three shells. But both still shoot wonderfully when loaded with only two shells. Frankly, I don't need three shots in a shotgun; two are just fine. So I am satisfied to let the guns—and me—grow old with dignity and, hopefully, a little grace. We have no need for rhino horn, tiger bones, or replacement parts as we move into our sunsets. I am satisfied for all of us to be what we are. Mostly, however, I just want us to be together for as long as we can.

The same goes for the old .30-06. It's a trusted friend that shoots better than *I* can. For example, sometimes I forget to load the rifle when I'm hunting. I have rounds in the magazine but not in the chamber of the rifle. It is a habit I picked up while living in Alaska. It is a good habit *up there*. In Alaska, one should never load a round into the chamber of a rifle until ready to shoot because if there's an accident, help probably isn't going to get there in time. But when I'm deer hunting in the Deep South, I need to remember to load my rifle after I get settled into my stand. As I've aged, the propensity to forget such things has evolved magnificently.

As I reflect on this business of hunting with an unloaded rifle, it dawns on me that doing so takes deer hunting to a higher realm of sport. And, truth be known, I'm not particularly uncomfortable operating within the framework of this higher realm. In recent years, and in concert with my aforementioned evolving neural circuitry, I've been able to conduct such hunts quite well . . . most of the time. I must admit, however, that a rifle that shoots itself is important on such hunts—if collecting venison appeals to you.

Here's an example of how an unloaded rifle hunt works: After I've carefully and silently slipped off the safety, slowly but deliberately put the crosshairs of the scope on the deer's chest, just behind the foreleg, and squeezed the trigger . . . the rifle goes "click" in the supercharged quiet of twilight's final flirtation with nightfall. The click of the rifle's firing pin disengaging on an empty chamber announces to the world and all its denizens that there is something lurking in yon dark woods, up in the trees, that is not healthy for deer.

The deer hears that audacious click and starts running. I give the deer a couple of seconds to get into good form, with afterburners fully engaged, then jack a round into the chamber, pretending to be astonished that a "dud" round doesn't eject from the rifle when I haul back the rifle's bolt and slam it forward again to get a round into the chamber. The rifle seems to sigh and say, "Well, here we go again!" And it goes ahead and shoots the deer for me.

It is a little embarrassing, actually, because it isn't me that shoots the deer. The rifle did it. It is like the two shotguns. It shoots itself. I'm just sort of "there" as a witness. Tough guns compensate for a hunter's shortcomings. Give them credit when and where due.

Anyway, at my age, it probably doesn't matter . . . getting the game, that is. I'm content to let the guns do the work for me. In fact, I actually don't shoot a lot of game anymore, just a couple of deer a year . . . sometimes three, plus twenty to forty ducks, and around a hundred quail, give or take a couple of dozen birds or so, and the odd woodcock and goose. And, of course, there's the foundation of squirrel hunting, which adds a few more critters to the pot, usually somewhere between twenty-five and thirty. Like I said, I've sort of backed away from shooting game much anymore.

Now, on my ventures into the hunter's world with one of my *tough* guns in hand, I tend to focus more on who I am and what I'm about out yonder, beyond the taking of game, and usually not very much on the gun—except for safety issues. But the gun's presence is always in my heart and mind. In fact, and as strange as it may seem, there are times when I can almost sense life and personality in these old guns as we go about our rambles together or share a bit of after-the-hunt time together with an oily rag before I put them to bed in their racks.

In this state of being, one that most old hunters have (*but damned few will admit to having*), there is quiet communication—graceful, smooth, spontaneous—between a hunter and gun. We come together, we *belong* together, in a strange sort of marriage. We know each other intimately. We accept each other for what we are and what we can and can't do. We do what we're supposed to be doing, *together*, and that's all that really matters. The special moments and the secrets are shared quietly and without fanfare. Our sacred bond is all about trust and respect. And sometimes I get the feeling . . . in fact, I am sure . . . that the forces that bond me with my *tough* guns flow both ways.

Postscript Quail Hunting

WE TOOK IT FOR GRANTED, ALL OF US. IN OUR YOUTH IT WAS always there for us, but we drifted from it, not fully realizing that the treasure we had was rapidly fading. As we prowled the woods and along the edges of fields and swamps, we were forever and again stepping into the middle of little brown bombshells that exploded in all directions.

Some of us had bird dogs, pointers and setters mostly, but we neglected them until late in the hunting season, after we'd saturated ourselves with squirrel hunts, duck hunts, and days in deer camps. We hunted birds but not seriously. We figured that the birds would always be there if ever we decided to transition from adventurers and explorers to gentlemen. And anyway, bird hunting was for "older hunters." We weren't there, yet—but the birds were.

That was back in the mid-1960s. The land was open to us. We could roam, ramble, and hunt practically anywhere. To be a teen-aged boy in the South back in the 1960s was magic. And if that boy had friends and access to a car, and perhaps a boat, the world was all before him.

We were consumed by hunting (and fishing) to the point of obsession. We felt occasional guilt for wasting good bird dogs as a result of pursuing other stuff, but we had no idea we were wasting the last breath of a dying sport—hunting wild bobwhites. We just didn't realize what was happening.

During those halcyon years, the nation arose from slumber, blinked, yawned, and began slowly, very slowly, to engage an environmental consciousness. "America the Beautiful" wiped the sleepers from its eyes, took a hard look at itself, and didn't like what it saw. Rivers had caught fire. Pesticides were killing eagles, pelicans, and God only knows what else. We were plagued by dam builders and flood-control advocates committed to the destruction of the nation's rivers. There were some fairly substantial and widespread agricultural and forestry practices that didn't quite seem to fit well on landscapes. Wetlands across the country, as well as the prairie provinces in Canada, were being drained. Hardwoods were being removed and land cleared to make way for pines, soybeans, and pasture. Duck seasons in the South were reduced to less than twenty days with limits of only one mallard a day. There were few deer, few wild turkey, almost no Canada geese, no bears to speak of, and elk were just a dream.

We lived in a ravaged land, but we had quail. We shot hawks, and we had quail. We shot owls and knocked down their big roost trees, and we had quail. We trapped very hard to meet the demand for fur: raccoon, fox, bobcat, skunk, opossum, mink, and otter—and we had quail. We killed every snake and every feral cat we saw, and we had quail. We ripped apart small streams and converted them to ditches with thick brambles along the banks, and we had quail. We raised chickens, shot more hawks and owls, killed more snakes, and we had quail. We had big gardens and pea patches with lots of bare ground and weedy spots scattered about, and we had quail. We burned the woods regularly, and we had quail.

Then, within a decade or so, by the mid-1970s, we shifted a little from being environmentally *conscious* and became environmentally *responsible* (sort of). The word "ecology" started being used outside of scientific circles. Congress had recently passed the Clean Water Act, the Clean Air Act, and the Endangered Species Act. We began taking better care of the land and the water and the grasslands and the woodlands and the wetlands. We quit shooting hawks and owls, quit killing snakes, drifted from trapping and the fur trade, stopped raising chickens in our back yards, stopped gardening at scales large enough to feed a family, started practicing "clean agriculture," modified a few forestry practices, and engaged in fire suppression on behalf of "Smoky the Bear." We invested in programs to enhance deer, wild turkey, bear, elk, and waterfowl and became legal minded, afraid of being sued, and seriously posted land, which, subsequently, made it virtually impossible for raccoon and other "varmint" hunters to prowl the countryside . . . *and the quail vanished.*

That's the nuts and bolts of it. We evolved as conservationists. We became more responsible citizens. And the quail paid the price. Now we all pay the price . . . *for doing the right thing.* Hunting wild quail in the South, for most of us anyway, has basically faded into history. But there is hope.

State fish and wildlife agencies throughout the South are working very hard at restoring quail, and they seem to be achieving some promising results. I'm cheering them on! But challenges still exist. Restoration of quail populations and quail hunting at a general regional scale is going to take time . . . a long time.

Patience is certainly a virtue. But I don't have a long time to wait. My white beard reminds me of this reality. I hear the clock ticking louder with each passing year. I know that if I'm going to hunt quail during these golden years, I need to do it *now.* Beyond time, however, what are some other reality checks?

To start with, quail hunting in the traditional style requires more than a twenty- or forty- or sixty- or eighty-acre tract of land. Unless there's access to a lot of land (hundreds, if not thousands, of acres) where the dog and the hunter can roam day after day, and where there are folks committed to managing access and harvest at a large scale, bird hunting in the traditional mode just can't happen. Gaining permission to cross fences is increasingly tough, if not virtually impossible, across most of the South. People are just scared to death of lawyers, and also they want their land and their hunting for themselves.

I absolutely understand. I'm a landowner, and I don't like having folks traipsing across my place, particularly when I'm not there. As a hunter, when I walk through my gate, I like knowing that the last person through that gate was me. Deer hunting and squirrel hunting, even duck hunting, can happen on smaller properties, but not quail hunting . . . at least not in the traditional sense.

So what is a quail hunter to do? Is there some way in today's world for a hunter to train and keep a bird dog tuned and to engage in the sport? Can we still witness the beauty and grace of a good dog working the landscape on a golden afternoon? Can we experience the thrill of the flush, the shot, and the retrieve? Can it be done on smaller properties? Is it prohibitively expensive? The answer to all of these questions, except the last one, is "yes." The answer to the last question is "no."

There are different ways to participate in bird hunting across the South, depending on how much you want to invest in time and money. First, the southern US has numerous outstanding shooting preserves that cater exclusively to quail hunters. They range from those with vast acreages and first-class accommodations, with fine dogs and guides and all the trimmings, to those that operate on a smaller scale with fewer amenities. If you only want to hunt a few times each year, perhaps only once or twice, going to a reputable hunting preserve is absolutely the way to go. Quail are stocked on these properties, and the shooting can be very good. There are very few wild birds on these hunts, but the stocked birds are flight conditioned and tend to flush and fly well. Prices vary. The more you pay, the better the experience, generally.

But I do it a different way. I buy 100 to 150 pen-raised birds every year, in 25-bird batches. I keep these batches of birds in a predator-proof cage located on my fifty-acre farm, just beyond the city of Starkville, Mississippi. Although I normally have two (and in some years three) small coveys of wild quail on my property, I do not shoot these wild quail. They are my treasures. I only shoot pen-raised birds. I also stay on my own land. I do not cross fences.

The pen-raised birds that I buy come from a very reputable shooting preserve and are all flight conditioned. The birds stay in good flight condition for a period of about seven to ten days. Beyond one week, the flushes begin to weaken and sometimes don't happen at all. But usually I've shot all twenty-five birds in a batch within a week of purchase.

When I'm ready for a hunt, I go to my bird cage and remove the feeders, the watering container, and the small square boards that I have on the bottom of the cage to give the birds something solid to stand on when roosting at night. This gives me room for capturing birds from the cage. Then I take a long-handled fish-landing net, open the main door of the cage, reach into the cage with the net, and catch and drag the birds, one at a time, across the floor of the cage and out onto the ground in front of the cage (still inside the net). The other birds will all be at the back of the cage, but sometimes a bird or two will flush and come toward the cage door. With a little practice, you'll learn how to catch your birds without having other birds in the cage escape. And if they do escape, it doesn't matter. Just hunt the escapees!

But back to the bird in the fish-landing net. It will flutter a bit and may get a little tangled in the netting. I reach down, control the bird from the outside of the net, slip my free hand under the net, grab the bird again, and place it into a bird-carrying bag. If it is tangled in the net, just take your time getting it free. You don't want an injured bird. Once the bird is in the bag, it will calm down. I continue this process until I have the birds that I want for that day's hunt.

I do not plant the birds. I've found that if I plant birds, my dog does not hunt well. He just trails where I've been walking as I planted the birds and goes directly to the birds. It becomes bird shooting rather than bird hunting. So I take the birds I want to shoot, usually five or six, out into the middle of a big pasture in the middle of my property, dump them out, and off they go in all directions . . . scattered to the four winds. Although they are pen-raised birds, they instinctively seem to go into the thickest cover available.

I give the released birds about thirty minutes to settle and rest, then I go get my dog, a wirehaired pointing griffon named Hank. Although I use him also as a retriever when hunting ducks, his first love is hunting and pointing quail. Usually, by the time I've released the birds and gone back to get him out of his kennel in my truck, he's frothing at the mouth and howling.

Hank hunts free-range quail differently than he does planted birds. He works free-range quail carefully and his points are firm—none of that "Hey, Boss, this ain't real" tail-wagging, shuffling stuff. Rather, he works them hard and sets them. We become a team, which is what quail hunting is all about.

The quail will be in some of the gosh awfullest places imaginable. The shooting can be tough, is usually fast, and generally has to be instinctive. The quail are in charge of the situations. I recommend that you save your fine double shotgun for a more controlled environment. I use a battle-scared old 20-gauge Remington with a variable choke set at "skeet." Be prepared to come home scratched and bleeding, with ripped shirts and britches, and also with a big smile and a happy dog.

Sure, it is fake. These are not wild quail. The land did not produce them. It couldn't! But if you get them from a good supplier and shoot them as soon as possible in the free-range mode, you can still capture something of the old bird-hunting tradition that echoes in your hunter's heart. You can do it on a small piece of property. Every batch of twenty-five quail provides me with four or five hunts (at five to six quail per hunt).

A six-bird hunt will take you all afternoon to pull off. And remember, pen-raised quail almost invariably refuse to flush after the sun sets. So if you release your birds around 1:30 p.m. and start your hunt around 2:15 p.m., you can have a three-hour hunt. That's a wonderful way to spend an afternoon. And think also of this: one hundred birds at five birds per hunt equates to twenty quail hunts per year. That's enough to keep both you and your dog happy.

And the cost? I budget about what I pay for my share of an annual duck-hunting lease over in Arkansas (split among four or five friends), or ten tanks of gas for my truck, or a month's worth of groceries for my wife and me. The key is to buy good birds, shoot them (or at them) within a week of purchase, and forget about the cost. If you start thinking about the cost of the birds, you will start planting them in spots where you'll be sure to get a good shot rather than releasing them into a free-range mode. That defeats the purpose of this whole thing. It isn't about quail shooting. It is about quail hunting.

So buy that bird-dog puppy. Let that puppy fill your heart. Train that puppy in your back yard. Build yourself a bird cage and put it out in a quiet spot on the land you want to share with that puppy. Find a local game-bird breeder. Read the old stories. Dream the old dreams. Fill that puppy with opportunities to become the dog it is bred to be. And, when you are both ready, *go quail hunting.*

Keep on Fishing

THERE ARE TIMES WHEN IT IS ABSOLUTELY NECESSARY TO GO fishing. Conditions, frankly, just don't matter. Furthermore, catching fish really has very little to do with it. In fact, if you aren't careful, catching fish can undermine your purposes. The trick is to do your best to stay focused on process and, if you do catch fish along the way, do so without interrupting your train of thought, or what you're really about.

I have a daughter who is a US Peace Corps volunteer developing and directing environmental education programs in a faraway land. Recently, the country where she's working erupted into chaos, with street demonstrations, riots, looting, and violent death. The Peace Corps told her that she, along with approximately two hundred other US Peace Corps volunteers, had to leave the country, at least for a while . . . until things settled.

If you live and work abroad, there is always a chance that you will encounter troubled waters. During my forty-year career as an international fisheries scientist, with multiple assignments on every continent except Antarctica, that has certainly been the case for me. On most of these assignments, I seemed to be in places that were either in some sort of turmoil or about to be. Only rarely was my work after the storm. Over the years, I found that the formula for getting my work done safely in such situations is to be alert, be absolutely aware of my surroundings, and never *ever* play mind games with myself. *When it is time to move, do it quickly and decisively.*

My daughter clearly understands these things. She's heard my old stories, is well trained, and is strong of body and mind. The one thing that I did not share with her, however, is that when the world around you starts to come apart, oftentimes you must leave much of what you love in place, including people. That's the painful lesson she's learning. But she knew this was coming. She could feel it building. It was just a matter of when.

As a father, it doesn't matter that I know she's capable of handling the situation she finds herself in. It doesn't matter that I know she's being helped by lots of people dedicated to keeping her safe. What matters is that my little girl is sad. She loved her work and the people she lived and worked with. Now she has to leave.

And then, it started raining . . .

It began with uncertainty. It was a teasing sort of rain. It unsettled me. Awash with emotions and concern about my daughter's safety, I knew, absolutely and in unequivocal terms, that I needed to get out of the house, to go fishing—or explode with anxiety.

But false starts plagued me. In fact, I made three separate trips from my house out to the crossroads, four miles away, that lead ultimately to my pond. I'd get to the crossroads, hesitate, then turn around and drive back home. Then I'd turn back around and go to the crossroads again. I think that the vultures that were on the side of the road eating a dead armadillo began to wonder if I'd ever quit messing with their dinner. I was wondering the same thing: would I, *could* I, settle on this rainy afternoon?

The rain played its games. But the deeper game was in my heart. I had every excuse *not to* go fishing . . . and every reason *to* go fishing. My heart and my mind and my soul could not get into synchrony. To top it all off, the wind was from the east. That's terrible for fishing in my pond and it makes me fidgety. Then the rain became ever more certain of what it wanted to become when it grew up. Conditions could not have been worse for fishing. But it didn't matter. Somewhere, in the deepest trenches of my soul, I knew that being on the water that rainy, windy afternoon just had to be.

On my third cycle from the crossroads to my house, I actually went back inside the house, got my raincoat, and declared myself a committed angler . . . despite my earlier reluctance and misgivings and despite an understanding of fish and water and wind and the spirit that lurks above it all, which all coalesced to remind me that fishing would be a fruitless exercise under these conditions—at least in terms of fish catching. But sometimes, such understanding and rational thought processes are trumped by other voices, other needs . . . other dimensions of the human condition.

Transcending reason, I forced myself to drive all the way to my farm's gate. As I did so, the rain gathered strength. I knew I was destined not only for a good soaking, but also for a good cleansing, a comprehensive cleansing.

Getting out of my truck and forging ahead, rod in hand, lures in my pocket, I could feel the water trickling off of my raincoat and onto the cotton trousers I wore. Then I could feel some of the trickles making it all the way down into my black rubber knee boots. I trudged on, crossed the bridges that span two little creeks, and began to hear birdsong. The rain came and went and with each coming was stronger than before. But the birdsong was continuous. It could not be dampened.

The woodlands were lush with new growth in every shade of green. Wildflowers filled the pastures with splashes of colors: pastel yellows, blues, purples, reds, and also white. They seemed to reach up, as if they were grabbing the raindrops, letting the water flow across their blossoms, cleaning them, enhancing their beauty. I too looked up, opening my eyes, my mouth, and my mind, letting the rain wash over me and into me. The rain was not cold. It was a spring rain, a life-giving rain, a rain to celebrate, to be out in, a rain that proclaims happiness and freshness and goodness . . . a rain that confirms that earth forces and those beyond are as they should be.

By the time I made it to the pond, its surface was pockmarked by large raindrops. The wind swirled. There was no shelter out there on the water. I knew that the only way I'd be able to fish was to go to spots in the middle of the pond, anchor, and do my best to keep position as I cast and retrieved my lure. It was then that I began to sense that my daughter was doing this exact same thing. Peace began to drift upon me. I felt her near to me. I could almost feel her breath. It was mixed with the wind.

I was under no illusion. Fish do not like all the splash and noise of a rain that's building up a head of steam. It scares them. It makes them nervous. I knew that they were out there, somewhere, but "hunkered down" for the duration. The thought crossed my mind that fish in the pond had more sense that I had. They were hunkered down as the world went wild around them, and I was not. I was out there in it all, subject to whatever the wind and the rain might throw at me. But the birds still sang and, when the wind on occasion stilled, tree frogs called. I obviously wasn't the only critter out yonder, engaging a world that was rumbling along at full-tilt boogie. I realized that I was happy to be exactly where I was, doing what I was doing, and I smiled. The smile became a quiet chuckle. Somehow . . . in ways I can't really describe or understand, the happiness I was experiencing out there, drenched by a spring rain, in a boat buffeted by the wind, listening to birdsong and frog calls, opened a door into my heart, and when that door opened I sensed a long-distance smile from my daughter.

The only lures I'd brought with me were soft plastic lures called Brush Hogs. They resembled some sort of cross between a lizard, a salamander, and a frog. Every part was designed to twitch, flutter, or tremble. At first, I tried casting without a slip sinker on the line. But that was pure, unadulterated folly. The wind just laughed, caught my lure in mid-cast, and threw it wherever it wanted. Additionally, without the weight and with my anchored boat spinning in the wind, I could not tell if or when a fish was nibbling at the lure. I had to face reality. I had to adapt to what was beyond my control.

My daughter smiled again and spoke . . . within my heart.

"Papa! Really! That's what you've always taught me!"

I'd caught nothing. I'd not had a strike or even a half-hearted nibble as far as I could tell. That didn't mean there'd been none. Rather, I just couldn't tell. So I put on a sinker and the fishing improved. At least I could cast and work the lure in a way that gave me a sense of what was happening out yonder in the deep.

"That-a-way, Papa . . . fish deep!"

I cast and I cast and I cast. The retrieves were dead slow as I crawled the lure across the bottom of my pond . . . time and again. The places where I knew bass liked to hang out produced nothing except the occasional snagged hook. Getting the hook off of a snag meant that particular spot was ruined, at least as far as fishing was concerned, for the rest of the day. There was simply too much commotion. I had to go someplace else to fish.

"Yes, Papa. And so do I."

But it didn't seem to matter one way or the other as far as fish catching was concerned. The only thing that came into the boat was rain and more rain. Water sloshed around my feet. The boat cushion I sat on was like a huge, wet sponge. The rain found the tiny pinholes where the raincoat hood was stitched to the rest of the coat. I could feel water trickling on my neck and between my shoulders. I just kept casting. With every cast I sent a prayer whirling away toward my daughter. I was like a monk with a prayer wheel and flags, with each spin of the wheel, each flap of the flag, sending its prayer. Cast, retrieve, cast, retrieve . . . my tears mingling with the rain flowing across my face.

"It's OK, Papa. I'm crying too."

I had a child in danger and that was all that mattered. But I'd felt it all before. I'd felt it when my eldest son parked his car and took off on an extended solo hike through badlands and desert in the American Southwest, and on the many occasions when he has ventured alone around the world for study, work, and adventure. I'd felt it when my middle son was at war in the Middle East, flying his bomber again and again into the maelstrom of battle, and again when he was flying in the Far East, responding to the whims of two presidents as they teased and insulted each other, playing a treacherous game that had every possibility of taking the world into nuclear war. Now my daughter, my youngest child, was carrying my nomadic genes out onto the currents of the world, aware, capable, and calm, a warrior of her own making, armed with compassion and competence, reaching out with a positive touch into the lives of people, giving them hope for a better future.

However, the world around her had other, stronger, currents . . . currents far beyond those upon which a twenty-three-year-old woman (or anyone else for that matter!) can safely ride. And when this happened, the safety net built by others thankfully opened for her. Her evacuation was ordered. She understood and obeyed. I heard her tears through the telephone, but also I heard the voice of a very strong and determined young woman telling me what she had to do and why.

The first strike came as a series of bumps. I knew I had to let the fish—and the world we shared out there on the pond—establish its own rhythm. No two situations are the same. The currents of inter-actions must be allowed to flow as they will, to define themselves, and then we respond as best we can. I let the bass run with the lure before I tightened the line and struck. Thousands of miles away my daughter was doing the very same thing in her world. Her line was tightening. She had to strike. But her fish were bigger . . . much, much bigger than mine.

I know, absolutely, that she is good at "fishing." She knows how and when to strike. She also plays her "fish" very well and can do so without interrupting her fishing . . . her focus on greater purposes. She's been *fishing* out yonder, across the vastness of planet Earth, since childhood, and most of it has been done alone. She is strategic and courageous . . . but also very careful. She pays attention to detail.

"Papa, I'm OK. I'm not scared. Trust in me. I'm your girl. I can do this."

The second fish hit hard, but I think that I probably hit it harder. I must have bounced the lead sinker off the top of the fish's head because it was immediately hooked and took to the air in what seemed to be a somewhat addled state. I tipped it off balance as it went airborne. That move put me in charge. It was a much larger fish than the first one I'd caught. It pulled very hard, but after I was able to get it past a snag beside one of my pond's islands, I knew that I would win the fight. And I did.

"Nice fish, Papa. You earned that one!"

As I eased the fish into the wire basket that trailed alongside my boat, the sky opened and the bottom fell out of it. I could no longer see to cast. I could no longer see the shoreline. What had just been heavy soaking rain suddenly became a chunk floater, a frog choker. The entire world around me went to flood . . . the pasture, the woods, the lane back to the gate, everything . . . including my heart. It was a fine flood—a blessing. And I sent a long-distance smile across the miles, into the realms of never-never land, to my daughter.

POSTSCRIPT

Just before noon on the day after my fishing trip in the rain, my daughter sent a follow-up message. She was packed and on her way to the staging location for evacuation. The trip would not be without a degree of danger, but she was prepared. She was now hooked to the biggest fish yet; and although it was "raining hard" and she was "very wet," she knew that she'd moved *her* "big fish" beyond the snag and that it would, eventually, come to her boat.

Then, later that same day, she sent another message. She said that she'd made it to the staging location for evacuation. The *big fish* was in the boat. All was safe and secure.

I took a deep breath and walked outside, wiping a tear in order to find my way through the doorway and past the patio gate. A gentle wind stirred the trees out in our lawn. Another very different wind stirred my soul. I listened to the wind in my soul very carefully. I could faintly hear a whisper. It came softly, fading in and out.

"Papa, I'm not done fishing. And I like the fishing best when I'm soaking wet, out in the rain . . . just like you. Without the rain there wouldn't be life."

Ten months after her evacuation she returned to the world and the way that she loves, on a new assignment in a different country as a seasoned and tempered Peace Corps volunteer. A faraway land had called her name. She knew how to listen to that call and how to respond to it. She didn't hesitate. It was time to go *fishing* again.

"Papa, it feels so right."

The Ones That Got Away

THERE IS AN OLD DUCK HUNTER'S STORY—FIRST COINED, AS I
recall, by the Cajun comedian Justin Wilson—about a grandfather
who took his very young grandson on a hunt somewhere down in
south Louisiana. Only the grandfather carried a shotgun. The boy
was still too small to shoot. The decoys were set and the hunters
were well hidden. Just at shooting time, a pair of mallard drakes
came floating into the decoys on set wings. The grandfather rose to
his feet, shot twice, and both ducks flew away.

The grandfather sat back in the duck blind, rested his shotgun
against one of the blind's supports, and called his grandson to him.
The little boy crawled up onto his grandfather's knee and snuggled
against the old man.

After a few moments the grandfather spoke. "Son, remember
this day, every detail of it. You have just witnessed a miracle." "What
miracle did I see, Grandpa?" the little boy asked. The grandfather
replied, "Son, you just witnessed two dead ducks flying away."

When I first heard this story a few years ago, I realized that,
more often than not, I've been blessed by similar miracles when
I've ventured afield with a rod or gun. Sometimes the magic is there.
Sometimes it isn't or . . . if it is . . . it comes in a different flavor that
bubbles up later on.

Like most sportsmen, when I'm sharing stories about my hunting and fishing experiences, I generally focus on the times when
game or fish were brought to hand. The other stories, those about
the ones that got away, are usually tucked into a secret corner of

my memories, waiting for me to work out the mysteries. They are the ones that haunt me. It's the critters that I did *not* get that are the immortal ones.

For example, there's a pet bass that lives in my pond. Her name is Eddie Joe. She's been living under a particular willow tree, at the edge of a drop-off, for a few years. Once upon a time she weighed almost eleven pounds. I know this because I caught, weighed, and released her. Now she's growing old and weighs between seven and eight pounds. She's deep into the process of ageing and losing body condition.

Eddie Joe and I hook up together once or twice every year. Sometimes she wins. Sometimes I win. I'll never take her from the pond, although I know, as a fisheries biologist, that removing her would be good for the rest of the bass that live there. It is her home, the only place in the entire world she's got to live, and I feel good about letting her live out her days there. Someday she'll be gone and a younger whipper snapper will take her place. I can relate to that. I'm retired . . . sort of. Like Eddie Joe, I pounce on a bait every once in a while, but mostly I just look them over and hunker down close to my own "willow tree."

The last time I hooked her I had, for all practical purposes, finished fishing for the day. I was out in my little boat and on my way back to the place where I drag it up onto the pond's bank. I had several bass in a wire basket that were destined for a fish fry that evening. As I recall, most were twelve to fifteen inches long and seemed to be in fairly decent body condition. It had been a good fishing trip.

I had a stiff bait-casting rod in the boat with me. As I approached Eddie Joe's willow tree, I decided to make one more cast just for the heck of it. I had not seen Eddie Joe for a very long time. The soft plastic Brush Hog plopped into the water just out from the willow tree and, before it settled, I saw a twitch in the line. The line began to move slowly out into the pond. I let the line tighten, lowered the tip of my rod, and then struck hard. Eddie Joe came completely out of the water (showing off!) and plunged into the mass of branches and roots that were in the water around her tree.

I could not get her out of that tangled mess. I'd pull and she'd pull. We kept this up for several minutes, until she came up to the surface and lay on her side, exhausted. I gave the rod one more strong pull and, of course, the line broke. It was tangled down in the brush. But Eddie Joe still lay flat on her side, on the surface and still connected to her end of the line, with the hook in the corner of her mouth (I could see the hook). When I got over to her, she saw me, swam down into the brush, and never came up. I could not get her out of that mess. I could not see her, but I could feel her swimming around down there.

Sick at heart, fearing for her life, I took the boat to the bank, stripped off all of my clothes, and swam out to the tangled brush by the willow tree. I located the line and followed it down, deeper and deeper until, finally, I found the hook. Eddie Joe wasn't there anymore. She'd managed to pull free from the hook and was gone. I whispered a prayer of thanksgiving. Losing a fish can be a blessing.

Once, after a successful black bear hunt in southeast Alaska, I went fishing in Prince William Sound. It was a fine spring day with broken clouds, mild temperatures, and very little wind. My friend Dean Rhine and I were fishing for rockfish. After a couple of hours of fishing I got hung up on the bottom. I pulled and pulled, trying to get unhung or perhaps break the line. It was then that the bottom of the ocean started moving. I wasn't hung at all. I was hooked to a huge fish.

This denizen of the deep was in absolute command of the situation. Whatever it was probably didn't even realize that it was hooked. I suspect that it was a big halibut. After what seemed like a very long time, but probably less than half an hour, the line snapped and, thankfully, we were free from the beast. I believe that some fish are supposed to stay in the ocean.

I've missed many a strike on my angling forays. I've had many a fine fish come completely out of the water and throw the lure back at me before I could rear back and pull the fish off balance. I've had big trout and char on the skinny end of a very fine tippet when the fish decided to jump, do a back flip on top of the taut micro-thread, and bust it to smithereens. When that happens, there ain't a dang thing that you can do about it! It all happens way too fast. You sit or stand where you are and the entire world around you goes still. You are like in some dream. One moment you have the fish of the day (or a lifetime) connected to you and the next moment everything is absolutely over and all you've got is a sort of sick feeling. You keep on fishing, but nothing is the same anymore.

Hunting misses have their own special rhythms . . . their own mysteries. Let's take deer hunting as a starter. In the far northwest corner of my farm I plant a little patch of winter wheat for the deer. It is a quiet place, the most remote of the property. I have a stand in a tree overlooking that food plot. I've killed lots of deer there over the years. Typically, I shoot one or two deer every year, then leave the rest of the deer out there in peace. When I hunt, I go about an hour before sunset. The deer come out at twilight.

On one late autumn afternoon, an afternoon so still I could hear robins turning over leaves, a fine big doe walked out into the middle of that little patch of wheat. She was about thirty-five yards from me, out in the open, completely unaware that I was up in the tree stand. It was a perfect setup. She stood broadside to me. The crosshairs of my rifle's scope settled on her chest, just behind and a little below her shoulder. I knew that the rifle was sighted in with precision. I squeezed off the shot. The doe stood there, turned, and *walked* back into the woods with her tail high. It was unbelievable! I searched the ground for any traces of blood or hair. There were none. I went into the woods looking for any sign of a hit. Nothing. Somehow, I'd missed that deer . . . at thirty-five yards.

The next day I checked my rifle. It was sighted in perfectly. The shots were well grouped (less than one-inch spread) and one inch high at eighty yards.

A week later I went back to the same stand. At twilight a doe walked out into the wheat, exactly like the doe had done the week before. As I watched her, I thought to myself that she sure did look like the previous deer, the one I'd missed. Just like the previous deer, she stopped and gave me a broadside shot. I took careful aim, steadied the crosshairs of the scope, and squeezed off the shot. The doe just stood there, looking up into the trees where I was hidden, trying to figure out the source of that loud noise. I'd missed again!

The doe turned, threw up her tail, and ran to the edge of the woods. Typically, a whitetail deer doesn't stop when it runs to the woods. But this one did. As she ran, I quickly rammed a fresh cartridge into my rifle. When the doe stopped, I put the crosshairs on her chest and dropped her in her tracks. When I went to her, I saw that the shot had been perfect. I have absolutely no idea how I'd missed what I think was the same deer twice in a period of one week.

Miracles prowl both ends of the spectrum. Once upon a time, back when I had a black beard and there was still hair on the top of my head, I was in western Alaska hunting caribou with my buddy Dean Rhine. We'd hunted several days without success. In fact, we'd only seen one caribou, and it was at least half a mile distant, running away from us. It was midday and we were hunkered down on the side of a mountain, eating lunch, when Dean whispered, "Don, there are two caribou bedded down right out in front of us!" I looked closely. Yes, indeed, there were two bulls about 150 yards away, curled up tightly amid a jumble of rocks down below us. Every now and then the larger of the two bulls would move its head. He had nice antlers.

We put down our sandwiches, grabbed and loaded our rifles, and took position behind one of the rocks in front of us. Our hunting coats were rolled up and placed on top of the rock to serve as steady rests for our rifles. Both of the bulls were now standing, fully exposed, out in the open. The setup was perfect. Dean said he'd take the one on the right. I'd take the one on the left. Both of our rifles were "spot on," zeroed to precision, adjusted to shoot four inches high at 100 yards. That means that we could hold directly on the center of the chest out to 200 yards and our bullets would hit in the killing zone.

At the count of three we both shot. Dean's caribou crumpled. Mine started running—fast—with its head held high, snorting steam in the crisp air, and covering ground as only caribou can do across rough mountain tundra terrain.

I've killed several caribou over the years, but this was my very first caribou hunt. As far as I knew at the time, it would be my only hunt for caribou. Thoughts of future caribou hunts were as yet not even in my dreams. And so, as that caribou was running off across the tundra, I thought to myself, "Well, Mister, you've just missed what might be your one and only chance to kill a caribou in your life!" I can remember Dean saying, "Don, do you want me to shoot it for you?!"

My response was to jack another round into the chamber of my rifle and get the sights back on my caribou. By then the caribou was more than 200 yards away and about ready to go out of my life forever. I pulled the crosshairs out to the forward edge of the caribou's chest and held six inches high. The bull had gained another 20 to 30 yards by then. There was no wind. I squeezed off the shot and—wonder of all wonders—the caribou bull flipped head over heels and landed on its back. It kicked once and was still. How I missed that first shot at 150 yards will always remain a mystery. How I *hit* that running bull at 250 yards is an even greater mystery!

Hitting moving targets is always gratifying, but especially so if they have feathers, are small and brown, and explode from under your feet. In this regard, one of life's absolute joys is a quail hunt with a good dog. Your heart pounds as you walk up to the dog on point, with your eyes looking straight ahead (never at the ground). You experience an adrenaline rush at the flush, mental focus and clarity like none other as the gun comes up and the target is selected, and deep satisfaction when there's a puff of feathers following the shot . . . then you start breathing again.

If I'm by myself and can take the wild shots safely, I tend to be able to hit a fair percentage of the quail that buzz up in front of me. At least I was doing this until about two years ago (before cataract surgery scrambled the equations). The little 20-gauge automatic that I typically use on bird hunts seemed to be connected to me in all dimensions . . . an extension of my mind and body. It almost shot itself. Even in the gosh-awfullest tangled mess of vines and thorn bushes a bird would get up, the gun would go off, and my old dog would retrieve the bird to hand. It was beyond miracle. It was magic.

Now it seems more common that when a bird flushes I might as well be throwing rocks at it. The chances of it gracing a dinner plate are remote. And when it comes to woodcock, I am increasingly convinced that they see the shot coming from behind them (their eyes are a bit far back on the head) and dodge it. But occasionally, when the stars, the moon, and the sun are aligned in proper order, the equations work themselves out, instinctive shooting kicks in, and this white-bearded hunter knocks down a few birds to go into the game pocket of his hunting vest. The misses are forgotten. The dog, bless his heart, forgives me for them. They enter into the realm of unspoken secrets and vanish like smoke in a windstorm.

Then, of course, there's the very serious business of shooting (at) waterfowl. Every year my goal is to kill twenty ducks and, hopefully, a couple of geese. That's enough for my wife and me to have a duck dinner once a month all through the year plus a goose or two for holidays. More typically, however, I shoot between thirty and forty ducks, plus the geese.

One season, when I was in my late forties, I hunted a lot with a friend named Randy Robinette. It was an exceptionally good year for ducks. I don't remember how many ducks I killed that season, but it was certainly in excess of forty. And that entire season *I did not miss a single duck that I shot at!*

The next season was an equally good year for ducks, but I was a nervous wreck. Prior to the beginning of the duck season, I could not sleep and, when I did, I missed ducks in my dreams. Duck heads would loom before me in those dreams, quacking and laughing. How would I be able to match what I'd done the previous year?

The truth is that I couldn't and didn't. I missed nearly every duck that I shot at! My shooting was horrible. I was using the same old pump gun as the previous year. The ducks came beautifully into our decoys, day after day. I think all season long I shot fewer than a dozen ducks. Search as I might, I could find no explanation for my poor shooting. It was a shooting slump of the most serious sort. My self-confidence plummeted to the bottom of a deep pit. I recovered somewhat after a few seasons, but never to the same level as that year before the slump hit. "Dead ducks," and particularly wood ducks (my favorite of all ducks to hunt), kept flying away! They still do.

And speaking of wood ducks—out on my farm I have a little brushy pond in the woods that wood ducks love. At first light they come twisting through the trees into that pond, giving me wonderful shots at twenty to twenty-five yards. It is a perfect set up. I've killed scores if not hundreds of wood ducks there over the years. But not anymore! No, siree. They come in beautifully, as they always have. I swing on them as I always have, make the shots, and watch as they go ripping off through the trees, untouched. I'm missing two out of every three that come! Nothing has changed in terms of the gun or the place or the ducks. But I can't hit them . . . at least not like before. They come slipping and darting through the shadows of early morning, giving me perfect opportunities. Sometimes, after I've missed them, they go ahead and land in front of me and swim around for a while, teasing me. Some of them actually swim right up to my feet and mock me. Then they flush in a wild flurry of wings, this time flying straight and steady. I shoot again, and miss again.

As I write this, the current duck season has a little more than one week left in it. So far this season I've killed twenty-four wood ducks while hunting on my little brushy pond in the woods. I've probably gone hunting thirty times. The ducks have come to the pond, and I've shot, on practically every hunt. It's just a guess, but I estimate that I've probably shot at sixty ducks. You can do the math if you wish.

I tell myself that it doesn't matter, that I've achieved a different (higher?) state in the hunter's evolutionary sojourn. After I've missed a shot, I discipline myself, trying to focus on the higher order of things. I take a breath, shake my head, and reload. I tell myself that missing doesn't affect the magic. It just deepens the mystery. I try to convince myself that maybe I'm "getting there" . . . finally . . . as a duck *hunter*, if not duck *shooter*. This works for a while. But then unexpected things happen to get this perspective, this sense of peace and acceptance, all discombobulated.

For example, during the recent Christmas holidays one of my sons went hunting with me—just to watch. He didn't even take a gun. I think he finds my shooting somewhat humorous (he's an excellent wing shot). The ducks came well to the little pond and were all over me, beating me with their wings. But I didn't shoot at them, not one single time. I simply could not get my gun up in time for shots as they came in. The ducks were already through the trees, zipping in and out of shadows, and on the water before I could do anything. They landed all around my feet. Then, when they flushed, they hugged the shadows until they were out of gun range. All I could do was watch them fly away. By sunrise I'd essentially surrendered.

It was then that I heard honking, serious honking, *close* honking. Low and behold, coming across the pond, a little above the treetops, were two Canada geese. There wasn't time to change from #4 shot to #2s. Plus, because I was hunting in close quarters, I had an improved cylinder choke in my shotgun's barrel. In spite of these handicaps, I swung on the near goose and shot.

I stood there in almost a state of shock, transfixed, as the goose folded and came crashing down through the tree branches. It hit the water very hard in the flooded woods just beyond the pond. The dogs were immediately on that goose, but the goose didn't need any additional grabbing. Those #4 steel shot had grabbed it enough. It was a dead goose.

Later that morning, when I cleaned the goose, I found that it wasn't just a lucky "head shot." To the contrary, that old goose had several "through-the-body" hits and two broken wings. It kind of puffed me up a little as a shotgunner. I thought to myself, "By golly, there may still be a little bit of lead in this old duck hunter's pencil!"

I've hunted a few times this season since killing that goose. During those hunts, I've shot *at* several more ducks and, as I recall, I think I've killed three or four of them. I tell myself that it doesn't really matter and that remembering hits and misses, keeping score, clutters up my mind. I push deeper into this mindset and tell myself that what I mostly care about is just being out yonder where I can watch the sunrise, listen to the whisper of wings, and witness ducks twisting through the tree branches as they dart through the shadows to land on my pond (which is true); and that dead ducks, regardless of whether or not they're belly up on the water or flying away, are always miracles (also true). I end the internal dialogue by telling myself that shooting the game or catching the fish I pursue doesn't matter anymore to this well-seasoned old sportsman. (That's a bold-faced lie. *Who am I trying to kid?!*)

Duck Tree

THERE IS A GENERAL AGREEMENT AMONG WATERFOWL HUNTERS that you will have more birds coming close to you if you are well hidden and less obvious. There are, of course, recognized and established exceptions.

Take snow geese, for example. If the geese seem hesitant to investigate your spread of decoys, you can set up white kites to flutter in the wind. Waving a white flag also can help. Perhaps the geese, being the socially conscious birds that they are, think you are surrendering and so come closer, honoring the code, to accept your sword. They complain bitterly about betrayal when you drop the flag and start shooting.

And then there's the long-lost art of trolling dogs. Ducks, being curious, albeit cautious birds, always seem to have an interest in what's happening on yon distant shoreline. A prowling critter like a bear, wolf, or fox can virtually suck a flock of ducks right up to the water's edge. Market hunters took notice. They bred and trained dogs that would march up and down the rocky beaches of New England, teasing the ducks until the ducks were so close that well-hidden market hunters could jump out of their covers and flush the ducks into huge capture nets. The nets were generally set upwind from the flushing spot so that the ducks would flush into the right direction: into the wind and into the nets.

I've experienced similar occurrences. Ducks that probably would not have given my decoys or call so much as a wing dip have spotted my dog walking the shoreline and wheeled in for a closer look. I've also had them try to land on top of my dog as he was making a retrieve. And what waterfowl hunter has not had a flock of ducks land all around him while he was sloshing about gathering decoys after a hunt?

The common denominator seems to be movement . . . of a certain sort. Otherwise you'd better be still, very still. Blink an eye as a pair of mallards or a flock of gadwalls circles your decoys and they will flare out of range and be gone forever. Fail to pick up a spent shotgun shell on a bright day with a little wind and you might as well be sitting in your duck blind knitting a sweater. Look up at the ducks as they pass overhead and they will spot your ruddy frostbitten face and flip over backwards under full power as they escape to never-never land.

The entire affair of attracting ducks into decent shotgun range becomes somewhat of an art form laced with a heavy sprinkling of magic. It is dependent on thinking like a duck, or at least trying to understand just a little about what is going on in a duck's brain. In this regard it seems to me that a duck's brain is all about sex and hunger and laziness and weather and wariness and bombasity and curiosity. It is the curiosity factor, however, that I think is often overlooked by hunters.

Ducks, particularly drakes, will throw caution to the wind in order to show off to their buddies or to impress their girlfriends—just like a bunch of teenaged boys on a tear, daring each other and proclaiming, "Hey, y'all . . . watch this!" The results are typically similar. If the stunt doesn't kill them, then the lady friends are impressed and they can strut among their pals. Ducks, just like teenaged boys, love to strut.

And so, while they are out carousing around, if they see something weird or out of place, ducks just can't seem to help themselves. They've got to check it out. If on close inspection of the curious thing they see other ducks (e.g., your decoys), they will literally sometimes try to land right on top of your head. I am convinced that under certain conditions I could lash a white teddy bear to a floating log, anchor the log out in the middle of my pond, twitch it occasionally with a long rope, and kill ducks. Those same ducks would flare if they saw a single small wad of duck down drifting with the wind across the pond's surface.

As a scientist, I know that some of the greatest achievements are accidental. A couple of inebriated geneticists staring into a fireplace while in a state of near stupor saw smoke curling and shouted, "Eureka!" Thus came the epiphany of the double helix in chromosome alignment. Another scientist I know, baffled as to why he couldn't get giant freshwater prawns to spawn in his laboratory, took a lunch break therein and accidently spilled soy sauce into an aquarium while trying to doctor his sandwich. The prawns in the tank immediately started to spawn—they needed just a little salt. In nature, they spawn in brackish water, not fresh. But before the soy sauce incident we didn't know that. Thus came the highly profitable freshwater prawn aquaculture industry. And so it goes.

I will never achieve a Nobel Prize in science. It is too late for that. I'm retired. Through the years, however, I've shared bourbon with many friends in front of fireplaces and I've spilled lots of soy sauce while making sandwiches. In these events I never experienced enlightenment beyond those of the common man . . . a tribe to which I identify greatly. My thoughts at the time were more focused on dogs and guns and fishing tackle and good times shared afield. And besides, Nobel Prizes are not awarded to a scientist for spending an entire career running trotlines and hoop nets to catch catfish in the rivers of the southern United States.

But, with humility, I must confess to being partner in a significant discovery that has great potential, scientifically and economically. To my knowledge, we were the first to the idea and we constructed the prototype. As is the case with most significant discoveries, it was purely accidental and the results were surprising. But upon discovery, we all immediately recognized what we had. Although we were (and are) just a ragtag assemblage of duck hunters, it was we who ushered into existence the genesis of the "Duck Tree."

The afternoon was gray and windy. The late December air had a bite to it. There were four of us: Don Flynn, Kevin O'Neal, my son Robert, and me. We had Kevin's dog, Rudy, with us. Although we were in the heartland of the South's best duck-hunting area, the eighty-acre field we'd leased was in more or less the lower reaches of the hunting spectrum. It was a partially flooded, sad-looking rice field with a brushy levee on one side. Most of the field was rice stubble and mud, but along the levee and down in one corner there was water. This was where we planned to hunt.

Getting to the hunting area required a long slog across the stubble and mud. Kevin had his four-wheel-drive all-terrain vehicle, and on this we piled our sacks of decoys. He churned his way to the setup spot and we followed on foot. There were a few ducks, mostly shovelers, on the water when we got there. They flushed at our approach. Overhead there were scattered flocks of geese, mostly snows and blues and a few white-fronted (speckle bellies). An occasional duck passed over. The prospects were not promising. There were too many other places, good places, for ducks to go for their afternoon feed. But this was all we had and we were committed to it. We'd do our best.

It took about thirty minutes for us to spread our decoys and for Kevin to go hide his little four-wheeler. There was really no place for us to hide other than down in the blackberry brambles that grew on the levee. We could not stand. There was nothing to stand by or in. We had to sit down among the thorns and vines and would have to shoot from sitting positions. That's tough to do . . . at least for me. There was one scraggly leafless tree on the levee nearby that was about twelve feet high. That was it. We had no blind. We were, for all practical purposes, exposed to the ducks. The only saving grace was that the wind was to our backs and the levee cut the wind. The ducks, if any came, would land into the wind in front of us—as they should.

As the afternoon aged, we began to hear shooting in the distance. There were ducks moving, somewhere. From time to time we could see small flocks of ducks, mostly gadwalls and mallards, passing along distant tree lines or high overhead. But nothing worked our field. We just sat there, listening, watching, and adjusting our sitting positions to avert cramps. There wasn't much talk.

A pair of mallards came over, full of chuckle. Kevin called. The ducks broke their course and started to circle around. Both were drakes. They circled twice, then locked up and drifted into the decoys. Kevin killed one. Don killed the other. The shooting intensified in the surrounding woods and fields. There were more ducks in the air, but they didn't show much interest in our place.

A flock of gadwalls whistled by overhead. We tried to bury ourselves deeper into the brambles. They swung far out over the field, then banked and circled back around over our decoys. They circled and circled, again and again, nervous and suspicious as only gadwalls can be. It was unlikely, from the way they were acting, that they'd ever come to our decoys. But they were getting lower with each pass. Kevin said to take shots as we could get them. So finally on one pass they were close enough for me to shoot. I killed one and Kevin got two.

Kevin hung his ducks in the forks of that scraggly tree on the levee so that they would cool. I questioned this to myself . . . but said nothing. Surely the ducks would see those dead ducks in the tree and flare. Just then another flock of ducks, mallards this time, skirted the far edge of our field, then turned inside out and made a beeline for us, passing right over the tree with the dead ducks hanging in it. They circled once then came in—directly in front of the tree. We killed three ducks from that flock. Kevin hung these ducks in the tree. We all contributed our other ducks to the tree, then hunkered down back into the brambles, all of us except Kevin. He stood beside the tree.

Another flock of gadwalls materialized out of nowhere, saw our Duck Tree, made one circle, and came directly to the tree, flaps down, wings locked. We wore them out and added more ducks to the tree. We all stood in position. It didn't matter. Ducks that on previous hunts would have paid no attention at all to our decoys spotted that tree full of dead ducks and immediately came to it. We tried to be selective regarding mallards and pintails: drakes only. We continued to fill the tree and then realized that we needed to do a count. We could have twenty-four ducks, of which sixteen could be mallards. We were close, very close, but still had a few ducks to go.

The Duck Tree worked its magic all the rest of the afternoon, and we kept shooting. At sunset, quitting time, when we had nearly all the ducks we were allowed, ducks were still coming to the tree. We took the dead ducks down from the tree and put them on stringers to carry out of the field. When we did, the ducks stopped coming to our decoys. They'd seen plenty of decoys in old rice fields before and simply were not interested in our setup. And when they saw us standing on the levee, as we'd been standing for at least the past hour shooting ducks as they came to the tree, the ducks passing over the field would immediately flare and be on their way.

After we got back to our trucks and had our gear and ducks loaded, we stood around and discussed our discovery and its potential. I proposed a possibility for consideration. We could get some of those dummy ducks used for retriever training and hang them from one of those artificial Christmas trees that's worn out and scraggly looking. Set the tree up, hang the dummies, and have at it. All agreed there was merit to the idea and possibly fortunes to be made. But then we had second thoughts.

A Duck Tree messes with the mind of ducks and makes them behave in unreasonable ways . . . just like duck hunters. For a duck hunt to have any purpose and meaning, it is important for at least one side of contenders in the match to exhibit some degree of sanity. If duck hunters can't do this (and we agreed they can't), then the ducks absolutely must. Thus, no more Duck Trees for us.

So take the idea and run with it if you wish. Make your fortune. Bask in glory. We relinquish all claims. We are not interested in fortune and glory. We prefer our insanity, the insanity of duck hunting.

Hooters Called Me Home

I'M AN ALASKAN IN EXILE. I BELONG THERE. I JUST DON'T GET to live there . . . at least not very much. But I'm there enough to keep the titer high in my soul. From time to time I get a good (although rarely enough) dose of that wonderful part of the world. The sweep of the land stirs me as does no other place on earth. The brittle silence of winter takes me into ethereal realms. The rush of a dogsled on a frozen river, the rush of a stream full of salmon, the rush of wings as ducks and geese swirl overhead, the rush of adrenaline as a brown bear or moose suddenly comes out of nearby brush . . . all fill my heart with joy beyond imagining. I stand in awe at the majesty of Alaska's mountains, the hush that settles across its nameless valleys when shadows are deep, the shimmering aurora in the heavens above it, and its rivers that flow wild and untamed to God only knows where.

I was confirmed an Alaskan as a young man in my twenties, but I'd been one in my heart since boyhood. I'd read the old stories of the far north; I'd dreamed the dreams. When I finally got there, I knew that I was where I belonged. The year was 1976. I'd spent nearly all the money I had to get a one-way ticket from Alabama to Anchorage. I landed on the sixth of June. Winter was just losing its grip on the interior. For nearly three months I rambled and roamed, probing the hidden pockets of "The Great Land" with a backpack on my back and a walking staff made from a hickory sapling I'd cut from an Ozark hillside. I still have that old staff. In fact, it is within arm's reach of me as I write. Just looking at it floods my heart and mind with emotion and memories.

For the first time in my life, the restlessness that had always plagued me was stilled, just a little bit . . . just for a while. When I breathed, the chilled air purged me physically and spiritually. Every step I took was familiar. I'd made every one of them thousands of times in my dreams. Every smell was recognizable. I explored mountains, tundra, forests, glaciers, rivers, and black spruce bogs. I was with the sheep, the caribou, the moose, the wolves, the bears, and the eagles. I fished for grayling. I was pounded by storms and attacked by mosquitoes. I fought wolves to save a moose calf that came running into my camp. Everything fit, including me. I camped in wilderness and on the outskirts of villages deep in the "bush." I met the wonderful people who live in this "Last Frontier." From my rhythms and speech, most of them recognized that Alaska was working its magic on me, engulfing me, bringing me into its arms, owning me.

My venture eventually took me over into Canada's Yukon Territory, and from there I made my way south by way of Lake Bennett, down and across the Chilcoot Trail, and to the port of Skagway back in Alaska. I took deck passage on ships, slowly discovering the world of southeast Alaska, the fishing and timber towns, the glaciers, the sea, the islands. I followed trails through its rainforests. I watched glaciers make icebergs. I saw whales spouting. I picked wild raspberries. Everything I had was soaked by rain and never really dried. But I was warm . . . warmer than I'd ever been in my life. There was a fire that burned in my gut, a fire that still burns within me. That was over forty years ago. The fire that Alaska kindled and stoked in me as a young man will persist for the duration of my mortal sojourn, and perhaps beyond it. Some fires, and particularly the most beautiful ones, are eternal. They are the fabric of the soul.

During those forty years, I've gone back to Alaska many times. I worked there for a while as a young assistant professor, teaching fisheries courses at the University of Alaska in Fairbanks. Over the years since then, I roamed the state, north to south, east to west. I hunted big game: caribou, moose, bear, wolf, and deer. I fished the rivers, the lakes, and the ocean. My ventures took me to the arctic, to and beyond the Brooks Range, deep into the vast expanse of the interior, a land laced with tundra and taiga, out onto the Alaskan Peninsula, and throughout the southeast. I fell head over heels in love with below-zero weather. I fell head over heels in love with the Alaskan people. And yet I could never find a way to stay there. God knows I tried. Every time I left Alaska, it reached out to me asking me, "Why?" I never had a good answer other than the stars just didn't line up in a way that let me do it . . . but there was something else.

I heard irresistible sirens calling me out into the world. Although I've always found internal peace when in Alaska, I was called every time to leave it . . . again and again and again. I was one of the restless men that the poet Robert Service wrote about. I was plagued by wanderlust. I could not sit still. And so I cast myself into the currents of the world beyond Alaska, time and again. Asia, Africa, Australia, Europe, South America, Central America, North America, and the Caribbean all became part of the sojourn. Oceans, deserts, forests of all kinds, rivers both great and small, swamps, marshes, mountains, hills, canyons, prairies, and coastlines of all sorts . . . I loved them all. I learned languages: Bahasa (Indonesian), Spanish, French, and enough Swahili, Vietnamese, and Serbo-Croatian to keep me on track and more or less safe. I stumbled into and out of wars. Once I was captured by enemy soldiers (and escaped). I have been shelled by artillery, held at gunpoint (many times), poisoned in the Himalayans, robbed, stabbed, beaten, and stoned. I've run out of money in far-off lands. Once I rented a jail cell in Kathmandu, Nepal, on a cold November night so that I would have a dry place to sleep out of the wind. The man in the cell next to mine died that night. I've slept on the streets with homeless travelers adrift on the currents of the world. I've met good people everywhere. I wouldn't trade any of it. Yet throughout the pilgrimage, I knew I had a home: Alaska. It was one of the few places in the entire world where I felt like I fit.

Eventually, however, I settled in the most "southern" place on earth, Mississippi. I am a southerner by birth and by the grace of

God. There was work to be done and a life to live in this remote corner of America's Deep South. In Mississippi, my lovely Chinese Panamanian wife and I raised three fine kids. In Mississippi I established and maintained a career as a university professor. And from Mississippi I was able to keep on launching myself back out into the far-flung corners of the world . . . including Alaska. Mostly, I went back there for professional ventures: meetings, presentations, fisheries research and surveys, and such. But somehow, when doing those things, I was usually able to work in a little fishing or a hunting trip of some sort, primarily for big game.

As the years passed, I began to drift away from hunting big game. It wasn't because I didn't love it anymore. I certainly did! I was particularly in love with Alaskan fly-in hunts . . . the kind where I'm dumped alone or with a friend on some remote gravel bar along a river, or on tundra, or at the edge of a lake. After the gear is unloaded, the pilot of the little bush plane usually says something like, "Hope to see you in a couple of weeks." I always hoped so too. The pilot then takes off—suddenly Alaska engulfs me. There's not much that's quieter or more lonely than some remote corner of Alaska after the bush plane that put you there vanishes over a distant mountain.

The first order of business once the plane is gone is to load the rifle and strap on my big .44 magnum revolver. There are critters in Alaska that stomp and bite. Then I begin working on the pile of gear before me, packing it to the spot that will be my camp. It has to be a place where I can see out yonder, a significant distance beyond the camp, just in case unwanted visitors (bears mostly) want to come take a peek at what I've got going on. Surprises are not fun.

I transition to another man, the one that resides in my heart between my ventures in Alaska. He awakens and rearranges my mind. I link with echoes from long ago. My senses sharpen. I feel stronger and *am* stronger. My resolution shifts to a larger scale. I become fully man again. I become the hunter again, matching wits with the great beasts, stalking, killing, and packing them out. A song fills my heart.

As the years marched on, however, feathers and shotguns started edging out hair and rifles, even on those big game hunts. I really don't know why. I found myself taking friends on big game hunts, but I was not really interested in shooting anything except camp meat. Frequently, I'd carry only my big revolver, especially if I was doing any fishing. In addition, I'd try to cram a shotgun into the little bush planes that transported me to my hunting areas. The pilots, in almost all cases, would say OK and give me those extra ten pounds for my old pump gun and a couple of boxes of shells.

Ptarmigan in the interior and waterfowl in the southeast became my game, my focus, when hunting in Alaska. My resident friends up there were making the same evolutionary shifts in their hunting. Like me, they had plenty of big game trophies hanging on their walls. None of us needed any more. Like me, they were entranced by feathers. Together, we had fabulous hunts in some gorgeous places.

During this transition to feathers, and particularly when hunting waterfowl and cranes down in the southeast, I started hearing about a very strange hunt. It was most commonly discussed in whispers, and then usually in a shadowy, secluded corner of a bar over a couple of beers. I'm no eavesdropper. But I kept hearing the word "hooters." I came to realize, eventually, that they were not talking about a restaurant full of pretty girls. From these muted conversations I slowly, ever so slowly, pieced together a picture of what is, for some folks, including me, one of Alaska's finest hunts. It is a hunt that very few people on the "outside" know about and fewer still engage: the springtime hunt for hooters.

Hooters are the males of sooty grouse (formerly called blue grouse). They are big birds, about the size of a three-quarter-grown chicken. In the early spring, hooters find a good perch in a tall tree and start calling, trying to attract a girlfriend. Typically, they give a deeply resonating six- to seven-note call that sounds sort of like an owl: *whoo-whoo-whoo . . . whoo-whoo-whoo-whoo*. Once they get cranked up, they rarely move from their calling perch. Sometimes there will be several hooters calling at the same time across the expanse of a mountainside or down along the steep slopes that flow into some valley.

The hunt is all about trying to locate the tree the bird is in and then trying to spot the bird up in that tree. In some respects, it is like a backward wild turkey hunt. Rather than the hunter calling the bird, the bird calls and the hunter tries to find it. That's easier said than done. First, you have to be able to tell direction using your ears. If you're an older hunter, at least one of your ears is probably not operating at 100 percent. You may find yourself whirling around in circles, like a moth around a light bulb, trying to figure out which way to go to get to that hooter. Then there's the terrain. Hooters rarely hang out in flat country. All I've ever seen (or heard) were in mountain country. They also are not usually in open terrain, but rather in rainforest that's thick, wet, covered by moss, and laced with icy cold streams and "train-wreck" log jams. Sometimes during hooter season there are still big patches of snow scattered about, especially early on.

To get to a hooter, you have to pick, and sometimes force, your way through the jungle that prevails in southeastern Alaska's rainforest. You've got to wade the streams, climb the mountains, and slog across bogs, snow, and spongy tundra. Your gun needs to double as a walking staff in order to help you scale some of the steeper terrain. And all the while . . . you must keep a keen lookout for brown bears that have just come out of hibernation and are *very* hungry and grumpy. Constant vigilance is required. With "Bruno" in mind, I hunt hooters with a 12-gauge pump shotgun; and most of the time, until I've found my hooter, I keep that old gun fully loaded with slugs.

If you are not in reasonably good physical condition, and if you don't like to be cold and wet most of the day, and if the thought of encountering a very large bear at very close range bothers you, and if there's any question about your ability to hit what you shoot at— when shooting fast and being accurate is *very* important (you can get the shakes later while skinning Bruno and explaining things to the troopers)—then I suggest that you invest your time visiting a salmon hatchery, watching a glacier, or going someplace with good food, a warm fire, and fine wine. Hooter hunting is probably not for you.

With regard to physical conditioning, the usual preparations for a wilderness hunt apply. Put thirty pounds of rocks into a backpack and walk five to ten miles a day with it strapped to your back for about three months before you go on your hunt. Once or twice a week during your training program, spend about an hour with that full pack, going up and down the stairs of a football stadium. Fill up your bathtub with cold water, pour in ten pounds of ice, and soak your feet in the water for about thirty minutes, every day for the three-month training period. Quit taking warm showers. Always take cold showers. This is called acclimation. Just grit your teeth and do it. And, finally, practice standing on the steps of your front porch, leaning backwards (wearing your backpack with the rocks inside), with your face looking straight up into the sky for thirty to forty-five minutes without stopping. Take a one-minute break and then arch your back and look at the sky again for another thirty to forty-five minutes. Do this until you fall backwards into your front yard. Practice rolling to minimize bruises and broken bones. I suggest you place a twelve- to twenty-inch-diameter log about six feet behind you so that you can practice your survival roll in a realistic fashion. Now that I think about it, perhaps it is better to begin training six months prior to the hunt rather than three months. That will give your broken bones an opportunity to heal.

One of the good things about this training program is that, by the time you've completed it, your spouse will happily tell you good-by, wish you well, and not ask you anything about your return date. This is important because you may need an extra bit of time (a few days or a couple of weeks) to hunt some mountainside or valley that you've discovered. The hooters are thick in your new discovery; and, if you leave them in peace, you will always question your sanity. The more time you can spend roaming in Alaska during springtime, regardless of your reason for being there, the better.

Spring is a lovely time of the year just about everywhere, but especially so in Alaska. The entire world up there seems to be yawning and rubbing the sleepers from its eyes. The ducks and geese are coming home. The bears are digging out of their winter hibernation dens. The fish are stirring in the ocean, and some are already heading up the creeks and rivers. There's a green blush dawning on the mountainsides and on tundra. The deer, the moose, and the caribou start having fawns and calves. Mama bears bring out their cubs to give them their first view of the world. The skunk cabbage is sprouting and blooming. Fiddler heads from ferns are curling up above the ground, ready to pick and add to your stir-fry dishes. There's new life everywhere. The sap is rising . . . in the trees . . . in the hooters. A fire still feels good, especially during evenings in a cabin, but when there's sun (a rare thing in southeast Alaska), the day can actually feel a little warm when you're stirring about outside. There's still a bit of snow in the shadowy places, but it's melting away quickly. The days get increasingly longer. Old shotguns get a good cleaning. Talk turns to hooters.

The email message from my friend Mark Stopha was short and to the point: "Come, as soon as you can. The hooters are hooting like crazy!"

Mark lives in Douglas, just across the channel from Juneau. We've known each other for over thirty years. We met when I was on the faculty of the University of Alaska. He then joined the Peace Corps (West Africa), and I moved to Mississippi. Shortly after he returned from the Peace Corps, he came to work with me on a graduate degree in fisheries at Mississippi State University. When he had his degree in hand, he returned to Alaska and quickly was hired by the Alaska Department of Fish and Game. He's been a biologist and commercial fisherman up there ever since. And from time to time I go up to pester him. We hunt and fish a little and fellowship a lot. His passion in spring is hunting hooters.

I immediately accepted his invitation. A week later we were in his boat, heading out to his cabin on an island about an hour's boat ride from Juneau. I'd been to the cabin before. I'd hunted black-tail deer with him in that area. My daughter (age ten years at the time) and a friend from Arkansas had joined us for that black-tail hunt. It was a successful hunt in every sense of the word. We got our deer, ran crab pots, engaged in beach combing, and had wonderful evenings in the cabin. He'd mentioned hooters during that deer hunt. As I listened, I became fascinated by what he was saying about them and about the hunt. Now we were together again, setting off on our hooter hunt.

When we got to the island, the tide was high. That made it easier for us to unload the boat. Once our gear was on the beach and the boat was pulled back out beyond the low tide zone and secured, we immediately started hauling our gear to the cabin. It was good to be back on the beach and back on the trail that leads to Mark's cabin. It was good to be back in that wonderful, moss-covered palace in the woods, a "man cave" well hidden from the outside by alder, birch, and spruce thickets. It was good to be back with Mark. And it was good to be back in Alaska.

We cooked supper, visited a little around the wood stove, and then crawled into our bunks. There was a damp chill outside the cabin, but the little stove kept it at bay inside. I lay there in the quiet, full of peace. The years raced through my mind. Alaska ventures swirled before me in a beautiful aurora of images and feelings. I drifted into never-never land. When I woke up, there was a faint light coming through the windows. It was an Alaskan dawn. And I heard hooters. There were at least three of the birds and they didn't seem to be very far away.

Mark was already stirring, getting the coffee pot going and gathering stuff for breakfast. I got up and helped tend the stove, cook the eggs, and pack the lunch that we'd carry. We would not be hunting this island, but rather a larger island across the strait, where we'd hunted black-tail deer. We also would not be using his large boat, but rather a skiff outfitted with a small, cantankerous, little two-stroke outboard motor.

The tide was falling as we walked down to the gravel beach. The rocks were smooth, gray, and wet. Mist swirled among the trees. The ocean was glassy smooth. Small flocks of ducks, divers mostly, buzzed past us, low to the water, the whisper of their wings only making the quiet that surrounded us that much thicker. The water was crystal clear. The air was pure. My heart was singing.

We loaded the skiff, donned our survival suits, and crawled on-board. The little motor was cold but, after a few pulls on the starter cord, began to sputter and smoke. Finally, it came to life and Mark let it warm up for a couple of minutes. Then he nodded his head and I pushed the little skiff away from the beach.

The sound of the outboard motor was swallowed by the vastness of Alaska. We had the world around us all to ourselves. We were just two tiny specks of life in a realm so huge that it is virtually impossible to comprehend. The reality is that people disappear in Alaska. Some disappear on purpose. I think that's why I go there. For a little while, a few days, a few weeks, I simply disappear. I move so deeply into Alaska . . . physically, spiritually . . . that the prospects for re-entry back into my other world are always questionable. There's no compromise in Alaska. When you're out there, you're on your own, in all dimensions. So far, from each of my ventures there, I've come back. So far . . .

We drove the skiff along the beach of the big island for a couple of miles and then beached it in a sheltered inlet where a small stream entered the ocean. We took off the motor and carried it and then the skiff about a hundred yards to higher ground, above the tideline. Lose that skiff and we'd be in very serious trouble. But the tide was not our only concern. If a bear came by (and they were most certainly out and about . . . we saw their tracks), curious or unhappy with the world, it could destroy that skiff in a matter of minutes. It could destroy our motor, destroy our fuel tank, eat the fuel lines, and leave us stranded. They do that sort of thing. But there wasn't much we could do to prevent a bear from doing any or all of the above. All risks can't be avoided. All you can do is try to minimize them.

We put on our packs, grabbed our shotguns, loaded them with slugs, and looked for a place to cross the stream. I was wearing good-quality, well-broken-in boots, guaranteed waterproof. For re-inforcement, Mark handed me a pair of portable, very light, wader socks to use when crossing streams. They worked very well for that purpose. But they were not something that could be worn during regular walking beyond streams. So I took them off after crossing that first stream.

The forest was soaking wet (it almost always is in southeast Alaska). Within ten minutes my "waterproof" boots were completely wet. They stayed that way for the duration of our hunt. I could have worn rubber boots and stayed dry, but climbing mountains in rubber boots is not something I recommend. It is better to walk wet and have ankle support than to be on a mountainside with dry feet but a sprained or broken ankle. The temperatures were in the mid-forties to low fifties, so, while uncomfortable, having wet feet was not particularly dangerous. There were several pairs of socks in my pack. I changed them about once every hour.

After crossing that first creek, we immediately went almost vertical, climbing up a heavily forested hillside. The ground was covered with ferns and moss. The trees were huge. I had to use my shotgun as a walking stick to help me get to a sort of plateau about a hundred yards up from that stream. Our climb was slow but steady. When we got to the top, we stopped and listened. In the distance, higher up, we could hear a hooter.

Fog swirled around us as we climbed to another plateau, and then another, and then one more. The hoots were louder and were coming nonstop. We edged closer, trying to determine which tree the bird was in. The hoots continued. There was a huge spruce ahead that seemed to be the source. We moved carefully, looking, listening, until we were under the tree. There was no question. The bird was up in it, somewhere.

Taking off our packs, we started looking. The hoots kept coming. For nearly an hour we looked, and looked, and looked. The bird never stopped hooting. We took out our binoculars and searched every limb of that tree, from the trunk out to the end of each branch. We circled. We stopped and ate a sandwich. The hoots kept coming. *Whoo-whoo-whoo . . . whoo-whoo-whoo.* We craned our necks backward until I felt that my head would never again sit correctly on top of my shoulders. Finally, Mark said, "Got him!"

Out about halfway on a limb, not sixty feet above us, was a dark blob. When the hoots came, one end of that blob moved. That was the bird's tail moving. We watched the bird for just a little while, making sure that the tail bobs came when there was hooting. Then Mark said, "Take him."

I unloaded the slugs from my shotgun and loaded three #6 shells. Carefully aiming at that blob, I pulled the trigger, and down came Mr. Hooter, all a flutter, hitting the deck with a heavy thump. My gosh, he was big. When I picked him up he felt like he weighed over two pounds, perhaps three.

After pictures were taken, Mark dressed the bird, taking the breast and legs and putting them into a plastic bag. There was no reason to be carrying around complete (and heavy) birds. There were more hooters up yonder on the mountain that we needed to go find.

We crossed an open area that was a mixture of tundra and bog. On the edge, across a fairly substantial snowfield, we could hear another hooter. It had picked just about the only spruce tree of substantial size, so we zeroed in on it. Still, it took us several minutes to locate that bird. It is amazing how well camouflaged they can be when tucked into the shadows of those branches. Basically, it seems that the trick is to find a dark blob and watch it to see if there's a tail flicker during the hoots. Except for the tail bob, the hooter doesn't move. It cares not a bit that there are two people below, spinning around, peering up, trying to sort out what's bird and what isn't. Finally, we spotted the hooter and added him to our bag.

Our third bird was back in the forest. When we finally found the tree, it again took us nearly one hour to see the bird. After thirty minutes of looking, we took a real lunch break. The hooter continued calling right over our heads as we ate. It is almost beyond comprehension that a bird can be so unconcerned about being watched, be hidden so well, and continue calling like that. After our lunch we pulled out binoculars and began a limb-by-limb search of the tree. I was first to spot the bird. And, after doing so, it seemed incredible that we'd not seen it before. It was almost directly over our heads, but nearly one hundred feet off the ground, on a branch a couple of feet from the trunk of the tree. I had to step away from the tree a few yards to get a good angle for the shot. When I shot, the bird came tumbling out of that tree, hit the ground, and started running down the side of the mountain. That hooter was one heck of a tough bird!

Mark started chasing it. That chase was something to behold! Mark is a big man, a *very* big man. Yet here he was, sprinting down that mountainside, jumping across logs and running through all manner of vegetation. The hooter knew that Mark was after it and increased its speed, even though it was crippled and could not fly. Every few feet Mark would stop and let fly with a load of #6 shot from his old double-barreled shotgun. After about the third or fourth shot, he connected and collected the bird. The way that Mark was able to move like he did in that jungle was amazing. It was like he had wings on his feet.

After that bird, we began making a large circle that would bring us back around to where we'd started the hunt. Some of the places we moved through were like fairylands. The moss, the ferns, the big roots and towering trees; the little seeps and streams, the larger creeks; the flat shelves with new growth in park-like areas with scattered aspens and birches . . . all coalesced into an almost spiritual current that picked me up and carried me.

I began to feel a lightness in my feet and thought again about Mark chasing that wounded hooter. I began to understand how people who have lived here awhile develop a rhythm that is in synchrony with the landscapes; and how, infused with this rhythm, they can move smoothly across those landscapes. I could, in fact, feel it happening in me . . . again.

I've always experienced this on my Alaskan ventures. It usually takes a few days. But now, after only one day of hunting hooters, I sensed the resurrection. I found myself again trusting my feet to find their footing as I plotted my courses through the various terrains. The only persistent challenges to break my rhythm seemed to be the "train wrecks," the crisscrossed jumbles of logs, where trees of all sizes have fallen against each other over the course of the years.

The older ones on the bottom would be in various states of decay, covered by moss and lichens, and appeared to be melting into the ground. But on top of them would be progressively fresher logs, all in a tangled mess. Picking one's way across and through the train wrecks takes time, balance, and nerve.

I'd just completed such a crossing when I heard a hooter right next to me. I stopped and called Mark. We stood there for about fifteen minutes searching for it. Then I backtracked around that train wreck, crossed a little draw, and worked my way up the side of a little hill to a position where I could get a different vantage point. Once there, it took me less than ten minutes to spot that bird. I could clearly see it. It kept calling. Every time it hooted, its tail bobbed strongly up and down. But from that hillside it was too far away for me to shoot. My old gun just won't kill a big bird cleanly beyond thirty-five or forty yards. I didn't want another hooter chase!

To shoot the thing, I'd have to go back down the hillside, across the draw and the train wreck, to my original position. But before doing it I marked the hooter's position, being careful to identify features of the branch where it was perched. I counted the number of branches from the bottom of the tree up to the bird's perch. When I got back to the place beside the tree where I could shoot, I located the branch that I'd mentally marked. It had a very distinctive twist to it. I made very sure it was the correct one. I cross-referenced all of the identifying features. But I could not spot that bird!! It kept on hooting. Mark and I searched for it another twenty minutes . . . looking up into that tree until we were sure that we'd never be able to get our necks straight again.

I *again* left Mark at the shooting spot below the tree and went *back* to the hillside. Once there, I could still see that bird on its branch. I coached Mark. We were absolutely certain we were looking at the same tree, the same branch, and the same spot on the branch. He still couldn't see it. I returned to Mark and *I* couldn't see it either! The situation was absurd. We knew the bird was there. I was able to spot it from the hill. The bird continued calling. But we could not locate it.

That bird never moved. But we did. We saluted Mr. Hooter, declared him the winner, and carefully made our way back down the side of the mountain toward where we'd left our skiff. How and why we were unable to spot that bird will always be a mystery to me.

Our circle back down the mountainside took us through some of the prettiest country I'd ever seen in Alaska. As we moved into the lower reaches, we entered a grove of birch trees mixed with aspen and an occasional spruce. Meandering through the grove, a beautiful little stream sparkled and rushed. Occasionally, along its course, it formed small ponds. The water in the stream and its ponds was exceptionally clear. I could see that the bottoms of the ponds were laced with tree branches. The stream itself had a bottom of pebbles and cobblestone. I looked for fish but could not spot any. I suspected that fish were there, but that they, like the hooters, were masters at hiding.

By this time, I was so thoroughly soaked that I didn't care a whit when it was necessary to ford that little stream. If the walking appeared to be easier on one side or the other, I just waded across. It didn't matter. What *did* matter was my tendency to forget that I needed to be ever watchful for bears. I became so enthralled by the beauty of the place that it took tripping over a deep impression in a silty bar alongside the creek to resurrect my focus. That impression was a huge bear track. It was wider than the length of the sole of my boot. And it was fresh. There was still a little loose dirt tumbling down the edges of the bear's tracks.

In Alaska, it is best not to have shells in the chamber of your gun. That way, if you stumble and fall, the gun will not discharge accidently. If there is an accident, it is unlikely that medical help will be able to come in time to do any good. So you keep the magazine full, the chamber empty, and stay prepared to work your gun's action and load quickly, if necessary. I checked my gun to be sure that there were four slug loads in the magazine and that the chamber was empty. That, and keeping a watchful eye and talking continuously with Mark so that the bear would know we were around, was all that I could do . . . all that either of us could do.

We never saw the bear, but the bear had found our skiff. In fact, it had been *inside* the skiff. Its muddy tracks were all over the bottom of it. It had also scooted that boat around some and rearranged the gear. But nothing was damaged except one thing—the paddle. The bear had snapped it into two pieces, either by stepping on it (unlikely) or biting it in two. Tooth marks in the wood told the tale. It was an old paddle, no doubt with many years' accumulation of impregnated fish slime mixed with sweat from human hands. We took the two pieces and lashed them back together with some rope we had with us. Although the lashings were tight, it was a pretty flimsy piece of engineering. We hoped we wouldn't need to use it.

After dragging the skiff back to the water and securing the outboard motor to the transom, we pushed off and were on our way . . . sort of. The motor wouldn't start. Try as he might, Mark couldn't get that thing to turn over. It wouldn't even sputter. I pulled out the paddle, such as it was, and started moving the boat toward the cabin, a bit over two miles away. There was a slight head wind, but we still made progress. I estimated that it probably wouldn't take more than three or four hours, perhaps just a little more, to make it back to the beach below the cabin. Mark continued working on that motor as I paddled from the bow. After about half a mile, which took nearly an hour to achieve, there was a cough, then a sputter, and then a cloud of blue smoke as that little motor came to life. Mark babied that motor just like a fire builder carefully tends the first little weak flames that come to his tinder during a rainstorm. The motor kept running. And we made it home, sailors home from the sea, hunters home from the hills.

But the reality was that I'd been "home" all day long and for several days prior to this one. Every part of every one of those days, every mountain slope, plateau, valley, and cove we ventured into . . . every whisper of wind, every stream crossing, every patch of snow, every hooter, every bear track, rock, log, train wreck, tree, and patch of ferns, every screaming eagle, flock of ducks, sparkling wave, and gravel beach . . . every smell from the dark, rich soil told me so.

A man with a home to go to, a home that always welcomes him back, is truly blessed. This is particularly true if that man is a restless sort of guy who roams the world at will, a man who has no choice but to do so—one who only gets back to his home occasionally. I am most certainly one of those blessed ramblers. And my home, the one I return to time and time again, is magnificent. It is, in fact, a huge cathedral, a cathedral graced by the beauty of wild and lonely places . . . a cathedral within which I hear my name whispered in quiet song by the winds and the waters. They remind me that I'm an Alaskan and confirm that I will be forever more. I may *live* someplace else, but Alaska is where I'm *alive*. This time, it was the hooters that called me home . . . just to remind me of that.

A Timeless Outdoor Tool

BEING A NATIVE SON OF THE SOUTH WITH A PROPENSITY TO venture off trails and into the forests, thickets, wetlands, and waters that bless this region, I've experienced a somewhat bell-shaped curve regarding accoutrements deemed critical to the enterprise. I started out with nothing and it has recently dawned on me that, with the passage of the decades, I am on track to end with nothing. I had no control over the start, but as I drift along that curve of the ages, I find myself moving increasingly toward simplicity.

Let's take boats, for example. At the tender age of eight years, I lashed sticks and boards together with baling twine to make rafts, and I used a smoothly trimmed trunk of a small sapling as a push pole to move about on the water. Needless to say, abandoning ship was a common occurrence. Eventually, I obtained a hammer, a rusty saw, and some nails. My rafts became more seaworthy. I also learned to fashion paddles using sections of stouter saplings to which I nailed a piece of inch-thick board.

When I approached my teens, I gained access to small boats. My parents gave me a real store-bought paddle! I paddled for a year or two but longed for an outboard motor. Then a much-loved and quite elderly uncle gave me his vintage three-horsepower Johnson outboard motor. That motor helped me move ever deeper into the realms of boating.

Eventually, as an adult, boats of all sorts became the platforms for a full career as a fisheries biologist. Many of the boats I used professionally were very specialized and were replete with gadgets for various purposes. Most had powerful motors. Of necessity, I spent considerable time deep in the guts of motors and boats, making sure that they were in proper condition to do the job required of them, including getting me back home from my sorties.

For the record, however, I've personally owned only four outboard motors. Two (including the little three horsepower) were given to me, and two I bought new. All have been good motors. And all now spend most of the time tucked away in the more remote corners of my shed or backyard. I rarely use them and, frankly, have a hard time imagining that I ever will again. I've gone back to paddles and am in love with canoes. The quieter way is winning.

My love affair with guns has traveled a similar path. I started with a cast-off BB gun that I found discarded in a pile of trash. I was seven years old when I dragged it out of that heap, took it home, and repaired it. It turned out to be a pretty good gun and shot where it was pointed. The feeding tube wouldn't work, so it had to be loaded one BB at a time, like a muzzle-loader, with a straightened coat hanger as a ramrod. That was OK with me. At least I had a gun!

Then at age eleven came a single-shot .22 rifle and a single-shot .410 shotgun . . . both old and somewhat beat up but beautiful in my eyes. They were gifts: the rifle a gift from a teenage girl in Kentucky and the shotgun a gift from the same elderly uncle in northeast Arkansas who'd given me that little three-horsepower outboard motor. At the age of fourteen I'd saved enough money from working my paper route to buy a new twelve-gauge Remington semi-automatic shotgun. Large-caliber rifles entered the scene about the time I graduated from high school. In college the handgun urge hit me and opened an entire new dimension of shooting into my life.

I wanted firepower, and so during my twenties I focused my attention on semi-automatic shotguns, rifles, and pistols. But by my thirties I'd drifted away from them and started focusing more and more on pump-action shotguns, revolvers, and bolt-action rifles. Simplicity and dependability trumped firepower. By my fifties, my shotguns were primarily double barreled, and I was hunting more and more with a single-shot rifle. Revolvers endured in spite of the evolution of fine semi-auto pistols over the years. Recently, in my sixties, I've come to realize that I've been moving along the curve as a hunter in ways I'd not anticipated. I'm actually back to shooting a single-shot air gun! I've found it to be just the ticket for squirrels. In fact, for the past several years I've killed more squirrels with that air gun than with any other gun I own . . . including a very fine (and expensive) bolt-action .22 rifle that is my treasure!

The same evolutionary process has occurred with camping, hiking, and fishing gear. My knives are durable, single-bladed affairs. I tried the multiple-tool models and gave them away. My tent (I only have one) is forty years old and still a fine thing. I've carried it all over the world, on every continent except Antarctica. It has sheltered me on many ventures, including many a hunt in Alaska when the weather turned sour (as it almost always does up yonder!). It weighs practically nothing and can sleep two comfortably and three if needed (including their packs and guns).

However, I actually prefer to leave the tent at home, making camp in front of my overturned canoe. A canoe reflects a campfire's heat superbly and provides good shelter. If I need more space (e.g., in rainy weather), I stretch a small tarp out from the canoe. As for fishing, although I am addicted to fly rods, I also love fishing with cane poles, and particularly those I've cut, seasoned, and rigged myself.

Boats, guns, and gear: they all seem to have followed the same curve toward a return to simplicity. But recently I've come to realize that there *is* an indispensable outdoor tool that is not subject to this evolutionary process. It introduces itself to us in elegant simplicity during our formative years and stays with us in its simplicity for the duration. It is little talked about but well known to persons who regularly venture forth into the southern wilds. Without this tool we risk suffering during all but the coldest months of the year.

I've never seen one for sale (amazing!). Perhaps this is because it costs nothing at all and is readily available to anyone with the gumption to reach out and snatch one. It is a tool that is used by children probing the bushy corners of backyards, by seasoned outdoor adventurers, and by the more reflective elders in our ranks (including me). Every manifestation of this tool has a unique configuration, but all maintain basic features of functionality. The tool I'm referencing is the spiderweb switch.

We are hardwired genetically to pick up and use sticks. Most children will naturally pick up a stick and reach out to the world with it, probing, prodding, striking, or stirring. Sticks were humankind's first tool and weapon. They become an extension of our bodies and help us during times of uncertainty. Larger ones help us walk, climb, wade, or navigate. In specialized form, they help us cast baits to fish. We tip sticks with sharp points and launch them at great speeds to down our prey.

Just like a fishing pole, an arrow, or a spear, a spiderweb switch is a stick modified to serve very specific, utilitarian purposes. It was as a youthful squirrel hunter in central Arkansas that I finally realized its value and deep-rooted connections to civilization's eternal forays into planet Earth's woodlands. Prior to my epiphany, I would enter the woods in the predawn darkness and was forever running into spiderwebs. Just about every time this happened, a spider would end up on my face or neck and crawl down the front of my shirt. Some were hard-shelled orb spiders, some were larger brown spiders, and occasionally I'd run smack dab into one of those big yellow garden spiders (the ones with black stripes). Spiders that got inside my shirt usually bit me. They're not particularly poisonous, but still the bite would hurt—much like a bee sting. Additionally, there'd be spiderweb fibers all over my face and on the outer surface of my glasses. This was aggravating, to say the least.

The challenges don't change much after sunrise. Unless the light is just right, you likely won't see the webs or the spiders in the shadowy woodlands. Then, suddenly, a web is wrapped around your face and the spider has either dropped to the ground or is on its way down underneath your shirt. This is particularly a challenge to squirrel hunters because they're focused on the tree branches as much or more than they are on the route before them. Deer hunters heading to their stands in the predawn darkness, early-season duck and upland game hunters, and creek anglers trying to find their way down to the water also face (no pun intended) the spiderweb issue. There's simply no way around the truth of the matter (as well as the webs). *Ventures into the southern wilds require a spiderweb switch.*

And yet not just any old switch will do. A proper switch must have particular features. It can't be too heavy or too light. It can't be too limber or too stiff. It's got to have a reach long enough to be effective, and terminate on the business end with an array of web-catching protrusions. It also needs to be a bit springy.

I've tried many varieties of switches. Pine has sticky sap and the needles offer too much wind resistance. Cane is either too stiff or too fragile, depending on where along the continuum you cut your switch. Cane switches are also better dried and seasoned than fresh. Plus, cane feels bulky to the hands and has knobs. Oak has a rough feel and doesn't tend to grow straight branches conducive to switch building. Osage orange is too curved and too hard to whittle. Locust has spines and also is too hard to cut with a pocket knife. Ash is too stiff. Maple is too brittle and will split. I've never tried walnut, pecan, hickory, or persimmon, but they seem to be in the same league as oaks, in that the potential switches, if they exist at all, are typically too high for me to reach.

It has been said that a curse can become a blessing, that dark clouds can have silver linings, and that the last shall be first. So it is with regard to materials for the crafter of spiderweb switches. Subsequently, and with full confidence, I present to you, for honest appraisal and consideration, what I consider to be the best source of spiderweb switches on planet Earth: the Chinese privet.

I admit that this immigrant to the North American continent has become the scourge of southern landscapes and should be eradicated. There's no question about that. I realize that birds relish the berries (and thereby scatter privet seeds here, there, and yonder) and that privet can provide windbreaks to protect God's creatures from winter's blue northern gales. But on the downside, privet will take over a woodland or an old field in pretty short order. Trim it back and it seems to double its density and growth rate. Goats and deer will eat privet, but there's so much of it that it is like a small

boy trying to eat his way out of a room full of chocolate chip cookies. Eventually, privet gets too large to provide decent browse. The
saving grace of privet (such as it may be), as far as I've been able to
discern, is that it makes the perfect spiderweb switch.

Of course, even with privet, there must be a craftsman's eye during the selection process. And every wielder of switches has her or
his preferences. I do not presume to advocate any particular style.
There is no plain vanilla flavor, no twelve-gauge pump with a modified choke and #6 shot, no six-foot spinning rig with ten-pound
test line, no one-size-fits-all knife handle, or fourteen-foot-long
aluminum flat-bottom boat. Nature simply doesn't work that way.
But seek and ye shall find. And if you don't like it, throw it away
and get another one.

With all due respect to individual preferences regarding construction of a spiderweb switch, I guess a primer is in order. If you
don't think so, I beg your indulgence . . . just for a little while. But
if by chance you've not yet become a crafter of spiderweb switches
made from privet, perhaps this will set the stage for you and get you
started. You will eventually fine tune. You may also develop diversity
expertise, crafting switches for specific domains.

First and foremost, the basic spiderweb switch needs to be about
three feet long and more or less straight. I prefer a little curve, but
that's just me. Go for straight and you more than likely won't be
disappointed. The terminal (distal) end needs a network of small
branches . . . not *too* small however or else they will not hold up to
the task. The fat (proximal) end needs to be no larger in diameter
than your little finger (left or right, it doesn't matter). I would suggest
your second toe, but to do so would reflect my cultural heritage.

Do not break the switch off of the bush! If you do this, it will
most likely split and all attributes of grip and balance will be lost.
You'll have to find another one. Take out your *single-bladed* knife
and carefully whittle your switch free from the bush. Whittle toward
the bush so that, when you've freed the switch, you've got a nice
pointed end. You may carve that back to a dull point if you desire. I
like mine sharp. That way I can more easily poke my switch into the

ground when I stop to look at things during my sojourns. A switch flat on the ground can be hard to relocate.

Now gently pluck off the leaves and small twigs along the main stem of the switch. You can do this with hands only, but frequently I use my knife. Don't cut them off—pluck them. As you move out to the end of your switch, remember that a network of smaller stems at the end is the critical web catcher. The object is to have a catcher twig network that is somewhat like your hand with fingers spread out. For this, put your knife to work again, but don't carve. Rather, go out four to six inches and bend those terminal twigs, one at a time, across the sharp edge of your knife. They will pop with a clean break.

Grab your switch and whip it up and down, then left to right . . . as if you are giving a blessing to the land, the day, or whatever. After you've practiced the vertical and horizontal moves, try circular moves, clockwise and counter clockwise. Some webs respond better to straight-line attacks, others to circular. Your switch has to be able to work both ways. If you don't feel like your switch can handle the anticipated challenges, discard it and start over. You will know when you've got the right switch. It is all about balance, just like a fine shotgun, fly rod, knife, or hand-crafted canoe paddle. It is your creation. When you get one that feels right, be proud of it.

A fine switch will last a full season, unless, of course, you lay it down on the ground and lose it. That's a heartbreaking event that can be averted by one simple embellishment: tie a small piece of brightly colored flagging tape to the main stem of your switch, just below the network of twigs on the distal end. The color is strictly a personal preference. I use orange, but I've seen some folks with blue or yellow. If it makes you happy, then that's the color for you.

Be warned about switch snatchers. Guests who accompany you on your ventures will steal switches. They are the same people who would not consider stealing vegetables from your garden or poaching your pond. But they *will* steal a good spiderweb switch—or worse, throw it away at the end of the trip!

That being the case, I keep a couple of "second-tier" switches in the bed of my old pickup truck. My guests never ask me whether or not I have switches for them. That's assumed. But they do ask, "Where's *my* switch?" . . . assuming that the ones I issue to them are theirs to keep. Sometimes I ask them to return the switches, but most of the time I just let them go, as tokens of good friendship in a spiderweb world. I never, however, loan my primary switch. Too much synergism has evolved between the switch and me over time to relinquish it.

The tool may not have evolved over time, but the user of the tool certainly does and has. In this regard, as the years have passed, I find myself more and more going afield as a hunter without a gun or an angler without a rod. I'm not exactly sure of the reasons why. I've thought about it, a lot, but have yet to settle on any answers. Physical limitations may have something to do with it. The coffee mug in my left hand doesn't leave room for a gun or a rod, and my right hand carries my spiderweb switch. I do not have a prehensile tail or a trunk to carry a gun or rod. Yet I still engage in my sports, deeper than ever. When I pass beside my pond and the bluegills dimple the surface, I raise my switch and set the imaginary hook. And when I stalk game to within reasonable range, I point my switch at the critter and quietly whisper, "Bang." Beyond timeless simplicity, a spiderweb switch is, quite frankly, a magic thing. I've never missed a strike or a shot with mine.

Prom Dance

THE MUSIC SEEMED TO COME FROM ALL DIRECTIONS. IT STIRRED something deep and primitive within me. A soft warm breath whispered in my ear and brushed the back of my neck. Delicate limbs swayed gracefully before me, in tempo with the music and the magic rhythms of spring. I was surrounded by the sparkle and flash of jewels as soft light played upon the scene. My feet seemed to glide in synchrony with the flow as I danced, somewhat cautiously, out into the open. I was completely absorbed by my surroundings and by the music and needed more room to move. And I knew, absolutely, at the tender age of eighteen, that I was in love . . . it was the evening of my high school senior prom.

A hawk screamed and a kingfisher rattled as I slapped a mosquito on my neck. I was knee deep in a shoal of Arkansas's Little Red River, fly rod in hand, fishing for rainbow trout as the evening hatch of mayflies created a twilight symphony. There was a gentle breeze drifting across the water that quietly called my name. Water willow moved in concert with the currents. The last rays of sunlight sparkled on the water in flashes of shimmering gold. I moved further out into the opening, to a place where I would have more room for my cast. I had to be careful as I waded in the currents across the rocky bottom. It required some very fancy steps because some of the stones were slippery. Yes, indeed, I was in love.

I could not imagine being any place else. I shuttered at the thought of being in a noisy crowd on so delicious an evening. My absence would not be noticed. And, frankly, I really didn't care. I liked girls and had some friends who were girls, but I did not like the places and activities that seemingly went into the equation of relationships. I had yet to find a girl that liked fly fishing, duck hunting, or canoeing. (That came later . . . thankfully!) I was a quiet, thin (but strong) boy who exercised a lot, spent his time outdoors, and did not care much for competitive sports or fast cars. Feminine eyes did not long linger on me. At least I didn't think they did. And besides, there was a war going on in Southeast Asia and odds were even that I'd eventually get into it. I needed to keep my focus, stay strong, and hone my skills as an outdoorsman.

For the record, I eventually *did* get into the war, but not in ways I'd anticipated. I became a Peace Corps volunteer in the middle of it all and, after the war, stayed active in the region my entire professional career, eventually, toward the end, teaching fisheries courses in Vietnam (where the entire mess started) at a university in the Mekong River Delta to the grandchildren of our former enemies, the Viet Cong (they called themselves "Night Dragons"), and drinking beer *with* those guys! We'd shake our heads, toast one another, and drift into memories. Those are stories for another time.

And so on this prom night, with all the world before me, my focus was fly fishing for rainbow trout on a gorgeous river. It never dawned on me that because I did not go to the prom, some girl didn't get to go. Back then nobody went to a high school prom without a date. But eighteen-year-old boys don't tend to think in those broader terms. They think mostly about themselves. I didn't want to go to the prom. I wanted to go fishing. And that's what I did. It haunts me to this day.

But it did not haunt me back then. It did not haunt me, or even enter my mind, when I waded out into that river, with the trout dimpling the water and mystery oozing from the shadows at twilight. I felt a thrill course its way through me and it caused me to shiver. To say that I was a happy boy would be an understatement. I was where I wanted to be . . . where I belonged.

My fishing gear was pretty rough: an old and beat-up fly rod (I think it was a 6-weight, perhaps a 7-weight) and a single-action reel that was somewhat off center on its spindle, passed down to me by an uncle. I didn't know much about lines and so used a level line. Ditto for leaders. All I did for leaders was tie on a length of four-pound monofilament. I don't think my line matched the rod weight. That relationship was still a mystery to me.

I had no coaches, no mentors. I'd read all I could about the craft, from outdoor magazines mostly, but without guidance I drifted into the lowest common denominator of fly fishing. I desperately wanted to do it right. I practiced casting in my front yard and fished for bluegill and small bass in a local lake to learn how to handle fish when hooked. I ordered flies from a sporting goods catalogue and based my selections on what I'd read in the magazines. My naivety was profound, but the visions, the images, and the dreams were powerful. When I got old enough to drive, I'd borrow our family car and drive to the Little Red River, a distance of about ninety miles from our home.

Somehow, some way, I learned to cast and how to present flies. I caught fish in that river. I caught lots of fish. I also spent a lot of time just watching the river and watching the fish, not casting, just watching. I began to recognize patterns of currents . . . how they move around structure and how fish use current and structure *synergistically*. I didn't know that word until I went to college. I'd never heard anyone use it and had never run across it in my reading. But I understood the principal of the word as a high school senior and applied it to my fishing. I learned that the mix also included me, the angler. I was part of the equation. How I conducted myself while fishing was the glue that held the entire enterprise together.

On this prom night, as the light faded from the sky and the may-fly hatch went crazy and the fish went crazy, I also started to go a little crazy. The trout were not spooky. They were focused . . . just like me. I was using a small, brownish-gray, dry fly and was, somehow, putting that fly and the line in the places I aimed for. My drifts were short before pickup, so there was little if any drag. My casts were not particularly long, so when I raised my rod the line came up gently and with minimal disturbance. I felt strangely as if I were engaged in some sort of waltz. I remember thinking that . . . that I *was*, in fact, dancing on my prom night.

I knew how to dance. My parents (a protestant minister and an elementary school teacher) had taught me how, secretly, on the linoleum floor in our house. I'd danced with my mother and with a broom. With their guidance I knew the moves and the flow and the gentleness: how to guide my partner and how to shift my moves smoothly in response to those of my partner. What I think they did not realize was that I applied those dancing lessons to fly fishing and the catching of trout. The trout became my partners in the dance, every one of them treasures.

When the trout took my fly and I pulled back, it was as if I were holding the hand of a beautiful girl. And when the trout jumped, it was like a girl twirling at my fingertips. Slowly, steadily, I'd bring the fish close to me and carefully hold it, as I would have held the waist of my dancing partner, lightly but with certainty. Then, the release . . . and echoes in the heart.

The dance ended. The symphony evaporated into the night. The mayfly hatch faded and then stopped entirely. There was still a little glow in the sky, but it was surrendering to the stars. The river murmured gently. The trout, my dancing partners, were back home safely.

I was alone. For a while I stood there, a solitary young man of eighteen years, at the edge of a river, a river much larger and deeper than the one that had orchestrated the evening's dance . . . and in the quiet, in the stillness, its currents swirled within my soul. Then a sweetness swelled from those currents. And I fell in love, all over again.

Now, fifty years later, it still happens *every time*.

About the Author

Photo courtesy of the author

Donald C. Jackson is the Sharp Distinguished Professor Emeritus of Fisheries at Mississippi State University. He served as a US Peace Corps volunteer in Malaysia, attended Lexington Theological Seminary in Kentucky, and was pastor of New Liberty Christian Church, Disciples of Christ (Owen County, Kentucky). He is a past president of the Mississippi Wildlife Federation and the American Fisheries Society and an ordained elder in the Presbyterian Church (USA). An avid hunter and fisherman, he is the author of *Deeper Currents*, *Tracks*, and *Wilder Ways*, all published by University Press of Mississippi.

Lightning Source UK Ltd.
Milton Keynes UK
UKHW041512151121
394001UK00001B/43

9 781496 835963